Small Business and Effective ICT

Small businesses make up some 90–95% of all global firms. Many undervalue the importance of information and communication technologies (ICT). Within the small business segment there can be significant differences amongst the avid early adopters of ICT and the laggards. Research on early adopters tends be more prevalent as they are perceived to have a more interesting and positive story. However, late adopters and 'laggards' also have their own interesting stories that are under-reported.

Small Business and Effective ICT draws on research undertaken over several years and documents the adoption/use of ICT across 'better' users of ICT (Leaders), typical ICT users (Operationals) and late adopters (Laggards). The findings are presented using a reformulation of the LIAISE framework which addresses a number of areas that include ICT literacy (L), information content/communication (I), Access (A), Infrastructure (I), Support (S) and Evaluation (E).

Some 60 businesses were investigated in Australia and the UK, with each business presented as a concise *vignette*. The vignettes serve to show that small businesses are not as conservative in their use of ICT as the literature suggests, with examples of innovative uses of ICT in small businesses provided. Lessons for the effective use of ICT by small businesses are presented.

The research design, methods adopted, presentation of findings through the vignettes, and 'take away' lessons have been written in a manner so as to appeal to a broad range of readers including academics, researchers, students and policy makers in the discipline.

Carmine Sellitto is a Senior Lecturer in the College of Business at Victoria University, Australia.

David A. Banks is an Adjunct Fellow in the College of Business at Victoria University, Australia.

Scott Bingley is a Lecturer in the College of Business at Victoria University, Australia.

Stephen Burgess is an Associate Professor in the College of Business at Victoria University, Australia.

Routledge Studies in Small Business

Edited by David J. Storey, School of Business, Management and Economics, University of Sussex

For a full list of titles in this series, please visit www.routledge.com

Small Business and Effective ICT

Stories and Practical Insights

Carmine Sellitto, David A. Banks,
Scott Bingley and Stephen Burgess

Routledge
Taylor & Francis Group

NEW YORK AND LONDON

First published 2017
by Routledge
711 Third Avenue, New York, NY 10017

and by Routledge
2 Park Square, Milton Park, Abingdon, Oxon OX14 4RN

Routledge is an imprint of the Taylor & Francis Group, an informa business

© 2017 Taylor & Francis

Library of Congress Cataloging-in-Publication Data
CIP data has been applied for.

ISBN: 978-1-138-93338-5 (hbk)
ISBN: 978-1-315-67409-4 (ebk)

Typeset in Sabon
by Apex CoVantage, LLC

Contents

Tables

Figures

Foreword

The small firm sector is hugely important to most economies. Furthermore, IT now touches many aspects of how all firms operate, and its rapid evolution provides new challenges for managers. Thus I welcome a book that focuses on IT in small firms, and especially one that offers something for both managers and researchers.

From my experiences as a researcher of SMEs, most owners and managers are very highly motivated and capable people. They are also very busy managing multiple aspects of the business, with IT being only one element to consider. The IT revolution for SMEs is about 30 years old, and the Internet has made it an even more important and complex aspect for managers to address. Thus SME managers need help and this book provides many insights, especially in the lessons learned, as discussed in Chapter 8. That material is aimed at managers of small firms. It is important that research results reach managers, so I hope the authors and many readers of this book will spread the word to managers. It is quite a challenge for such insights to reach managers. While I expect few managers will attempt to read the whole book, there is wisdom, especially in the lessons learned, that managers should be exposed to.

This book should appeal to researchers of IT in SMEs, and especially those relatively new to research, for example, those undertaking thesis research, who need guidance and something to aspire to. The authors provide many examples of how IT fits within specific small firms, and how such case evidence can be analysed. When I started my research journey, nearly all research involved numbers, i.e., the quantitative approach was the dominant paradigm. That suited me as I had studied statistics at university. I had also taught quantitative methods to business studies students. However, during my PhD research in the 1980s, I began to recognise the limitations of survey research. As a result, I included face-to-face interviews with managers of small firms, and these interviews provided rich pictures that helped me publish in high-quality journals. The stories from individual firms proved to be full of important insights, and I can still remember some of them, especially those that showed that IT could be strategic, i.e., IT helped the firms compete. For example, I remember the interviews with a pharmaceutical wholesaler who bit by bit took over most of its regional competitors, primarily because the firm had created IT links with pharmacies that helped the firm provide a 24-hour delivery service. There was also the three-person fire/safety business that used a simple database application to record sales, and subsequently reminded customers that a six-month or annual inspection was due. Also, a very small aluminium window manufacturer used IT to do something that none of its competitors could, by providing an immediate price quote over the phone, through a simple, graphical application, that linked sizes and lengths of materials with costs. I have been a strong advocate for case research ever since.

Much of the book's analysis is based on the LIAISE framework, which provides a multifaceted framework. Rather than focus on one aspect of IT, the framework encourages the examination of use, skills, support, governance and impact. I see this as a strength of the research approach, that could inspire future studies of IT in SMEs. It is not rocket science, and there are lots of issues to be researched.

Paul Cragg
February 2016

After about five years in industry, Paul Cragg became a teacher and researcher in 1975. Most recently he was Professor of Information Systems at the University of Canterbury, New Zealand. Prior to Canterbury, he taught at the University of Waikato (NZ), and Leicester Polytechnic (England). He received his PhD from Loughborough University, England. He taught the management of IS across a wide range of courses from undergraduate through to PhD. He has published his research on IS in small and medium-sized enterprises in numerous journals, including Information & Management, MIS Quarterly, European Journal of Information Systems, Journal of Strategic Information Systems, Journal of Small Business Management, International Small Business Journal *and* Total Quality Management and Business Excellence.

Preface

Academic conferences can be quite collegial and instrumental in initiating the foundations for new ideas. From about 2002 to 2007, David Banks and Ann Monday from the University of South Australia and Stephen Burgess and Carmine Sellitto from Victoria University met on a number of occasions at conferences and realised that they shared a common interest in the use of Information and Communications Technologies (ICT) by small businesses.

Around 2008 they decided to apply for a research grant from the Sustainable Tourism Cooperative Research Centre (STCRC), which had been established under the Australian Government's Cooperative Research Centre's program in 1997. The STCRC undertook research into the strategic challenges facing Australian tourism and operated until 2010.

The research grant project involved an in-depth investigation into the use of ICT by small tourism businesses. The STCRC application was successful; however the project involved the merger of our grant application with another from the University of Queensland, making the project bigger than originally anticipated. After completing the final project, the academic team published for the STCRC "Helping Tourism SMEs Plan and Implement Information and Communication Technology" (Scott, Burgess, Monday, O'Brien, Baggio, Sellitto, & Banks, 2010). This report included a literature review, reference to skills capabilities assessment tools (contributed by the University of Queensland) and data collected from a focus group and interviews conducted in South Australia and Victoria (states of Australia) by the academics affiliated with the University of South Australia and Victoria University. The final STCRC report, which contains some of the early analysis that informed the data collection and analysis in this book, can be downloaded from the STCRC website: http://www.crctourism.com.au/BookShop/BookDetail.aspx?d=696

Whilst the research conducted as part of the STCRC project provided insights on the use of ICT by small tourism businesses, the authors of this book felt that there were lessons learned that could apply to small businesses in general. However, the two limitations that were faced when this idea was conceived were, firstly, that the initial data collection was restricted to tourism small business and, secondly, one of the researchers had moved to the UK, and another had moved to the USA for six months as a visiting research scholar after which he also moved to the UK. However, the latter event provided us with a further opportunity. We decided that a further round of data collection was needed that not only refreshed the original data, but was targeted towards small businesses in general rather than just small tourism businesses. To provide some extra variation from our initial sample, David was able to facilitate further data collection in the UK. We selected a small coastal town to collect that data and this occurred in 2011 and 2012, whilst the Australian authors were visiting the UK.

Scott Bingley, now a lecturer at Victoria University, had been a PhD student at the time of the first round of data collection in South Australia and had been involved as a research assistant in the data collection in both States. Scott was also heavily involved in the data collection in the UK. Having a keen understanding of the data, Scott was an ideal person to also have as an author of this book.

The authors are all keen researchers and authors in the area of small business use of ICT. They have seen first-hand the challenges that still face small businesses in their use of ICT and how, with just a little effort, many of them could use ICT much more effectively within their businesses.

A multifaceted lens of analysis that is used in this book is the LIAISE framework. This framework was proposed by Schauder, Johanson, Denison, and Stillman (2005) to guide non-profit businesses in the adoption of ICT. The stages of LIAISE (Literacy, Infrastructure, Access, Information and Content, Support and Evaluation) represent important stages that a small business could expect to go through to use ICT effectively. LIAISE is introduced in Chapter 2 and is then referred to throughout the book.

The idea behind the book is to underline the importance of small businesses taking a 'holistic' approach to the adoption of ICT. We achieve this by:

- Initially representing the activities of the small businesses according to the LIAISE framework and by contrasting the behaviours of successful ICT users against unsuccessful users;
- Telling the individual stories of each of the small businesses that participated in our research. We want to show that although ICT lessons can be learned by examining trends regarding ICT use that might be reflected in statistical data and analysis, ICT adoption in small business can also be informed by a narrative for each individual small business. In doing this, it will be shown that small businesses are not as conservative in their use of ICT as the literature might suggest. There are seemingly many examples of innovative uses of ICT in the small business environment, of which a number are documented in the book.
- Providing a set of lessons learned in regards to how small businesses can use ICT that we believe will be of interest and use to the majority of small businesses. The lessons learned may also provide a platform for further investigations of ICT use in the small business domain by academics, vendors and consultants.

References

Schauder, D., Johanson, G., Denison, T., & Stillman, L. (2005). *Draft information economy strategy for Australian civil society.* Melbourne, Australia: Centre for Community Networking Research, Monash University.

Scott, N., Burgess, S., Monday, A., O'Brien, P., Baggio, R., Sellitto, C., & Banks, D. (2010). *Helping tourism SMEs plan and implement information and communication technology.* Queensland, Australia: Sustainable Tourism Cooperative Research Centre.

References

Contributors

Carmine Sellitto is a Senior Academic in the College of Business at Victoria University in Melbourne, Australia. He is also aligned as a Research Associate with Victoria University's Institute of Sport, Exercise and Active Living (ISEAL). He received his PhD from RMIT University, Australia, where he was awarded the business PhD student prize for innovation. He has published widely on topics associated with e-business, enterprise systems, information management and technology, tourism and IT, Internet marketing, information quality and small business technology adoption. His articles have appeared in the *Australasian Journal of Information Systems, Information Technology and Management, Information Systems Frontiers, Information Research, International Journal of Tourism Research, The Journal of the American Society for Information Science and Technology* and *International Journal of Retail and Distribution Management*.

David A. Banks is an Adjunct Fellow in the College of Business at Victoria University in Melbourne, Australia. He has taught and researched in universities in the UK, New Zealand, Australia, Hong Kong and the USA. His main interests are in project management, e-business, collaborative information systems, information systems development and learning processes in higher education. The latter two topics formed the focus of his PhD at the University of Manchester (UK). He has a long-standing interest in Audience Response technology and has used a number of systems to support his teaching and research since 1995. He has authored/edited two books, contributed chapters to a number of books and published in a range of peer-reviewed journals and conferences. He has served on a number of advisory panels and editorial boards since 1988. He is a member of the British Computer Society and holds Chartered IT Professional status.

Scott Bingley is an Academic in the College of Business at Victoria University in Australia. His research areas involve small business and the use of computer systems, technology adoption in sport, and social media use in small business. Scott completed his PhD at Victoria University, Australia, in 2012. His topic was centred on adapting a technology adoption model for local (grassroots) sporting clubs and associations to explain how they are adopting Internet applications, and how beneficial these applications are. Scott teaches in the Masters of Enterprise Resource Planning (ERP). Some of the units he has taught are The Information Systems Professional, Management of Information Technology, Business Analytics, and Strategic Use of ERP.

Stephen Burgess is an Associate Professor in the College of Business at Victoria University, Australia. He has research and teaching interests that include the use of ICT in small businesses (particularly in the tourism field), the websites of community-based organisations, and the use of user-generated content in tourism and B2C electronic commerce. He has received a number of competitive research grants in these areas. He has completed several studies related to website features in small business and how well websites function over time, including his PhD from Monash University, Australia. More recently he has pursued research that examines participation in grassroots sport and the use of ICT in local sporting organisations. He has authored/edited three books and special editions of journals in topics related to the use of ICT in small business and been track chair at international conferences in related areas. He has published in journals such as the *European Journal of Information Systems, International Journal of Information Management, Journal of Information Science, Information Systems Frontiers, Tourism Analysis, International Journal of Tourism Research, Journal of Hospitality Marketing & Management* and *Education + Training.*

Part I
Overview

1 Introduction

Preamble

Small businesses make up some 90–95% of all global businesses. Many of these businesses undervalue the importance of information and communication technologies (ICT). Research on ICT use in large businesses does not translate easily to the highly disparate small business environment. Even within the small business segment there can be significant differences amongst the avid early adopters of ICT and the ICT laggards. Research on early adopters tends be more prevalent as they are perceived to have a more interesting and positive story. However, late adopters and laggards also have their own interesting stories that are under-reported. This represents a gap in the business and ICT literature.

This book draws on research undertaken over several years and documents three different categories of adopters: early adopters of ICT (which have been labelled as ICT Leaders), businesses who adopt ICT later and use it mainly for operational purposes (ICT Operationals) and late or non-adopters of ICT (ICT Laggards). The findings are presented using a reformulation of the LIAISE framework that was developed for the non-profit sector. LIAISE addresses a number of adoption areas that include ICT Literacy (L), Information content/communication (I), Access (A), Infrastructure (I), Support (S) and Evaluation (E). The use of the LIAISE framework for evaluation and presentation purposes is original and gives the book a novel and creative perspective.

Sixty businesses were investigated, with each individual business presented as a concise vignette, another distinguishing aspect of the book. The vignettes serve to show that small businesses are not as conservative in their use of ICT as the literature suggests, with many examples of innovative uses of ICT in small businesses provided.

The book focuses on two disciplines, small business and information and communications technologies. The main aim of the findings presented in the book is to provide a resource for academics in these disciplines to inform their research in the area and, amongst industry, for small businesses to facilitate good ICT practice.

Businesses in the UK and Australia were sourced for the research. The Australian-based businesses are drawn mainly from the tourism sector, whilst the UK-based businesses are more diverse.

The research design, presentation of findings through the vignettes and 'take away' lessons have been written in a manner to appeal to the general reader. There is limited statistical analysis with an interpretive narrative used to explain findings.

The book underlines the importance of small businesses taking a 'holistic' approach to the adoption of ICT and, through the LIAISE framework, identifies the need for Literacy, Infrastructure, Access, Information and Content, Support and Evaluation.

The book draws on investigations that have been undertaken in the field and is not an aggregation of the extant literature into themes supported by cases studies sourced from secondary parties. This will appeal and be of value to readers, as will the concise vignettes highlighting the adoption stories of the different adopter groups.

Small Business Definitions

There is a great deal of variation in the practical and academic literature about what constitutes a 'small' business. Definitions vary on factors such as the number of employees, the number of full-time employees, annual turnover, asset levels and so forth. Different regions of the world, and their governments, will generally employ a combination of these to determine whether a business is 'small'. Other terms that are related to this discussion are 'micro' businesses (the smallest of small businesses) and 'medium'-sized businesses (usually larger than small businesses but smaller than large businesses), as well as the term 'small and medium-sized enterprises' (or 'SME'), which refers to small and medium-sized businesses together.

We have a preference for using the number of employees to determine business size, as we feel that it is easier to ask businesses for that information when conducting studies. For this book we adopt the following definitions as used in Burgess, Sellitto, and Karanasios (2009, p. 3):

A **micro business** is any business with 1–5 regular employees.
A **small business** is any business with 1–20 regular employees. This obviously includes micro businesses.
A **medium-sized** business is any business with 21–50 regular employees.
Therefore, a **small to medium-sized enterprise** (SME) is any business with 1–50 regular employees.

ICT Use in Small Business

The reason that we have written this book is that we see a significant gap in relation to how small businesses may be assisted to use the Internet and set up their web presence effectively. This section provides an introduction to the issues faced by small businesses when they adopt and subsequently use ICT.

Various researchers have reported that small business technology adoption requirements will invariably be influenced by their operating environment (Arbore & Ordanini, 2006; Fillis & Wagner, 2005; Peltier, Zhao, & Schibrowsky, 2012), with the benefits being specific to the areas that the technology is applied. A number of factors influence the small business operating environment. Some of these will now be discussed.

Resource Availability/Poverty

Small business growth, operations and adoption activities are traditionally shaped by the resources that they have available to them, which are reflected by the attributes of available time, money and skill base (Gnyawali & Park, 2009; Hunter, 2012; Peltier, Schibrowsky, & Zhao, 2009). This resource poverty (as it is sometimes referred to) is one of the primary issues that restrict the small business from adopting emerging technologies (MacGregor & Vrazalic, 2005). Montazemi (2006) suggested that resource poverty impacts on small business owners in that they do not appropriately consider new or emerging technology for their business, the allocation of suitable resources for training of staff to use the technology, and a cost recovery phase that may arise due to a poorly executed strategy in regards to initial adoption. Burgess et al. (2009) identified limited resources as one of the main reasons associated with adoption inertia when it comes to newer ICT, whilst Peltier et al. (2012) highlighted 'switching costs' as an important factor that small business owners seldom consider when moving from one adopted technology to another. Goode and Gregor (2009) indicated that smaller business entities tend to have fewer structural resources and employees, be less experienced and have a lower degree of investment when it comes to ICT adoption.

Management/Owner Support and Understanding

The perceptions of small business owners to new or emerging technologies can offer an understanding of how they might use such technology as a substitute over an existing application (Peltier et al., 2012). Lee (2004) identified that the expertise and knowledge that a small business owner possessed was an important factor associated with the adoption of new computer technology. Indeed, the extent of ICT success and financial advantage is associated with small business management competencies (Dibrell, Davis, & Craig, 2008). Burgess et al. (2009) argued that the small business manager's appreciation, enthusiasm, awareness and perceived value of a proposed new web technology was a quintessential factor that contributed to the small business being positioned for success. Small business owner/managers are a significant element in the adoption process, given that they are the primary decision-makers to which problem and challenges are referred (Hunter, 2012; Peltier et al., 2009). Underpinning this decision-making issue when it comes to technology is that many small business owners tend to have a centralised management style with short-term planning perspectives (Bunker & MacGregor, 2000; Hunter, 2012). Other traits that are affiliated with the decision to adopt technological innovations by small businesses include the owner's age, educational level and gender (Fillis, Johansson, & Wagner, 2003), whilst Woznica and Healy (2009) reiterated that managerial knowledge, skills and experience are all important key factors in allowing the advantages of ICT to be fully exploited by the business.

Strategic Outlook

General business strategy and ICT adoption are directly interrelated. Henderson and Venkatraman (1999) indicated that the alignment between ICT requirements and business strategy affected business performance by improving organisational competitiveness and governance practices. In the small business setting, the co-alignment of business strategy and ICT adoption has been shown to result in such businesses improving and enhancing performance (Bergeron, Raymond, & Rivard, 2004; Burgess et al., 2009). Business strategy and ICT adoption can also be based on perceived enhancement to the company's image, where a small business might be seen as technologically aware, potentially raising its status (Lee, 2004). Burgess et al. (2009) suggested that small business strategy, when associated with adopting a web presence, should be premised on seeking clearly defined competitive advantage, where the business may wish to either differentiate itself, be a low-cost entity and/or use the technological innovation for engaging a specific niche market.

Employee Skills

A particular element of resource poverty relates to employee skills. Small businesses traditionally lack appropriate skills and/or have limited access to specialist staff when it comes to using ICT (Burgess et al., 2009; Hunter, 2012). Furthermore they tend not to be in a position to provide the required or necessary training for existing staff (MacGregor & Vrazalic, 2005). The opportunity for small business employees to gain knowledge about a newly adopted technology can be limited due to owner/managers having concerns that staff might be absent from important daily duties whilst at training as well as concerns that newly acquired skills could take too long to be used in the business (Parker & Castleman, 2007). Marmaridis and Unhelkar (2005) reiterated the view that the loss of experienced ICT staff or an individual power user can have a detrimental effect on the business. Existing employees can, in fact, influence the adoption of new ideas and technology in a small business (Hunter, 2012). These employees act as a form of change agent or technology champion that tend to potentially speed up the adoption process in a classic diffusion scenario (Rogers, 1995), the inherent knowledge and skill set possessed by these employees speeding up the adoption of the innovation. Various authors have reported the influence of employees promoting technology adoption to small business managers as a significant conduit that shapes the adoption process (see Parker and Castleman (2007) for a summary of this issue).

Existing ICT Systems

An important issue when adopting any new form of computer technology is considering how the new system will interact with other existing small business systems, applications and infrastructure (Burgess et al., 2009). Lee (2004) identified that computer systems' compatibility was an important factor that was associated with the adoption of Internet technology by small businesses. Marmaridis and Unhelkar (2005) suggested that ICT adoption tends to be mainly ad-hoc, with many off-the-shelf solutions in place that potentially act to restrict future systems integration. Indeed, the use of different types of applications, with potentially different operating standards, can further hinder small business systems consolidation or even intra-application data exchanges. Arguably, the small business computing environment could generally be considered as islands of legacy systems, potentially not sharing data and being a disincentive to integration. In ICT in general, such integration becomes important for the small business when needing to connect to important partners (Strüker & Gille, 2010). It is recognised by the authors that internal infrastructure issues, such as setting up local networks, are less of an issue for small businesses these days than they were in the past.

Supply Chain Influences: Customer and Suppliers

For the small businesses, the demands and behaviour of customers can be a central determinant in considering the implementation of new technology (Burgess et al., 2009). Hence, a small business might have customers in the form of larger and powerful retailers that can exert pressure on a business to adopt a specific technology (DCITA, 2006; Strüker & Gille, 2010). Indeed, this type of adoptive action can be easily enforced through the use of commercial contracts that mandate the use of a specific technology when dealing with the larger retailer. This economic pressure placed on small business entities by their customers, suppliers or trading partners is commonly encountered and can lead to the forced adoption of specific technology (Duan, Deng, & Corbitt, 2012).

Competitors

Small business managers tend to be more reactive rather than proactive when it comes to the adoption of new technologies, innovations or practices. This approach fits with their decision-making that is typically a sequential process in considering such options (Hunter, 2012). Competitors can influence how and when a small business considers new ICT applications (Burgess et al., 2009; Duan et al., 2012). Parker and Castleman (2007) suggested that small business goals and objectives can be influenced by the industry environment in which they operate. The example they allude to relates to a perceived pressure associated with intra-industry competitors potentially driving the adoption of electronic business activities. Gnyawali and Park (2009) propose that cooperation between small business entities through the practice of co-opetition will strengthen their ability to adopt new forms of technological innovations.

Government

Government or industry regulations that apply to the sector in which a small business operates can impact the specific information that needs to be collected (DCITA, 2006). In many instances, the implementation of a specific ICT application allows this regulatory data to be more readily captured. Clearly, regulatory compliance requiring the capture of important data will invariably necessitate that a small business is forced to adopt a specific software application/technology for it to operate in that industry sector. For example, in the food and health sector, various food and drug regulations require important information capture at different points of the supply chain for business compliance. Hence, for any small business operating in this sector, such data-capturing technology will be advantageous (Sellitto, 2009). Arguably, this is also a barrier for any new business to enter that industry sector. Consequently, the technology can also be viewed as something that keeps new entrants out, imparting a form of technological protection for existing small businesses.

Small business adoption of new forms of technology can also be influenced by government policy and associated support (Duan et al., 2012; Tan, Fischer, Mitchell, & Phan, 2009). For example, governments can impact on small business uptake of new technologies through supportive small business technology policies, providing incentive schemes for small businesses to use ICT and/or by mandating that a specific technology be used as part of small business interaction with government (Parker & Castleman, 2007).

Data Privacy

Burgess et al. (2009) indicated that small business owners will have traditionally been accustomed to collecting customer information and that they will understand the importance of making sure that information is kept confidential. Furthermore, they highlight the importance of having a clear privacy policy that is easily accessible on the small business website as an important good practice that builds customer trust. Duan et al. (2012) alluded to the concept of secure transaction systems as an important element of small businesses wanting to participate in e-marketplaces. Secure systems are important in establishing trust between customers. Bunduchi, Weisshaar, and Smart (2011) suggested that data security is an ICT maintenance activity that small businesses can cost-effectively access through an external provider. Implicit in this data security process is the maintenance of client data privacy.

The LIAISE Framework

The LIAISE framework was originally developed for the non-profit sector providing guidelines for addressing various aspects of ICT adoption and use, including gaining access to ICT (through ICT infrastructure, literacy and support), how to use ICT, and how to evaluate its effectiveness. The framework is used in this book to allow us to categorise ICT adoption by a group of small businesses. The framework provides us with a means to understand and map the experiences of businesses in their use of ICT. In this book, the views of small business participants in Australia and the UK were analysed and classified according to the LIAISE framework. This was an informative exercise as it assisted in identifying processes related to ICT adoption that small businesses could target to potentially improve their ICT performance. Additionally, many factors that were raised in the previous section that relate to the adoption and use of ICT by small businesses were evident.

The ultimate aim of the book, through analysing the stories of each of the participating small businesses, was to identifying a series of 'take-away lessons' that could be applied by any small business to assist them in the adoption and use of ICT. Whilst these lessons are discussed in detail in Chapter 8, they are introduced briefly here.

Takeaway ICT Lessons for Small Businesses

Lesson 1: Match ICT Aims and Strategies to Business Aims and Strategies

A business will need to consider where it wants to be in three to five years time, whether it is looking to expand or is happy with the existing customer base or whether the business supports a particular lifestyle. All of these questions will influence the short- to long-term strategy of the business. This book is about the use of ICT and not specifically about business planning. However, if there is a business plan for the small business that sets out the business aims and its short- and longer-term objectives then it is going to be much easier to develop ICT aims and strategies to match.

Lesson 2: Think About the Readiness of the Business to Adopt ICT

Many businesses suffer from resource poverty (limited time, limited knowledge, limited finances) in relation to the use of ICT. The business needs to consider devoting the time to properly learn about ICT capabilities and what they can do for the business. If ICT is thought about as a strategic resource rather than as a cost then it is easier to justify the time spent on this task.

Lesson 3: Know About Established and Newer ICT

A business should have an idea of what ICT is currently available and affordable for the business and how it might be able to be employed effectively.

Lesson 4: Possess Appropriate Skills to Use ICT Effectively in the Business

Once the knowledge of ICT is gained and the decision to adopt or upgrade is made, it is important that the relevant skills to use the ICT are available to the business.

Lesson 5: Know How to Access ICT Skills From Reliable Sources

ICT skills can be brought into the business by hiring consultants or hiring employees with ICT skills. However, it is known that small businesses often use other approaches to source their ICT skills, especially using family and friends as they offer a low-cost alternative to gaining expertise. One of the risks of this strategy is that these people, whilst well-intentioned, may not have the level of ICT expertise required (for instance, they might be hobby users of the technology) or enough understanding of the business context to be able to offer advice that is of value. It is for this reason that we caution the use of family and friends as a single source of ICT expertise, or at least recommend that the small business owner/manager should carefully consider the training and background of the person from whom the advice is being sought.

Lesson 6: Know Something About Added-Value Uses of ICT in Addition to Regular Uses of ICT

The business should know what ICT applications are available for the business and how they can add value.

Lesson 7: Consider Upgrading ICT Resources at Least Every Five Years

Small businesses should consider upgrading their ICT resource on a reasonably regular basis. They should, however, only do so if there are demonstrable benefits available to the business by doing so.

Lesson 8: Develop ICT Recovery Plans That Enable Functioning Hardware and Software and Access to Data to the Extent That Operations Will Not Be Adversely Affected If Something Fails

Small businesses should have a regular routine of at least backing up important data, should store programs away safely and know how to restore them, and should know where and how to source hardware quickly should it fail.

Lesson 9: Evaluate, on a Regular Basis, the Success of ICT Investments

Although not always easy to quantify, this requires a small business to identify appropriate ways to measure the success of their investment.

Lesson 10: Develop Formal Measures to Evaluate the Success of ICT That Relate to the Achievement of Business Aims

Not only should small businesses regularly evaluate the success of the ICT according to their business aims, wherever possible, they should develop formal measures to do so.

Outline of the Book

The book is comprised of three major sections.

Part I: Background

This section of the book provides an introduction to the use of ICT in small business and outlines the LIAISE framework.

Chapter 1: Introduction

This chapter explains the origins of the research reported in the book and the types of businesses included. It gives an overview of the Australian-based small tourism businesses that form the basis of findings in the first part of the book and the UK-based coastal businesses reported in the second part of the book. The focus of each chapter is presented in a concise manner to highlight the content.

Chapter 2: Small Business and LIAISE

The LIAISE framework was originally developed for the non-profit sector, providing guidelines for appropriate ICT adoption. The chapter highlights the similarities between small businesses and non-profits when it comes to ICT adoption and argues that the LIAISE framework is a suitable vehicle for understanding and mapping the experiences of businesses in their use of technology. The LIAISE framework is briefly explained and then a reformulated version is developed to be used in the small business domain addressing the areas of ICT Literacy (L), Information Content and Communication (I), Access to ICT-based resources (A), the intrinsic availability of ICT Infrastructure (I), ICT Support (S) and ICT Evaluation (E).

Part II: A Study of Australian Small Tourism Businesses

This section introduces the Australian-based small businesses. One chapter records the individual ICT adoption stories of each of the businesses, whilst a second chapter presents an analysis of the findings according to the LIAISE framework.

Chapter 3: The Australian Small Tourism Business Cases

This chapter reports upon the first phase of the study that examined the ICT practices of 41 small tourism businesses. It considers why tourism businesses were selected and how they were identified. Using the LIAISE framework for analysis presents the findings according to the three adopter categories (ICT Leaders, ICT Operationals or ICT Laggards). The latter part of the chapter brings together 41 short vignettes describing the ICT experiences of each business.

Chapter 4: Australian Small Tourism Businesses and LIAISE

In the previous chapter each individual ICT business 'story' was presented through the use of concise vignettes. In this chapter the data underpinning the vignettes, derived from the individual businesses, is used to present an analytical perspective to the study, shedding further understanding on some of the overarching aspects of ICT adoption. The findings are presented using the areas of the LIAISE framework. The chapter also includes a summary commentary on the findings based around the three adopter categories.

Part III: A Study of UK Small Coastal Businesses

This section of the book introduces the UK businesses. It follows the same format as Part II.

Chapter 5: The UK Small Coastal Business Cases

This chapter reports upon the second phase of the research study that examined the ICT practices of small businesses in a UK coastal township. The same model developed in previous chapters, aligning the LIAISE framework and small business domains into the various adopter categories, is used.

Nineteen concise vignettes reflecting the experiences of the ICT Leaders, ICT Operationals and ICT Laggards are recorded.

Chapter 6: Small UK Coastal Businesses and LIAISE

This chapter presents analysis of the data underpinning the UK-based businesses to further expand on the understanding of ICT adoption. The findings are presented using the areas of the LIAISE framework.

Part IV: Afterword

This section draws together the findings of the Australian and UK-based study.

Chapter 7: The Overall Story

This chapter brings together the UK and Australian studies and presents the salient issues encountered across both locations. The timeline between studies enables a retrospective on the progress (or lack of progress) of businesses in their ICT adoption. The stories and results presented in the book are reflected upon.

Chapter 8: Take-Away Lessons for Small Businesses

This chapter provides an overview of the challenges facing small businesses in the current ICT environment. It provides a summary of unique 'take-away ICT lessons' for small businesses that result in sound ICT practices that will be applicable into the future as technology changes. Small businesses will be able to pick and choose between these lessons depending upon what particular situation they are in. For instance, an early adopter of ICT may not need to be advised on where to source knowledge of how to use a particular technology, whereas an ICT laggard may find this useful. However, our findings suggest that any small business can benefit from advice on how to effectively assess the success of their ICT applications.

Conclusion

This chapter has introduced the idea behind the development of this book. The chapter commenced with a preamble before defining the term 'small business'. Factors that influence the adoption and use of ICT by small businesses were then introduced followed by the LIAISE framework, which will be used throughout the book to examine and classify ICT use by our 60 participant small businesses. Ten 'takeaway' lessons for ICT use by small businesses were proposed. Finally, an outline of the book was presented.

References

Arbore, A., & Ordanini, A. (2006). Broadband divide among SMEs: The role of size, location and outsourcing strategies. *International Small Business Journal, 24*(1), 83–99.

Bergeron, F., Raymond, L., & Rivard, S. (2004). Ideal patterns of strategic alignment and business performance. *Information and Management, 41*(8), 1003–1020. doi: 10.1016/j.im.2003.10.004

Bunduchi, R., Weisshaar, C., & Smart, A. U. (2011). Mapping the benefits and costs associated with process innovation: The case of RFID adoption. *Technovation, 31*(9), 505–551.

Bunker, D. J., & MacGregor, R. C. (2000). *Successful generation of Information Technology (IT) requirements for Small/medium Enterprises (SME's): Cases from regional Australia.* Paper presented at the Proceedings of SMEs in a Global Economy, Wollongong, NSW.

Burgess, S., Sellitto, C., & Karanasios, S. (2009). *Effective web presence solutions for small businesses: Strategies for successful implementation.* Hershey, PA: IGI Global.

DCITA. (2006). *Getting the most out of RFID: A starting guide to radio frequency indentification for SMEs.* Barton: Department of Communications, Information Technology and the Arts (DICTA)-Australian Government.

Dibrell, C., Davis, P. S., & Craig, J. (2008). Fueling innovation through information technology in SMEs. *Journal of Small Business Management, 46*(2), 203–218.

Duan, X., Deng, H., & Corbitt, B. (2012, 3–5 December). *What drives the adoption of electronic markets in Australian small-and- medium sized enterprises?—An empirical study.* Proceedings of the 23rd Australasian Conference on Information Systems (ACIS 2012), Geelong, Australia.

Fillis, I., Johansson, U., & Wagner, B. (2003). A conceptualisation of the opportunities and barriers to e-business development in the smaller firm. *Journal of Small Business and Enterprise Development, 10*(3), 336–344. doi: 10.1108/14626000310489808

Fillis, I., & Wagner, B. (2005). E-business development: An exploratory investigation of the small firm. *International Small Business Journal, 23*(6), 604–634. doi: 10.1177/0266242605057655

Gnyawali, D. R., & Park, B.-J. R. (2009). Co-opetition and technological innovation in small and medium-sized enterprises: A multilevel conceptual model. *Journal of Small Business Management, 47*(3), 308–330.

Goode, S., & Gregor, S. (2009). Rethinking organisational size in IS research: Meaning, measurement and redevelopment. *European Journal of Information Systems, 18*(1), 4–25.

Henderson, J. C., & Venkatraman, N. (1999). Strategic alignment: Leveraging information technology for transforming organizations. *IBM Systems Journal, 38*(2–3), 472–484.

Hunter, G. M. (2012). Conducting information systems research using narrative inquiry. In Y. K. Dwivedi, M. R. Wade, & S. L. Schneberger (Eds.), *Information systems theory: Explaining and predicting our digital society* (Vol. 2, pp. 349–365). New York: Springer Science+Business Media.

Lee, J. (2004). Discriminant analysis of technology adoption behavior: A case of internet technologies II small businesses. *The Journal of Computer Information Systems, 13*(2), 57–66.

MacGregor, R. C., & Vrazalic, L. (2005). A basic model of electronic commerce adoption barriers: A study of regional small businesses in Sweden and Australia. *Journal of Small Business and Enterprise Development, 12*(4), 510–527. doi: 10.1108/14626000510628199

Marmaridis, I., & Unhelkar, B. (2005). *Challenges in mobile transformations: A requirements modeling prospective for small and medium enterprises.* Proceedings of the International Conference on Mobile Business, Sydney, Australia.

Montazemi, A. (2006). How they manage IT: SMEs in Canada and the U.S. *Communications of the ACM, 19*(12), 109–112.

Parker, C., & Castleman, T. (2007, 5–7 December). *Why should small firms adopt e-business? A framework for understanding the SME e-business context.* Proceedings of the 18th Australasian Conference on Information Systems (ACIS). Research, Relevance and Rigour: Coming of Age (CD-ROM), Toowoomba, Queensland.

Peltier, J. W., Schibrowsky, J. A., & Zhao, Y. (2009). Understanding the antecedents to the adoption of CRM technology by small retailers: Entrepreneurs vs owner-Managers. *International Small Business Journal, 27*(3), 307–336.

Peltier, J. W., Zhao, Y., & Schibrowsky, J. A. (2012). Technology adoption by small businesses: An exploratory study of the interrelationships of owner and environmental factors. *International Small Business Journal, 30*(4), 406–431.

Rogers, E. (1995). *Diffusion of innovations* (4th ed.). New York: Free Press.

Sellitto, C. (2009). A study of RFID adoption in the Wine Industry supply chain. *International Journal of Economic and Business Research, 1*(2), 214–227.

Strüker, J., & Gille, D. (2010). RFID adoption and the role of organisational size. *Business Process Management Journal, 16*(6), 972–990.

Tan, J., Fischer, E., Mitchell, R., & Phan, P. (2009). At the center of the action: Innovation and technology strategy research in the small business setting. *Journal of Small Business Management, 47*(3), 233–262.

Woznica, J., & Healy, K. (2009). The level of information systems integration in SMEs in Irish manufacturing sector. *Journal of Small Business and Enterprise Development, 16*(1), 115–130. doi: 10.1108/14626000910932917

2 Small Business and the LIAISE Framework

Introduction

This chapter introduces information and communications technologies (ICT) and their use by small businesses, before introducing the LIAISE framework in detail and discussing how it will be applied throughout the book.

Information and Communications Technologies (ICT)

Before considering the use of information and communications technologies (ICT) by small businesses, it is useful to explore the notion of ICT and their contribution to organisations generally. The World Bank Group (2011) described ICT as consisting of "the hardware, software, networks and media for the collection, storage, processing, transmission and presentation of information (voice, data, text, images), as well as related services".

ICT for the company have to eventuate in increases in profit (or for non-profit organisations, achievement of their goals). Whilst ICT may benefit a business in a manner that may not directly result in extra value to the customer (and increased sales), they should at least improve an organisation's abilities to meets its goals.

Tiernan and Peppard (2004) examined the value to an organisation of spending on ICT (which they called 'IT') and noted that the simple possession of ICT generated no value to the organisation itself. The authors suggested that value only emerged by judging how it is used ". . . both operationally and strategically, including in its interactions with customers, suppliers and perhaps even regulatory authorities" (Tiernan & Peppard, 2004, pp. 3–4). In their well-known article, Porter and Millar (1985) identified three ways that organisations could use ICT to assist them to compete with other businesses:

- Be the low-cost producer. In this instance an organisation produces a product or service of similar quality to competitors, but at a lower cost. This allows businesses to sell their goods at a lower price, or to achieve a greater margin from sales.

- Produce a unique or differentiated product. This involves providing value in a product or service that a competitor cannot provide or match. This is so that customers will consider factors other than price when making purchase decisions.
- Provide a product or service that meets the requirements of a specialised market. A business identifies a particular niche market for its products and/or services. The advantage of targeting such a market is that there may be less competition than the organisation is currently experiencing in the more 'general' market.

How then, can ICT add value? Recently the term has been used extensively to describe different business activities, including describing the effects of ICT use in organisations, with researchers not necessarily describing what is meant by the term. Some, however, have offered hints as to its meaning. Miyazaki, Idota, & Miyoshi (2011) related corporate productivity to different stages of ICT application development and related the stages of development to 'added value productivity'. In this case productivity (and thus, added value) was determined by a formula related to factors such as general capital, software capital and total number of employees.

Small Business and ICT

There is a lack of research into ICT use by small businesses when compared with their larger counterparts (Bayo-Moriones, Billón, & Lera-López, 2013). One of the problems with studies that examine the use of ICT by small businesses is that there is not a standard definition of small business that is universally applied around the world (Burgess et al., 2009). Terms such as 'small business', 'micro business' and 'SME' (small and medium-sized enterprises) can be readily found in the literature. SMEs make up the vast majority of enterprises worldwide (for instance, 98% of businesses in Europe). As such, they are critical to economic growth (Apulu, Latham, & Moreton, 2011). For the purposes of this book, that sector includes any business with up to 20 regular employees. The small business sector is typically characterised by a number of special features (Schlenker & Crocker, 2003):

- Many small businesses are primarily concerned with 'quality of life' and are not a source of growth either in relation to their number of employees or in annual turnover. They typically choose to remain at a constant size for management reasons, such as maintaining quality of life, or other reasons such as not wishing to manage and employ more staff (Burgess, Sellitto, & Karanasios, 2009).
- Many small businesses are lacking one or more major processes that are seen to be core to the tasks of 'doing business' (such as product conception, manufacturing, sales, delivery and/or post-sales service). As such, they are required to turn to other businesses to supply these missing processes.

Within the small business sector there has been a general characterisation of a group of entrepreneurial small business owners who are orientated to risk-taking activity, being strategic and/or embracing innovation (Mazzarol, 2005). This orientation potentially drives the small business to grow and prosper. This leading group is a direct contrast with the majority of small business owners with a lifestyle and/or task-processing orientation, which can potentially relegate the importance of activities associated with growth and innovation (Mazzarol, 2006).

Arguably, the leading entrepreneurial business owners (with their focus on growth, risk-taking and strategy) will tend to have a greater propensity to extend their innovative behaviour to the realms of ICT adoption and application. Such a group could be expected to be proactive when compared with their competitors, being creative with respect to adopting or even considering newly emerging technologies and their applications. Rogers' (2003) classic innovation adoption theory alludes to a small group of leading innovators as being the early users of new ideas and technology, a trait that sets them aside from later adopters and allows them to gain comparable relative advantage within the environment they might share.

Added Value Benefits of ICT to Small Businesses

Historically, small businesses have primarily used their computers for administrative and operational purposes such as accounting, budgeting and payroll. For instance, del Mar, Alonso-Almeida, and Llach (2011, p. 3) examined ICT use by small travel agents in Spain and suggested that the use of ICT could eliminate the need for unskilled workers in areas, "for it automates the most routine tasks with little or no added value". Modimogale and Kroeze (2011) examined SMEs in South Africa and also differentiated between the use of ICT for cost reduction or efficiency improvements and their potential to add value. The authors suggested that more entrepreneurial businesses recognised the potential for ICT to assist in providing information for decision-making and to help 'add value' to small business offerings.

In a comprehensive study of UK small businesses, Higón (2012) noted that benefits of ICT use could be classified into product innovation and process innovation. Whilst most ICT applications affected process innovation, those that were specifically designed for research and development purposes (such as computer-aided design) assisted with product innovation. Also, businesses with a website were seen to be more likely to innovate in regards to products. It was also determined that businesses with a higher number of ICT applications were more likely to experience process innovation.

Mpofu and Watkins-Mathys (2011) developed a framework from the literature to represent the key stages and of ICT adoption in small businesses and the factors that affect these stages. The stages are:

- **Pre-stage** (uninvolved business: may be influenced by government policy)
- Stage 1: **threshold** (keen to try ICT but unsure how to: may be influenced by business environment, suppliers, customers and so forth)

- Stage 2: **beginner** (online recently but unsure how to proceed: driven at this stage by characteristics of owner/manager)
- Stage 3: **intermediate** (has Internet, a website, email but no definite ICT strategy: influenced at this stage by organisational factors such as readiness for ICT; business size, ICT expertise and so forth)
- Stage 4: **advanced** (ICT is integral to business strategy: influenced by the perceived benefits that ICT can provide)
- Stage 5: **innovative** (capability to exploit ICT for both product and process innovation: influenced by formal and informal social networks)

Gilmore, Carson, O'Donnell, and Cummins (1999) examined the types of added value that marketing provided for 60 SMEs in a regional area of Northern Ireland and classified the business aspects of added value across several areas. It is interesting to consider how these areas could apply to ICT use:

- Product-related aspects of added value—where small businesses are able to use ICT to offer a wider range of goods than their competitors.
- Price-related aspects of added value—where businesses competed on price. This would be similar to Porter and Millar's (1985) concept of using ICT to being a low-cost producer.
- Delivery/Distribution-related aspects of added value—the use of ICT to contribute to safe and timely delivery of products.
- Other aspects of added value—other areas of ICT use that might assist in improving business reputation.

What form do ICT applications take when they add value to the activities of an organisation? Ritchie and Brindley (2005) outlined a framework for ICT adoption that identified 'added value' outcomes of ICT use in SMEs. Similarly, Tiernan and Peppard (2004, p. 5) identified a number of ways in which ICT could be employed "on the journey of creating value". Summarised, these ICT applications covered most aspects of business operations, such as the use of ICT to:

- search for information
- improve communications
- improve decision-making
- improve automated recording and monitoring of business processes
- improve work practices
- improve business relationships, and
- make larger-scale business improvements (such as making organisations more flexible or extending the scope of the business).

The work of Gilmore et al. (1999), Ritchie and Brindley (2005) and Tiernan and Peppard (2004) can be used to synthesise a matrix that allows the classification of ICT applications into different types of ICT applications and different forms of added value. Table 2.1 summarises the Matrix of ICT Applications

Table 2.1 Matrix of ICT Applications for Added Value

ICT Applications		Generic Added Value	Added Value (Customer) Benefits (Gilmore et al., 1999)			
Type of ICT Application	Description Source: Ritchie and Brindley (2005); Tiernan and Peppard (2004)		Product Related	Price Related	Delivery and/ or Distribution Related	Other
Improved Information Search	Information search and knowledge acquisition; Reducing search cost					
Improved Communications	Effective communications					
Improved decision Support	Problem-solving capability; Better decision-making					
Improved Recording and Monitoring	Transaction efficiency and effectiveness; Monitoring evaluation and control					
Improved Work Practices	Improved working practices; Improving quality and delivery; Redesigning business processes to improve efficiencies; Facilitating development of new products or services; Enhancing existing products and services; Delivering improved manufacturing techniques; Redesigning workflows					
Improved Relationships	Relationship development; Coordinating supplier linkages; Establishing and sustaining customer relationships					
Improving the Big Picture	Enhancing organisational flexibility; Reconfiguring business networks; Extending the scope of the business.					

Source: Gilmore et al. (1999), Ritchie and Brindley (2005), Tiernan and Peppard (2004)

for Added Value. The idea behind the matrix is that an ICT application can be classified by the type of application (first column in Table 2.1) and its added value benefit. The types of ICT application are derived from Ritchie and Brindley's (2005) added value outcomes of ICT use in SMEs and Tiernan and Peppard's (2004) uses of ICT for creating value. The added-value benefits are based on Gilmore et al.'s (1999), with an extra column included to cater for applications that provide 'generic' added value (that is, value to the business that cannot specifically be translated into direct value to the customer).

Although the classification of ICT usage by small businesses as described in the Matrix of ICT Applications for Added Value is important, there are a range of issues that small businesses need to consider before they are able to use ICT to add value to their businesses. The next section examines some of these through the LIAISE framework.

The LIAISE Framework

Having examined literature pertaining to small business use of ICT, the aim of the remainder of this chapter is to introduce the LIAISE framework, which will be used throughout the rest of the book for analysis of the small business cases.

Supporting Small Business Use of ICT

There has been a growing body of research that suggests that the use of ICT in small businesses is not similar to its usage by larger businesses. Welsh and White (1981) were the first to articulate that small businesses were not really a micro version of their large business counterparts; they had their own style of management and intrinsic operational peculiarities. These defining peculiarities make them the focus of distinct government support structures, regulations and funding provisions (Dennis, 2011). Small business uptake of ICT is a prevalent focus of governments and one that is reflected in the number of official policies developed to support and facilitate such uptake (Burgess et al., 2009). Arguably, the uptake of ICT by small businesses, as promoted through government-based schemes and policies, benefit not only the businesses themselves but positively contribute to the overall economy.

Indeed, the issue of small business adoption of ICT is a consistent focus of governments, industry representatives, small business groups, practitioners and academics (Sellitto, 2011). Within the realms of government activity, various support structures and incentive schemes have been used to encourage the adoption of newly emerging and/or innovative technologies by small businesses. For instance, the United Kingdom's Department of Trade and Industry proposed an e-business adoption ladder that can be used to classify small and medium-sized enterprises (SME) as a result of their Internet adaptability (Department of Trade and Industry, 2004). Another UK government body (Business Link) provided a significant information resource aimed at small businesses to inform them how and why they should utilise online business opportunities. The Canadian government, through the Industry Canada Department, developed a support program to promote the uptake and utilisation of small business online activities (Industry Canada, 2007). The Malaysian government promoted the uptake of ICT by small businesses through the provision of loans and funding opportunities to promote capacity-building, whilst the Singaporean government supported small enterprises by financially contributing to the training of employees of these businesses (Burgess et al., 2009). In an endeavour to encourage small businesses to move to the online environment, Australia's Department of Communications, Information Technology and the Arts (DCITA) produced a six-stage guide in promoting e-business development (DCITA, 2004), allowing small businesses to understand, build and manage their e-business presence.

Another Australian-based initiative that informed the application of ICT across Australian civil society was termed the LIAISE framework, which was originally used in the non-profit sector of the economy (Denison, 2009). This framework provides a guide for addressing various aspects of ICT adoption and use, including gaining access to ICT (through ICT infrastructure, literacy and support), how to use ICT and how to evaluate its effectiveness. Although developed for use by non-profit and resource-poor groups, there are common influencing factors that are shared by small businesses and non-profits when it comes to ICT use (Bingley, Urwin, Hunter, & Burgess, 2010), that is, they both suffer from resource poverty in relation to ICT use in regards to lack of finances to devote to ICT, lack of expertise in its use and lack of time to devote to its use.

The rest of this book aims to use the LIAISE framework to take a holistic approach to examine the use of ICT by small businesses in two countries on either side of the world, Australia and the UK. The notion of a holistic approach is in contrast to many small business studies that examine limited or selective aspects of ICT adoption. The book draws on a set of small business experiences in these countries in regards to ICT adoption and use and maps these to the various components of LIAISE. Another aspect of the book is that it examines the individual stories of these small businesses and how they employ ICT. In order to do this, it is first necessary to introduce the LIAISE framework.

LIAISE—A Framework to Represent the Effective Use of ICT

Early work by Schauder, Johanson, Denison, and Stillman (2005) helped to inform the Australian government's non-profit ICT adoption strategy. Schauder and colleagues proposed the LIAISE framework that was seen as an enabler for non-profits in guiding the adoption and diffusion of ICT, implicitly addressing the important areas of:

- ICT Literacy (L)
- Information Content and Communication (I)

- Access to ICT-based resources (A)
- The Availability of ICT Infrastructure (I)
- ICT Support (S)
- ICT Evaluation (E)

Denison (2009) later used the LIAISE framework to explore ICT adoption amongst community-based organisations, extending the framework to incorporate aspects of specific computer support, networks of people and applications.

The non-profit sector, represented through the range of smaller community-based organisations, has been shown to have common similarities with the workings of the small business sector (Bingley, Urwin, Hunter, & Burgess, 2010; Burgess & Bingley, 2008; Burgess, Johanson, Schauder, Karanasios, Sellitto, & Stillman, 2006; Karanasios, Sellitto, Burgess, Johanson, Schauder, & Denison, 2006). Clearly the framework that was developed for the non-profit sector has relevance and applicability to ICT adoption within the small business domain.

In suggesting a draft information economy strategy for Australian civil society, a report prepared for the Australian Government Department of Communications, Information Technology and the Arts (Schauder et al., 2005) suggested LIAISE to guide the application of ICT across Australian civil society and non-profits in particular. Karanasios et al. (2006) suggested that each aspect of LIAISE should be in place to enable the successful use of ICT. Denison (2009) subsequently evaluated the LIAISE framework through a series of interviews with community-sector organisations in Australia and Italy. The study found that the LIAISE framework provided a useful taxonomy of the factors important to the take-up of ICT. Furthermore, Denison (2009) formulated and projected the different elements of LIAISE framework as shown in Figure 2 interrelating the framework's six defining elements.

Burgess et al. (2006) suggested that the LIAISE framework could be applied to categorising the ICT needs of small businesses. The remainder of this chapter discusses literature related to each aspect of the LIAISE framework with regard to the small business arena.

Infrastructure

The infrastructure component of the LIAISE framework reflects the technological infrastructure that is in place enabling ICT access for an organisation. Examples of infrastructure can refer to broadband Internet availability in a particular geographical area, access to suitable hardware, installation of internal networks where appropriate, opportunities to source external suppliers of infrastructure services and the ability to share ICT resources within the organisation.

Small businesses typically rely on governments or large private businesses to provide the external infrastructure to allow the delivery of services such as telecommunications and Internet access. A number of studies (for

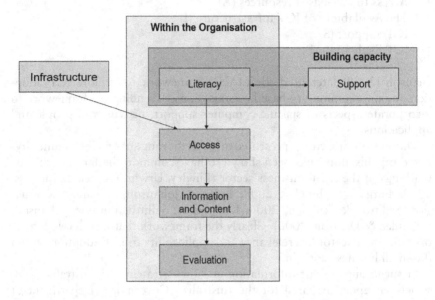

Figure 2.1 LIAISE Framework Components (adapted from Denison, 2009)

instance: Oliveira & Martins, 2010; Sanders & Galloway, 2013) discussed the difficulties caused by lack of infrastructure in developing countries and rural and remote regions of developed countries. For instance, Apulu et al. (2011) found that insufficient infrastructure (including poor service from Internet Service Providers [ISPs]) and unreliable electricity supply were major impediments to effective use of ICT by Nigerian SMEs. A study of Australian small businesses (Kimber & Mason, 2013) found that ISPs that assisted small businesses to move online was a driver in them moving online. The authors also identified lack of support from governments (in regards to policy and initiatives) and lack of loans from banks as limiting factors. Mpofu and Watkins-Mathys (2011) found that when compared to Botswana and Zimbabwe, South Africa had a more competitive business environment, more ISPs and more technology suppliers, and this lead to a faster increase in connectivity by small businesses in that area.

Internal infrastructure issues (such as setting up local networks and print-ers) are less of an issue for small businesses these days than they were in the past since the advent of mobile and wireless networks, although security remained a concern (Brockett, Golden, & Song, 2012).

Literacy and Support

The next aspects of the LIAISE framework to be examined are Literacy and Support, that is, how to access and use ICT effectively and where to source the support services needed when there is a literacy shortfall in the business.

(L)ITERACY

The Literacy element associated with the framework reflects an organisation's understanding of ICT capabilities, allowing it to know how to access ICT and subsequently be able to use the technology. Literacy tends to be governed by the availability of appropriate skills to allow an organisation to realise relevant ICT benefits. Such skill sets might be internal to an organisation and thus readily available or, if not, will need to be sourced externally (see (S)upport). Invariably the availability of ICT-related skills will have a bearing on the understanding of ICT by small businesses and how they can be accessed and used.

Cragg, Caldeira, & Ward (2011) identified access to relevant and appropriate information systems knowledge as one of the important elements associated with ICT adoption and use by SMEs. However, Burgess et al. (2006) noted that in regards to literacy there was a barrier to the general understanding of the importance of ICT in small businesses, as well as how they might access and use technology. Kimber and Mason (2013) noted that lack of awareness of how to use ICT effectively was a barrier to small businesses adopting an online presence. The authors also cited lack of awareness of the benefits and no desire to change as barriers to online engagement. The development of knowledge and organisational learning is critical to realising the benefits of ICT and the Internet (Beckinsale, Levy, & Powell, 2006). A major issue facing many small businesses is that they lack the basic knowledge of how to use ICT effectively, do not know how to evaluate the performance of their ICT and lack the skills to plan for the long-term use of ICT in the business (Burgess, 2008; Denison, 2009). All of these issues were found to limit the adoption of ICT by Nigerian SMEs, who were hindered by a combination of lack of awareness and education about ICT, lack of skills and knowledge-sharing about ICT within businesses (Apulu et al., 2011). In a study of Malaysian SMEs, Tan, Chong, Lin, and Eze (2010) found that smaller businesses were often unaware of the level of financial and technical support that may be offered by government and the private sector.

(S)UPPORT

The Support component of the framework is all-encompassing and reflects the continuous activities that an organisation needs to have in place to support and operate the ICT applications implemented. Sources of ICT support can be external consultants, training courses, technical manuals and so forth. Support activities are broadly focussed and might include knowing where to source upgrades associated with hardware and software, how to implement a website redesign, supporting technical services or knowledge support services for ICT (knowing how to set up, use and maintain ICT systems) or engaging contracted support services where required. In Figure 2.1, Support is positioned to allow the organisation to build internal capacity through improved ICT Literacy.

Burgess et al. (2006) found that small businesses were often unsure of where and how to source ICT expertise when it was not available within the business. Many small business owners relied on informal networks such as family and friends for ICT support. Formal training (such as that provided by consultants) can be perceived to be expensive and may take employees away from their everyday work (Burgess & Sellitto, 2005). Nigerian owner/managers of SMEs were found to be reluctant to invest in employee training for fear of losing them afterwards (Apulu et al., 2011). In a study of African small businesses, Mpofu and Watkins-Mathys (2011) found that small businesses that took advantage of training and support offered by technology suppliers were able to reduce problems with regard to lack of internal ICT expertise.

Taylor, McWilliam, England, and Akomode (2004) noted that small and medium-sized businesses used a range of approaches to developing the skills they needed to use e- business, including gaining 'hands-on' experience, attending short courses, enrolling in higher education courses and consulting experienced staff, such as external consultants. However, there was also a fear that vendors and consultants may not adequately understand the requirements of individual small businesses (Burgess et al., 2009).

Access

The term 'digital divide' is often used to refer to the gap between those who have access to ICT and those who do not. Srinuan and Bohlin (2011) examined digital divide research and found that early research examined the notion of having physical access to technology as driving the digital divide. More recently, socio-economic status and having adequate ICT knowledge/skills were found to also contribute to the digital divide. Thus, the notion of a digital divide can be examined in regards to both access and use of ICT. In the LIAISE framework, Access acts as a milestone which is achieved when both the appropriate levels of Infrastructure (effectively physical access to ICT) and Literacy (knowing how to source and use ICT) are attained and the business has the adequate resources (time, money, skills) in place allowing them to adopt and implement ICT effectively. Effective access to ICT will often be restricted due to the limited small business resource base (Burgess et al., 2006). For instance, Kimber and Mason (2013) noted that lack of time to research, set up or maintain ICT applications, as well as their cost, was an impediment to Australian small businesses moving online.

Typically, finance is needed to purchase technology-related products, whilst time needs to be made available for staff to use and exploit ICT capabilities. Organisations within the small business sector are generally regarded as being resource-poor, exacerbating the ability to access/adopt ICT and moving it further down any priority list they may have. For example, Apulu et al. (2011) found that financial constraints and the cost of implementation of ICT limited the adoption of ICT by Nigerian SMEs.

Jones, Simmons, Packham, Beynon-Davies, and Pickernell (2014) found similar barriers to adoption in micro businesses.

From a small business viewpoint, it is well known that their rate of adoption of ICT as a whole is lower than that of larger businesses (Barba-Sánchez, Martínez-Ruiz, & Jimenez-Zarco, 2007; Deakins, Mochrie, & Galloway, 2004). Any differences between large and small businesses can usually be related to the human and financial resources that are available to devote to the use of ICT. Also, delays in the adoption of ICT generally can be related to a lack of appreciation by small businesses of the benefits that they can offer (Corso, Martini, Paolucci, & Pellegrini, 2001).

Information and Content

This aspect of the LIAISE framework is concerned with *how* ICT can be implemented in the small business environment by managers and owners. The Information and content element associated with the LIAISE framework reflects the ability of an organisation to implement ICT applications. Such applications might be broadly implemented (for instance, email) or can be utilised for a specific purpose by a business (for instance, using a website as a medium to engage a target group). The ability to implement relevant and appropriate ICT applications reflects activities associated with knowing how to find information on using ICT effectively, delivering electronic content to an organisation's constituency and being able to utilise ICT for communication purposes. This aspect of the framework can reflect the creation of electronic data (content) using applications, with the subsequent use of this content to facilitate communication or inform decision-making.

The Matrix of ICT applications for added value introduced earlier in the chapter (refer to Table 2.1) will allow us to classify the various ICT applications adopted by businesses examined in this book according to the specific benefits and the types of added value that they provide for the businesses.

USES OF ICT BY SMALL BUSINESSES

The Sensis study of ICT use by Australian SMEs (Telstra Corporation, 2013) found that 98% of SMEs had some type of computer (desktop or laptop), some seven out of 10 possessed a smartphone and two out of five businesses possessed a tablet computer.

Sellitto, Banks, Monday, and Burgess (2009) reported that small businesses primarily use computers for administrative and operational purposes, noting applications in areas such as accounting, home office, budgeting, payroll management and inventory control. These applications are usually purchased 'off the shelf' rather than customised for specific small businesses purposes (McDonagh & Prothero, 2000). In their literature review of ICT use in rural areas, Galloway and Mochrie (2005) highlighted a number of studies that referred to the use of ICT to automate standard administrative functions. A study of US-based micro businesses by Muske, Stanforth, and

Woods (2004) examined the use of different computer applications within the businesses. The most commonly used applications were the Internet (89%), word processing (87%), financial record-keeping (80%), graphic design (62%) and databases (59%).

Lockett, Brown, and Kaewkitipong (2006) suggested that basic applications like email and Internet access were commonly used by small businesses. However, there was a lower uptake of more complex software, such as financial ledger, supply chain and customer relationship management applications. Similarly, Schubert and Leimstoll's (2007) study of over 1,100 small business (with 10–249 employees) in Switzerland revealed that ICT was used predominantly to support activities such as finance and accounting, HRM (human resources management) and management. Lesser-adopted applications were those related to customer service and marketing/distribution, procurement/purchasing and other activities. There was also some evidence of small businesses using strategic ICT applications, predominantly in the areas of forecasting sales and customer analysis. Jarvis, Dunham, and Ilbery (2006) examined the use of Internet technologies in manufacturing SMEs, noting that seven out of 10 businesses suggested that email use was commonplace and a driver of supply chain relationships to undertake electronic transfer of designs, orders and invoices. Internal use of email amongst employees was also important.

The Sensis study of Australian SMEs (Telstra Corporation, 2013) found that most businesses (96%) were connected to the Internet, just over two-thirds of the businesses had a website and a just over one-third had a social media presence. The most commonly used online applications were email (92%), online banking (86%) and accessing directories (77%). Whilst 35% of SMEs used social networking (the vast majority using Facebook), only 20% of these businesses (7% of overall businesses) updated their social media presence on a daily basis.

Levenburg and Klein (2006) examined the online delivery of customer services in 395 SMEs in the USA, reporting that eight out of 10 of these businesses used the Internet. The authors segmented the SMEs into micro (1–10 employees), small (11–50 employees) and medium-sized (51–250 employees) for comparison purposes. They found that the small and medium-sized businesses used ICT in a similar manner, whilst the micro businesses appeared to "do things differently" (Levenburg & Klein, 2006, p. 143). One reason given by the authors for this observation was that micro businesses were mainly retail and service in nature. These types of businesses tended to deal directly with customers, with high levels of interpersonal contact being considered to be the norm. Levenburg and Klein (2006) found that micro businesses were more likely to use the Internet for research, whereas the small and medium-sized businesses were more likely to use it for providing added value or enhancing customer service. Email represented an important communication tool for all types of businesses. In a study of UK SMEs, Higón (2012) found that adoption rates of PC applications, email, business website, e-commerce and ICT used for research and development purposes increased as business size moved from sole proprietors to medium-sized businesses. For instance, PC applications had been adopted by 66% of sole proprietors, 82% of micro businesses, 90% of small businesses and 95% of medium-sized businesses.

Small business use of ICT is also affected by the industry sector that it is involved in. The Sensis study (Telstra Corporation, 2013) of Australian small businesses found differing adoption rates of ICT across industry sectors. A study of Malaysian small businesses (Tan, Chong, Lin, & Eze, 2010) noted that service-based SMEs were usually smaller in size and manufacturing SMEs were more capital- and human resource–intensive. Service-based SMEs were more likely to adopt ICT to improve coordination with value chain partners.

Evaluation

The Evaluation component of the LIAISE framework reflects organisational activities that measure or seek feedback from the implementation of ICT. This allows an organisation to determine if the initial objectives of introducing ICT have been achieved, as well as identify any problems or issues that may arise. Invariably, the limited resource base of small businesses will preclude them from necessarily having formal processes in place, and informal approaches will be the norm. However, knowing how to evaluate the success of ICT use and performance can provide particular value to small businesses (Burgess et al., 2009).

Small businesses and even researchers examining the activities of small businesses are often not proficient at measuring the benefits of their ICT systems (Bayo-Moriones et al., 2013) and have been noted to have limited understanding and knowledge about how to evaluate the success of ICT usage (Burgess et al., 2006). They tend to lack strategic vision when it comes to ICT evaluation and the capital resources needed to carry it out. These are two important factors that act as inhibitors for many businesses to carry out ICT evaluations (Lin, Lin, & Tsao, 2005). The problem of evaluating ICT effectiveness can be because the adoption of ICT involves costs that may be difficult to document as well as business benefits that are difficult to quantify (Caldeira & Ward, 2002). For example, Eikebrokk and Olsen (2007) focussed on e-business competencies amongst SMEs, indicating that the difficulty of measuring e-business success was one of the limitations of their study. They suggested that the heterogeneous nature of e-business participation was not easy to measure at the individual business level, so success might need to be evaluated across different e-business entities. Burgess (2002) reported three methods, sourced from the literature, that have traditionally been used by small businesses to evaluate ICT use/adoption success:

- *Measures of system usage.* These measures centre on examining data that has automatically been generated from the ICT system. Measures could include the number of transactions generated from use of the system, reports generated by the system and so forth. Measures of usage of systems are perhaps the easiest to measure, but do not always relate to improved productivity or performance.

- *Measures of impact upon organisational performance.* The problem with attempting to measure the impact of ICT systems on business performance in general are that systems are often integrated with other organisational changes (such as improvements in businesses processes) that can affect performance. It is difficult to extract the benefits that ICT provide from benefits provided by other changes in the business.
- *Measures of User Satisfaction.* This is the most common method used to assess the level of ICT success. It usually occurs by asking users or even owner/managers their opinion of the success of a new system. However, such measures are tied to expectations, which may vary between different users and stakeholders, although Bayo-Moriones et al. (2013) discussed literature that found that owner/manager perceptions do constitute a suitable approach to assessing the effect of ICT.

Most research projects that have attempted to evaluate the success of ICT projects in small businesses have surveyed the information satisfaction levels of the owner/ manager. Caldeira and Ward (2002) have also identified approaches that measure the success of ICT in small business, with the use of more strategically oriented systems being able to potentially deliver greater success. Bayo-Moriones et al. (2013) examined Spanish SMEs and found that use of computers and the Internet have an immediate, positive effect in regards to improved communications, both internal and external to the business. They also found that ICT generally has to be in operation for at least one year to realise its potential.

In relation to online activities, Stockdale, Ahmed, and Scheepers (2012) noted that customer engagement and the flow of traffic to a business website were the most frequently cited benefits of social media. The authors examined successful social media use by US businesses and found that they used a combination of quantitative measures (website traffic, time spent online by users, expenditure on marketing, revenue growth) and qualitative measures (insights into success of social media use) to judge its success.

Conclusion

Based on an examination of ICT adoption and use amongst small business entities within the groupings of the LIAISE framework as described in the previous sections, it is possible to add further detail for each component of the framework to reflect the ICT issues faced by small businesses. Figure 2.2 depict the LIAISE framework, which has been annotated with ICT adoption factors that are particular to many small businesses. These include their limited resources, lack of strategic vision, conservative nature, tendency to rely on informal networks for ICT support, use of ICT to undertake

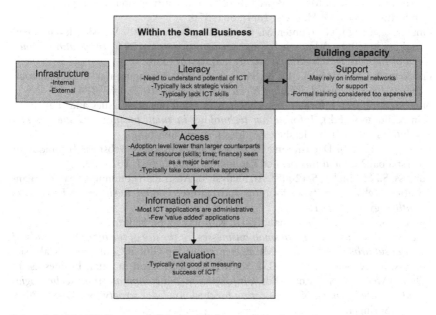

Figure 2.2 LIAISE Framework (adapted for small businesses)

predominantly administrative applications and general lack of knowledge and awareness of how to evaluate the implementation of ICT they might adopt.

This inclusion of important small business ICT adoption factors builds on Denison's (2009) visualisation of the framework. The next section of the book reports on a study that explores the use and uptake of ICT by a group of small business enterprises in the tourism sector, the findings of which are subsequently mapped to the LIAISE framework.

References

Alonso-Almeida, M. D. M., & Llach, J. (2013). Adoption and use of technology in small business environments. *The Service Industries Journal*, 33(15–16), 1456–1472.

Apulu, I., Latham, A., & Moreton, R. (2011). Factors affecting the effective utilisation and adoption of sophisticated ICT solutions: Case studies of SMEs in Lagos, Nigeria. *Journal of Systems and Information Technology*, 13(2), 125–143.

Barba-Sánchez, V., Martínez-Ruiz, M. P., & Jimenez-Zarco, A. I. (2007). Drivers, benefits and challenges of ICT adoption by small and medium sized enterprises (SMEs): A literature review. *Problems and Perspectives in Management*, 5(1), 104–115.

Bayo-Moriones, A., Billón, M., & Lera-López, F. (2013). Perceived performance effects of ICT in manufacturing SMEs. *Industrial Management & Data Systems*, 113(1), 117–135.

Beckinsale, M., Levy, M., & Powell, P. (2006). Exploring internet adoption drivers in SMEs. *Electronic Markets, 16*(4), 361–370.

Bingley, S., Urwin, G., Hunter, M. G., & Burgess, S. (2010). Website development and use in CBOs: A knowledge management perspective. *The International Journal of Interdisciplinary Social Sciences, 5*(5), 327–338.

Brockett, P. L., Golden, L. L., & Song, A. (2012). Managing risk in mobile commerce. *International Journal of Electronic Business, 10*(2), 167–184.

Burgess, S. (2002). Information technology in small business: Issues and challenges. In S. Burgess (Ed.), *Information technology in small business: Challenges and solutions* (pp. 1–17). Hershey, PA: Idea Group Publishing.

Burgess, S. (2008). Determining the cost of small business websites: Technique or crystal ball? *Global Business & Economics Anthology, I*, 202–209.

Burgess, S., & Bingley, S. (2008). An analysis of Australian community based organisation websites by type, location and feature. *Global Business & Economics Anthology, I*, 86–101.

Burgess, S., Johanson, G., Schauder, D., Karanasios, S., Sellitto, C., & Stillman, L. (2006). *Building capacity in small businesses for the use of the internet: A study of 'outer'suburbs in Australia.* SME Entrepreneurship Global Conference, Malaysia.

Burgess, S., & Sellitto, C. (2005). Knowledge acquisition in small businesses. In T. van Weert, & A. Tatnall (Eds.), *Information and communications technologies and real-life learning: New education for the knowledge society* (pp. 47–54). New York: Springer.

Burgess, S., Sellitto, C., & Karanasios, S. (2009). *Effective web presence solutions for small businesses: Strategies for successful implementation.* Hershey, PA: Information Science Reference.

Caldeira, M. M., & Ward, J. M. (2002). Understanding the successful adoption and use of IS/IT in SMEs: An explanation from Portuguese manufacturing industries. *Information Systems Journal, 12*(2), 121–152.

Corso, M., Martini, A., Paolucci, E., & Pellegrini, L. (2001). Information and communication technologies in product innovation within SMEs—The role of product complexity. *Enterprise and Innovation Management Studies, 2*(1), 35–48.

Cragg, P., Caldeira, M., & Ward, J. (2011). Organizational information systems competences in small and medium-sized enterprises. *Information & Management, 48*(8), 353–363.

DCITA. (2004). *E-business guide: An Australian business guide for doing business online.* Canberra: Department of Communications, Information Technology and the Arts (DCITA).

Deakins, D., Mochrie, R., & Galloway, L. (2004). Rural business use of information and communications technologies (ICT): A study of the relative impact of collective activity in rural Scotland. *Strategic Change, 13*(3), 139–150.

Denison, T. (2009). *Diffusion and sustainability of information and communications technologies in community-based non-profit organisations: An exploratory study of Victoria and Tuscany* (PhD). Monash University, Melbourne, Australia.

Dennis, W. (2011). Entrepreneurship, small business and public policy levers. *Journal of Small Business Management, 49*(1), 92–106.

Department of Trade and Industry. (2004). *Business in the information age—International benchmarking study.* London, UK: UK Department of Trade and Industry. Retrieved 15 December 2015 from http://webarchive.nationalarchives.gov.uk/2012 0823131012/http://www.businesslink.gov.uk/Growth_and_Innovation_files/ibs 2004.pdf

Eikebrokk, T., & Olsen, D. (2007). An empirical investigation of competency factors affecting e-business success in European SMEs. *Information & Management, 44*(4), 364–383.

Galloway, L., & Mochrie, R. (2005). The use of ICT in rural firms: A policy-orientated literature review. *Info, 7*(3), 33–46.

Gilmore, A., Carson, D., O'Donnell, A., & Cummins, D. (1999). Added value: A qualitative assessment of SME marketing. *Irish Marketing Review, 12*(1), 27–35.

Higón, D. A. (2012). The impact of ICT on innovation activities: Evidence for UK SMEs. *International Small Business Journal, 30*(6), 684–699.

Industry Canada. (2007). *Ebiz. enable—Where to start.* Industry Canada.

Jarvis, D., Dunham, P., & Ilbery, B. (2006). Local rural labour markets: Enterprising or constraining? *Local Economy, 21*(2), 151–165.

Jones, P., Simmons, G., Packham, G., Beynon-Davies, P., & Pickernell, D. (2014). An exploration of the attitudes and strategic responses of sole-proprietor micro-enterprises in adopting information and communication technology. *International Small Business Journal, 32*(3), 285–306.

Karanasios, S., Sellitto, C., Burgess, S., Johanson, G., Schauder, D., & Denison, T. (2006). *The role of the internet in building capacity: Small businesses and community based organisations in Australia.* 7th Working for E-Business Conference, Victoria University, Melbourne, Australia.

Kimber, J., & Mason, C. (2013). *Internet use by small business: An exploratory study in regional Australia.* Australia: CSIRO.

Levenburg, N. M., & Klein, H. A. (2006). Delivering customer services online: Identifying best practices of medium-sized enterprises. *Information Systems Journal, 16*(2), 135–155.

Lin, K., Lin, C., & Tsao, H. (2005). IS/IT investment evaluation and benefit realization practices in Taiwanese SMEs. *Journal of Information Science and Technology, 2*(4), 44–71.

Lockett, N., Brown, D. H., & Kaewkitipong, L. (2006). The use of hosted enterprise applications by SMEs: A dual market and user perspective. *Electronic Markets, 16*(1), 85–96.

Mazzarol, T. (2005). A proposed framework for the strategic management of small entrepreneurial firms. *Small Enterprise Research: The Journal of SEAANZ, 13*(1), 37–53.

Mazzarol, T. (2006). *Entrepreneurship and innovation: A manager's perspective.* Victoria, Australia: University Press.

McDonagh, P., & Prothero, A. (2000). Euroclicking and the Irish SME: Prepared for E-commerce and the single currency? *Irish Marketing Review, 13*(1), 21–33.

Miyazaki, S., Idota, H., & Miyoshi, H. (2011). Corporate productivity and the stages of ICT development. *Information Technology and Management, 13*(1), 17–26.

Modimogale, L., & Kroeze, J. H. (2011). The role of ICT within small and medium enterprises in Gauteng. *Communications of the IBIMA,* Vol 2011, Article ID 3692988, doi:10.5171/2011.369288

Mpofu, K. C., & Watkins-Mathys, L. (2011). Understanding ICT adoption in the small firm sector in Southern Africa. *Journal of Systems and Information Technology, 13*(2), 179–199.

Muske, G., Stanforth, N., & Woods, M. D. (2004). Micro business use of technology and extension's role. *Journal of Extension, 42*(1).

Oliveira, T., & Martins, M. F. (2010). Understanding e-business adoption across industries in European countries. *Industrial Management & Data Systems, 110*(9), 1337–1354.

Porter, M. E., & Millar, V. E. (1985). How information gives you competitive advantage. *Harvard Business Review, 63*(4), 149–174.

Ritchie, B., & Brindley, C. (2005). ICT adoption by SMEs: Implications for relationships and management. *New Technology, Work & Employment, 20*(3), 205–217.

Rogers, E. M. (2003). *Diffusion of innovations* (5th ed.). New York: The Free Press.

Sanders, J., & Galloway, L. (2013). Rural small firms' website quality in transition and market economies. *Journal of Small Business and Enterprise Development, 20*(4), 788–806.

Schauder, D., Johanson, G., Denison, T., & Stillman, L. (2005). *Draft information economy strategy for Australian civil society*. Melbourne, Australia: Centre for Community Networking Research, Monash University.

Schlenker, L., & Crocker, N. (2003). Building an e-business scenario for small business: The IBM SME gateway project. *Qualitative Market Research: An International Journal, 6*(1), 7–17.

Schubert, P., & Leimstoll, U. (2007). Importance and use of information technology in small and medium-sized companies. *Electronic Markets, 17*(1), 38–55.

Sellitto, C. (2011). *An analysis of information and communication technology (ICT) articles published in leading small business and entrepreneurship journals*. Proceedings of the 34th Institute for Small Business & Entrepreneurship Conference (ISBE 2011), Sheffield, UK.

Sellitto, C., Banks, D., Monday, A., & Burgess, S. (2009). A study of Australian small to medium tourism enterprises (SMTEs) and their ICT adoption. *The International Journal of Knowledge, Culture and Change Management, 9*(6), 1–14.

Srinuan, C., & Bohlin, E. (2011). *Understanding the digital divide: A literature survey and ways forward*. 22nd European Regional Conference of the International Telecommunications Society (ITS2011), Budapest, Hungary.

Stockdale, R., Ahmed, A., & Scheepers, H. (2012). *Identifying business value from the use of social media: An SME perspective*. Pacific Asia Conference on Information Systems (PACIS), Hochiminh City, Vietnam.

Tan, K. S., Chong, S. C., Lin, B., & Eze, U. C. (2010). Internet-based ICT adoption among SMEs: Demographic versus benefits, barriers, and adoption intention. *Journal of Enterprise Information Management, 23*(1), 27–55.

Taylor, M. J., McWilliam, J., England, D., & Akomode, J. (2004). Skills required in developing electronic commerce for small and medium enterprises: Case based generalization approach. *Electronic Commerce Research and Applications, 3*(3), 253–265.

Telstra Corporation. (2013). *Sensis e-business report: The online experience of small and medium enterprises*. Australia: Sensis.

Tiernan, C., & Peppard, J. (2004). Information technology: Of value or a vulture? *European Management Journal, 22*(6), 609–623.

Welsh, J., & White, J. (1981). A small business is not a little big business. *Harvard Business Review, 59*(4), 18–32.

World Bank Group. (2011). *ICT glossary guide*, [http://web.worldbank.org/WBSITE/EXTERNAL/TOPICS/EXTINFORMATIONANDCOMMUNICATIONANDTECHNOLOGIES/0,,contentMDK:21035032~menuPK:282850~pagePK:210058~piPK:210062~theSitePK:282823,00.html#I], Accessed 14 December 2015.

Part II

A Study of Australian Small Tourism Businesses

3 The Australian Small Tourism Business Vignettes

Introduction

A key narrative element of this book is the summary output of semi-structured interviews that were carried out with 21 businesses in South Australia, 20 businesses in Victoria and, subsequently, 15 businesses in the UK. The aim of the interviews was to determine ways in which a representative sample of small businesses were using and managing information and communication technologies (ICT). The interviews were carried out by a number of researchers who used an interview guidance form that had been developed from the literature search phase of the research and refined by means of focus group activity.

We have labelled the reported outcomes of these interviews as 'vignettes'. This term vignette is typically used in social science research to indicate a tool or approach where respondents rate "brief texts depicting hypothetical individuals who manifest the trait of interest (e.g., health) to a lesser or greater degree" on the same scale as their own self-rating (Grol-Prokopczyk, Freese, & Hauser, 2011), but here we are using the term in a more reflective way. We are using the term vignette to denote factual summaries that have been "softened away or shaded at the edges, leaving only the central portions" (Velupillai, 2004, p. 1). This allows us to present the salient issues for each business interviewed in a way that:

- Provides a summary description of the type and nature of the business investigated
- Identifies the broad nature and ICT issues facing the participant organisations
- Removes peripheral conversations from the interview transcripts that do not have direct relevance to the issues at hand
- Protects the identity of the participant organisations, in line with the ethics requirements of such research projects and
- Permits analysis within the LIAISE framework.

The vignettes are reported in historical (or narrative) present tense as they are drawn directly from actual interview transcripts or reports. To further expand on the story, there is one slightly 'extended' vignette provided for each adopter category. Each vignette is appended with an indication of the status of the web presence of each business at the time of completion of this book. Of course, small businesses are known to have a high failure rate, so some of them had not survived at the time of writing this book. This chapter reports upon the first phase of the study that examined the ICT practices of small tourism businesses in Australia.

Background

Why tourism businesses? The initial funding for this study came from the Australian Sustainable Tourism Collaborative Research Centre, who provided funding for a research project to examine the ICT practices of Australian small businesses.

The data collection occurred across two States of Australia, South Australia (SA) and Victoria, examining small businesses located around the capital cities of both States (Adelaide and Melbourne), as well as rural areas.

The investigators targeted small tourism enterprises in conducting the research, many of which tended to be family-run businesses (Getz & Carlsen, 2005). Indeed, tourism is composed of interrelated sectors that include retail, sports, cuisine, agriculture, heritage and regional bodies, many of which are classified as small and medium-sized tourism enterprises (Liu, 2000), with a high proportion being located in regional areas (Morrison & King, 2002). These allowed a range of different types of small businesses to be sampled that were all from the same sector, providing a readily available group of businesses to examine with the LIAISE framework as a mapping tool.

The data for Victoria was collected in the period November 2007 to January 2008. A series of interview questions were identified from the literature. Initially, however, the intention was to hold two focus groups of small businesses to assist in teasing out any further issues surrounding ICT adoption and usage that may have been worth raising in the interviews. Whilst it was intended to hold a focus group in both metropolitan and rural Victoria, the logistics of gathering businesses together near the Christmas period in 2007 meant that it was only possible to hold one focus group, in a rural Victorian town. The remainder of the data collection occurred via interviews with small businesses in surrounding areas of the rural town and in and around the Melbourne CBD (Central Business District) area. Businesses were sourced from online and offline business directories.

The focus group was facilitated by the researchers from SA and the data collection was supported by the use of Audience Response System (ARS) technology, which allowed participants to 'vote' or 'select' from a preselected range of responses and then instantly 'view' group responses to particular questions on a large screen (Banks, Monday, Burgess, & Sellitto, 2010). The use of ARS technology proved to be particularly beneficial to the participating businesses because the group process allowed them to transparently note how others were managing their ICT and to discuss any emerging issues. From this focus group, the researchers slightly modified the questions to be asked during the interviews. Five businesses participated in the focus group and 15 other businesses (five rural and 10 metropolitan) were interviewed in Victoria.

The data for SA was collected in the period December 2007 to February 2008. Businesses were selected from rural areas in South Australia and the capital city, Adelaide. Business details were gathered from a range of sources obtained from local tourism offices and the SA Tourism business website.

As with the Victorian data collection, all the interviews (which typically lasted between 30–60 minutes) were arranged so as to accommodate individual businesses' availabilities, with the interviewers travelling to each business or to a convenient local location (such as a coffee shop). In total, 21 SMTEs were interviewed in SA. Ten of the businesses were in rural parts of SA, the remainder being metropolitan.

Although surveys were considered for the study, the researchers felt that it was not only necessary to examine the factors affecting adoption and use of ICT in some depth, but also to explore the reasons behind the decisions that businesses make in regards to ICT adoption.

In total, the data collection for Victoria and South Australia consisted of 41 businesses, 21 being metropolitan businesses and 20 rural businesses.

The initial focus group and subsequent interview questions allowed the researchers to categorise findings using the various components of the LIAISE framework. For all but the infrastructure element of LIAISE, open-ended questions were used, allowing the capture of ICT adoption themes that could subsequently be categorised. For instance, under the framework's component of:

- Literacy—questions were employed to gain a broad understanding of how ICT were used and availability of ICT skills within the business.
- Support—questions examined how skills in relation to the effective use of ICT were sourced, such as through training and the use of external consultants.
- Access—questions focussed on the resources available for accessing ICT effectively (adequate finance to fund ICT and available time to devote to their setup and use). The questions exploring this category were closely aligned with questions that examined Literacy and Support.
- Information and Content—questions related to how ICT were being employed within the SMTEs.
- Evaluation—questions focussed on how a small business judged the success of ICT use within the business.

The results of the interviews were analysed for ICT themes that were able to be categorised under the general categories of the LIAISE framework.

The research was of an exploratory nature and called for careful sifting and examination of data, a process that does not easily allow data to be automated and computerised, hence manual data analysis was used in preference to using qualitative data analysis software. Collectively the researchers had some 35 years of experience between them in the area of small business ICT adoption/use, reinforcing the themes identified and adding a reliability element to the interview analysis.

Demographics

Table 3.1 summarises the different types of businesses that participated in the study. Tourism businesses that were affiliated with the attraction and tour domains made up over 60% of study participants.

There was a reasonably equal split between the states, although there were over double the number of metropolitan than rural *tour* businesses.

The number of people employed by the businesses that participated in the study is summarised in Table 3.2. Some 71% of business had only 1–5 employees, which is consistent with the notion that businesses engaged in tourism-affiliated industries are predominantly micro businesses.

Table 3.1 Variety and Geographical Location of Participating Businesses

Type of Business	State		Area		Total	Overall Percentage
	Vic	SA	Metropolitan	Rural		
Attraction	8	7	7	8	15	37
Tour	4	6	7	3	10	24
Accommodation	2	5	3	4	7	17
Event	3	1	1	3	4	10
Other	3	2	3	2	5	12
Total	20	20	21	20	41	100

Table 3.2 Type and Location of Participating Businesses

Number of Employees	State		Area		Total	Overall Percentage
	Vic	SA	Metropolitan	Rural		
1–5 (Micro Businesses)	17	12	13	16	29	71
6–19 (Other Small Businesses)	3	9	8	4	12	29
Total	20	21	21	20	41	100

General Background

Most of the businesses (88%) that participated in the study had been in operation for three or more years. There are some interesting observations to be made when examining how long the participating businesses had actually been in operation and comparing this to how they had been using ICT. The majority of the businesses indicated that they had been using ICT for as long as they had been in operation. All the businesses that had been in existence for five years or less indicated that they had been using ICT for the life of the business. One Victorian business did not use ICT at all despite the fact that it had been in operation for over 10 years. In a number of cases the proprietors had been using ICT before they started their businesses, usually in prior employment.

In regard to the sector, the tourism industry is an information-intense sector that has traditionally used a broad and diverse range of information and communications technologies (ICT) to facilitate the capture, collation and subsequent dissemination of information (Sellitto, Banks, Monday, & Burgess, 2009). As such, it might be expected that ICT applications would be important for individual businesses (Buhalis & Law, 2008), perhaps more so than for similarly sized businesses in other sectors. Arguably, with the tourism industry and ICT being so well suited to each other, many technology applications have the potential to be used innovatively to derive strategic and tactical benefits.

As mentioned earlier, another important aspect of the global tourism industry is the high proportion of small businesses that are interlinked to provide the range of products, services and support structures that enables the industry to function. Proprietors and families are often drawn to the industry for lifestyle reasons and often to regional areas, the industry being relatively easy to break into as it does not really require specific or previous experience (Getz & Carlsen, 2005; Liu, 2000; Morrison & King, 2002). This is also the case in Australia, with tourism-based activities being viewed as a significant contributor to a regional area's development (Jackson & Murphy, 2006; Liu, 2000; Sellitto et al., 2009).

Having set the scene for small tourism businesses and provided some of the background of the participants in this first data collection phase, the rest of this chapter tells the individual stories of the participating businesses in regards to how they used ICT in their operations.

The Australian Business Cases

In the previous chapter, the conceptualised LIAISE framework was proposed as an enabler for non-profits to guide them through the adoption of information and communication technology (Schauder, Johanson, Denison, & Stillman, 2005). The conceptual framework identified several areas of ICT that included ICT Literacy (L), Information Content and Communication

(I), Access to ICT-based resources (A), the intrinsic availability of ICT Infrastructure (I), ICT Support (S) and ICT Evaluation (E).

In examining the adoption of ICT by small business entities, it is notable that not all businesses have adopted technology to the same degree. This diversity would be expected, as not all small businesses have the same level of need, skills and entrepreneurial abilities in regards to ICT. Hence, three domains associated with ICT uptake were used to group small businesses into lower, middle or upper categories in regards to ICT. This grouping also serves to provide a common presentation summary for the vignettes that follow. Furthermore, these three domains also align with several areas of the LIAISE framework. A description of the three domains used to group the small businesses relating to their uptake of ICT were:

- *Use and Innovation* in regards to ICT. This domain related to how ICT was being employed within the business. As might be expected, record-keeping and accounting were fundamental elements of ICT available to business, being implemented through the purchase of off-the-shelf software packages (McDonagh & Prothero, 2000). Some businesses were found to also garner better than expected efficiencies after the uptake of ICT in various operational areas, whilst others were noted to achieve baseline results or barely any improvements. Various businesses found that they could be innovative in their application and use of ICT with a number of novel applications within the business. In regards to the LIAISE framework, Use and Innovation of ICT aligns with the Information Content and Communication (I) area. The Information and Content element of LIAISE reflects how the organisation has implemented ICT applications and whether they are broadly based, or specifically applied to certain functions. This area of LIAISE tends to include how ICT can be potentially used in creative and novel situations.

- *ICT Skills.* This domain related to the ability of small businesses to have the available skills to deal with not only the initial adoption of ICT, but also the ability to use existing skills to then fully leverage the value of the technology (Burgess, Sellitto, Banks, & Monday, 2009; Peltier, Schibrowsky, & Zhao, 2009). The skill proficiency amongst businesses varied, and their grouping was based on their perceived practical understanding and familiarity with ICT activities as well as the total number of years they indicated they had used ICT. The businesses having been grouped to the lower classification could be viewed as reflecting naïve ICT users whilst those classified at the highest level are relatively more expert in understanding ICT. In regards to the LIAISE framework, ICT skills aligns with Literacy (L). Literacy reflects an understanding of ICT capabilities and the skills associated with being able to subsequently use various types of computer technology. Where suitable skills are not available within the business they need to be sourced externally, which is an activity that reflects the ICT Support area in the LIAISE framework. In the context of the ICT Skills domain, Support (S) is grouped as a sub-area under Literacy even though it appears as a distinct entity in the original LIAISE framework. Effective access to ICT relies not only on having access to the technology (for instance, Internet access requires the use of an ICT device to access the Internet and effective ICT Infrastructure (I) to deliver the service), but also having the skill (ICT Literacy (L) to use it. Literacy is reliant on access to, or availability of, appropriate skills to derive relevant and appropriate ICT benefits.

- *Governance.* This domain related to small businesses identifying the benefits derived from using of ICT, where benefits were noted as being a direct measure of the ICT performance. There was variability in the benefits reported by businesses with enhanced operational effectiveness being commonly encountered as being significant in cost saving (Burgess et al., 2009; Cragg, Caldeira, & Ward, 2011). However, numerous businesses mentioned increased revenue, extra value for customers and improved decision-making as important business benefits they derived from ICT. In regards to the LIAISE framework, Governance aligns with Evaluation (E). The evaluation area of LIAISE reflects activities that identify, measure and record the organisational value of ICT. Such activities place an organisation in the position of being able to gauge whether ICT objectives and aims have been addressed, and which derived benefits received, which is arguably an intrinsic measure.

Figure 3.1 depicts the association between the LIAISE areas and the small business domains used to group the small businesses.

The rationale for the grouping of small businesses into a lower, middle and upper category in regards to business ICT domain also lends itself to being able to collectively classify each business to an adopter category. Hence, before presenting vignettes, the grouping of small businesses in regards to their ICT adoption has been undertaken to identify those that can be viewed as Leaders, Operationals and Laggards in regards to ICT adoption, with

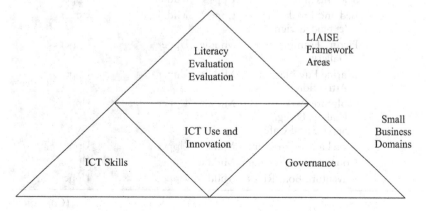

Figure 3.1 The LIAISE Framework's Alignment With Business ICT Domains

the work of Rogers (2003) being used to inform these naming conventions. Rogers (2003) proposed five groups of adopters. The innovators and early adopters were typically the first to try a new idea, technology, process or innovation; this allowed them to gain competitive advantage to lead their rivals. Then followed the majority of adopters that were happy to copy or imitate what the early group of adopters were doing. The Laggards were typically the non-adopters or the last to use new innovations. In this work the Leaders are not so much the first to adopt but the ones that are using ICT at a level that would allow them to gain some form of advantage; the Operationals are small businesses that are using the ICT for standard operational activities; the Laggards are the slow adopters of ICT and when adoption occurs it could be viewed as potential impediment given their dislike for change. Table 3.3 summarises the grouping of the South Australian and Victorian businesses into adopter categories.

Table 3.3 Adopter Categories and the ICT Domains

Adopter Category	Business Name	ICT SKILLS	ICT GOVERNANCE	ICT USE AND INNOVATION
ICT Leaders	Market Tours	Upper	Upper	Upper
	Recreation and Nature Park	Upper	Upper	Upper
	Nautical Craft Company	Upper	Upper	Middle
	Chinese Philosophy	Upper	Upper	Middle
	Holiday Tours	Upper	Upper	Middle
	Inner City Tour Company	Upper	Middle	Upper
	Cherry Growing and Marketing	Upper	Middle	Upper
	Sea Museum	Upper	Middle	Upper
	Bed and Breakfast (extended vignette)	Upper	Middle	Upper
	Picture Framing and Gallery	Middle	Upper	Upper
	Marine Life Nature Attraction	Middle	Upper	Upper
	Sculpture Park, Gallery, Design Service and Café	Middle	Upper	Upper
	Motel and Apartments	Middle	Upper	Upper
	Country Hairdressing	Middle	Upper	Upper
	Adventure Boat Rides	Middle	Upper	Upper

(Continued)

Table 3.3 (Continued)

Adopter Category	Business Name	ICT SKILLS	ICT GOVERNANCE	ICT USE AND INNOVATION
ICT Operationals	Beach Hostel	Upper	Middle	Middle
	Aromatherapy	Upper	Middle	Middle
	Weddings and Events Planning	Middle	Upper	Middle
	Country Club and Golf Course	Middle	Upper	Middle
	Booking Office	Middle	Upper	Middle
	Tour Company (extended vignette)	Middle	Middle	Upper
	Corporate Catering	Middle	Middle	Middle
	Indigenous Art Gallery	Middle	Middle	Middle
	Period Farm and Cottage	Middle	Middle	Middle
	Country Trips	Middle	Middle	Middle
	Spa and Coffee Shop	Middle	Middle	Middle
	Mini Tours	Middle	Middle	Middle
	Motel	Middle	Middle	Middle
	Children's Entertainment	Upper	Middle	Lower
	Backpacker Company	Middle	Lower	Upper
	Farmers Market	Upper	Lower	Middle
ICT Laggards	Guided Tours	Lower	Upper	Lower
	Rural Market	Middle	Lower	Lower
	Beauty Salon	Middle	Middle	Lower
	Australiana	Middle	Middle	Lower
	City-Based Walking Tours	Lower	Middle	Lower
	Rural Riding Academy	Lower	Middle	Lower
	Personalised Tours	Lower	Middle	Lower
	Airport Passenger Transport	Lower	Middle	Lower
	Aboriginal Artwork	Lower	Lower	Lower
	Guided Golf Tours (extended vignette)	Lower	Lower	Lower

The grouping of businesses in Table 3.3 is visually depicted using a black-grey-white visualisation, with black shading reflecting an upper ICT rating, grey a middle level and white a lower one. The original scheme used traffic light colours of green (upper), amber (middle) and red (lower). The use of a black-grey-white visual was directed by publishing limitations. The allocation of each business into the three respective adoption groups was based on a numerical scoring approach collectively determined by the researchers. The Laggards had a cumulative score range of 0–2, the Operationals scored 3–4 and the Leaders scored 5–6. An upper-black rating was allocated 2 points, a middle-grey rating 1 point and a lower-white rating was allocated 0 points.

The ICT Leaders

Market Tours

Background

The owner of this five-year-old business has a long history as a chef and has maintained a stall at the city's local fresh food and gourmet produce market for 20 years. The business offers a number of walking tours of the local market, allowing people to sample and learn about various culinary produce. There are several types of culinary tours offered, either at breakfast time or during the morning, which take around two hours to complete. People who participate in the tour receive a history of the market and an overview of its products and are also provided with an opportunity to interact with suppliers, retailers and producers. The tour serves the national and international tourism market, and the business has expanded in line with a general growth in tourism to the state.

The Use of ICT

ICT has been used by the business since its inception, and the business currently uses a desktop PC (personal computer) and laptop running Windows XP, plus mobile phones and PDA (personal digital assistant). The computers are backed up on a daily basis to different types of media that include an external disk drive and compact disc, with important financial data being moved to an off-site location weekly.

The owner was quite enthusiastic about the role of ICT in the tourism sector in general, and for his business in particular. By gathering and recording information from people during tours, he has been able to use various computer applications to analyse and subsequently identify what makes a tour successful. It is these types of insights that have allowed him to generally improve the experience of people on future tours, or be in a position to more appropriately align them to specific visitor and tourist groups.

Potential customers are able to make a tour booking via the website, at which point an SMS (text message) is sent to his PDA phone advising him of relevant details. This same information is sent to the calendar stored on his computer at his central office. At the same time, his bank receives the money and the person who has made a booking receives confirmation information.

He is keen to expand his use of ICT in the business and has been exploring the possibilities of being able to better communicate with larger tour groups, where there is a risk that some of the people in the group do not clearly hear the story he is telling. He is interested in using similar technology to that used in art galleries where individuals carry a small mobile device that contains a recorded commentary, possibly in different languages.

One problem that he faced was the increased volume of work generated by electronic communications. This has demanded more of his time and he is conscious that potential customers increasingly expect an immediate response to their queries. He would prefer that all customers would use the electronic booking and payment system but is aware that older age groups, who make up a significant portion of his customer base, are not always willing to use the technology. The current business website is accessed via the larger market website and provides for electronic bookings.

The business uses several social media platforms (Twitter, Facebook and Instagram) allowing it to interact with followers through posts related to the walking tours, the promotion of the food market where the stall is located and related culinary events that might be promoted by tourism entities.

Current Status

The range of tours and events offered by this business has expanded and the website is now considerably richer in terms of links to external sites. Most social media are accessible from the site.

Recreation and Nature Park

Background

This business was approximately 10 years old and comprises two interrelated and complementary entities, namely a wildlife nature park and a café. Although the owner originally became involved in the business to accommodate a lifestyle choice, he has now adopted a growth strategy that has seen a 17–20% increase in visitor turnover in the 24-month period prior to the interview. The business draws its customer base mainly from within state boundaries, with regular visitors from the local region. The owner indicated that it had been difficult to attract international and out-of-state visitors because Internet access was restricted to a telephone dial-up mode due to the physical location of the business. It is anticipated that once broadband became available within the next couple of years, a new avenue for attracting clients would emerge.

The Use of ICT

The owner has had many years of experience in ICT that was gained working for a large Australia-wide business and he is confident that he could quickly learn about new technologies if they were required or were appropriate to use in the business. ICT was not seen as a major tool for competitive advantage, there being only a very small number of other locations in Australia that feature the particular wildlife that were the central focus of the nature park. The owner suggested that ICT may in the future offer opportunities for collaborative ventures with the other similar attractions in other parts of Australia.

The business uses two linked Point of Sale (POS) computers (Windows 2000) in the café, with a separate laptop being used for the wildlife attraction side of the business. Twenty people are engaged to act as part-time guides to run the park's activities, with ICT being instrumental in determining work rosters and for contacting people by SMS to advise them of when they are required. This relatively high number of part-time staff has led to the development of formal backup and contingency policies to ensure business continuity even with guides who have little ICT experience. The POS data is backed up daily to hard disk and flash drive, the laptop being backed up to flash drive also on daily routine.

The business has also installed webcams after initial requests from customers. The animals that form the focus of the wildlife attraction are mainly nocturnal, spending their days in burrows. They are sensitive to bright light, and they do not react well to flash light emitted from cameras. The installation of webcams in the burrows allowed the animals to be viewed from either the park proper or the nearby café. Once broadband becomes available, the owner is planning to stream live images and video from the webcams on the business's website. The current website features both the café and the attractions associated with the nature park, and a three-minute YouTube clip is used to promote all the attractions at the venue. The business was yet to adopt the prominent social media channels such as Twitter and Facebook for business purposes, however presence on open review sites such as TripAdvisor has resulted in the business being highly rated by people.

Current Status

The café side of the business appears to have closed down, but the nature park is still active. The website for the nature park provides access to considerable literature about the particular wildlife at the nature park, but it appears that bookings are only possible by phone. The YouTube links are no longer evident on the website.

Nautical Craft Company

Background

This two-person business, based in a busy city-centre market, has been selling wooden craft items for the past 28 years. The owner indicated that the company is at the mercy of seasonal buying and commented that business was "very slow until October, and then it took off over Christmas". Their aim for this business is to maintain and then improve their current lifestyle.

The Use of ICT

The market the business operates from has no electricity so paper records are created at the market with subsequent data entry performed at home. When questioned about the use of a portable computer, he commented that he could not justify the cost of a laptop, and that bookkeeping only takes around one hour per week.

Internet is used from home to research design possibilities for new products for the market stall. The owner is competent with ICT, having used computers since the start of the business and also having written an Apple-based cash register system. He is self-taught, largely from books and magazines, and can call upon his son, a web designer, when required. There is a formal data recovery plan with backup taking place monthly.

The business has a professionally developed commercial website with the aim of capturing a worldwide market. This strategy has paid dividends with most of their business coming from state and/or international clientele. One feature of the website is the ability for customers to pay via credit card or PayPal, but the owner noted that no one has ever paid for a product using PayPal. He has received positive feedback about his website, with some customers expressing surprise that this small market-based business has such a good website.

This company has not explored social media tools; however, the owner did not rule out the possibility of using them in the future. The owner commented that they "don't need them at the moment". Other than the lack of power to his shop, the main barrier that would limit adoption of other ICT is cost. Although he updates his hardware every one to three years, he does not feel that investment in a laptop would offer any significant benefits for the shop.

Overall, this business may not be seen as being innovative in their use of ICT, but they are very efficient in the way they employ them. They run a 'tight ship' and have developed a professional-looking website, and successfully generated another stream of revenue.

Current Status

The website design is virtually identical although payment is now only via credit card, not PayPal. The business has a Facebook page that is quite active. The business is also listed in a number of local business directories.

Chinese Philosophy

Background

This eight-year old business is located in the city and sells products and consultation services related to the Chinese Feng Shui system. This is a small business, comprising a husband and wife whose main aim is to run an efficient business. The wife is much more technically astute than the husband, joking that "my husband is very low-tech, so I keep things low-tech for him".

The Use of ICT

The business has a PC running Windows XP and has just bought a new laptop. It reviews its need for hardware upgrades every few years. The business feels that computers can provide value in marketing, record-keeping and supply chain areas.

The business requires all its record-keeping and communications to be electronic. It has been using computers for the past 10 years (not just for this business) and has developed an online version of the physical shop. However, when asked how closely the virtual and the physical shops were, the owner stated that although the business sells the same products and services, these were not linked electronically. Each face of the business uses different software and databases are not linked.

The business has investigated social media, incorporating Google blogs and YouTube videos on their website. It generally does not like YouTube videos, as advertising on them takes the focus off the products and services. The business also has a Facebook fan page with a few hundred followers.

The business backs up its computers every month to an external hard drive. The business feels that it has the computer skills necessary for both now and in the future, although it has, in the past, hired external consultants to help develop the website and computer systems.

Current Status

At the time of writing the business website had been simplified, but the functionality was similar. There was no indication that the business had a social media presence.

Holiday Tours

Background

This small metropolitan tour business had been operating for over a decade. Originally the business operated 'high end' tours, but had changed to offer more popular tours to the younger market, and the business had expanded as a result. The interviewee was the owner of the business.

The Use of ICT

The business has been using ICT for almost a decade, mainly for accounting-related matters, such as invoicing, and relied heavily on online banking, making direct deposits to suppliers and placing orders online. The business operated with one PC and one laptop.

The business had a basic 'brochureware' website (that it, the website only showed information and had no other features) and had no interest in social networking.

The current low-level use of ICT within the business is interesting as the owner is rated as having a very high level of ICT expertise. In this instance the usage is perhaps reflected in the often-conservative nature of small business owners rather than the level of ICT knowledge. The owner suggested that customers are asking for an online booking option and, interestingly, the business has been pushing suppliers to adopt online transactions. Also, the business is moving towards introducing a loyalty program that represents a more advanced ICT use. This would improve the business rating for ICT Use and innovation in the future. Also, the business is rated highly in regards to ICT governance, with regular, off-site backup of vital business data, regular measurement of the benefits that ICT provide and a review of the suitability of ICT every one to two years.

Current Status

No details could be found about this business online at the time of writing.

Inner City Tour Company

Background

This business was established in early 2004 by the owner, who identified that the centre of the city had a plethora of small laneways, nooks and curios that could provide visitors with an assortment of different experiences associated with history, fashion, cafés and shopping. She used her local knowledge of the inner city to devise guided walking tours that are predominantly aimed at the international tourist. One of her strategic aims in the beginning was to tap into the international market and to grow the client base. This is important, as tourism per se appeared to target new customers rather than accommodating the needs of repeat customers. Initially a solo operation, the business now has at least 10 people that are involved in delivering tourism-related products.

The Use of ICT

The business has made good use of communication technology in order to achieve some of the primary business objectives of growth and efficiency.

Mobile devices allow the owner to be constantly on the move as a tour guide but to also remain in touch with other aspects of the business.

The business uses a single PC running Windows XP and an assortment of computer applications to maintain scheduling and also to apply costing models to the tours that operate. This prevents over-booking of tours and identifies when a second tour should be organised to accommodate demand.

The business's website is important in providing information about all the tours offered as well as focusing on the city as a destination city. The website assists with promoting tours through testimonials and relevant photos. Importantly, the interactive website allows the company to directly manage customer enquiries and capture bookings, thus negating the use of an intermediary. Indeed, the Internet provides a major booking source (70% of business) and has allowed the business to grow quickly. The website allows the business to attract international customers before they arrive in the city. Previously, the business used a third-party booking service which was found to be cumbersome and prevented the business from running cohesively. The owner noted that the website booking system allowed the business to gain an edge over competing tour businesses that did not have this facility directly on their website. The website also links to affiliate tourism sites to provide increased opportunities and assist prospective customers with a broad range of information. Furthermore, the owner uses the Internet proactively to research competitors to see how they compare to the business's own products. The adoption of the website also allows the business to offer tour gift vouchers, a feature that was triggered by customer enquiries. It would appear that the gift voucher offering allows the business to generate positive cash flow well in advance of delivering the tour service.

Current Status

The website is still vibrant and rich with links. The business originally had both Facebook and MySpace sites which provided their first foray into using social media. MySpace has since been dispensed with, whilst Facebook has become a platform that is used to profile the business's tour offerings as well as identify and link to various city events and activities. By 2013, the Facebook fan base had attributed over 1,000 likes to the business's content. The business adopted YouTube in early 2010, which contributed to expanding the business's social media activities. Not one of the uploaded videos was created by the business, the majority of uploaded videos originating with past customers who captured their own video views of the tours offered by the company. Over the years, the business has been featured on several local, national and international TV media programs and has links to these clips via its YouTube presence, allowing professionally created content to be used for promotion purposes. The Twitter social media platform has also been adopted and has built up over 3,500 followers, providing the business with another social media marketing channel.

Cherry Growing and Marketing

Background

This is a rural micro business that has been in operation for more than two decades selling cherries directly to the public and via markets. They have two main growing areas that are roughly 50 km apart, providing different 'micro climates' that allow for diversification in their product offerings. The extra location also provides an alternative if the main crop fails. The business normally functions with two employees (the full-time owner and one part-time employee), but at harvesting time approximately 30 people are employed. The business mainly operates as a lifestyle business, although, especially during harvesting time, there is an emphasis on efficiency.

The Use of ICT

The owner of the business was trained in computer use in his previous employment and this knowledge has carried through to the current business, where computers have been in operation for over a decade. ICT are used for basic tasks such has record-keeping, but there are also a number of innovative uses; for example, the Internet is used to research growing techniques and to source employees. The business has an information-based website but no social media presence.

The business has established a remote ICT system at the alternate site to notify the owner (by telephone call) when the temperature gets too low so that he can travel to the site to protect the crop against frost. However, he commented that this could be a very time-consuming aspect of the business and deflected attention from other aspects of the business. The business viewed the systems that had been set up as crucial but identified finding support when it is needed at short notice as a major problem with ICT use in the business. Thus, whilst it would generally be regarded that having strong ICT skills is a bonus to a business, the owner would have preferred to be able to turn to someone else when there was a problem.

Whilst the ICT skill levels and innovation of the owner are impressive, the business was only assessed as being average in regards to ICT governance. They consider upgrading their ICT every 3–5 years, with the owner commenting that 15 years earlier he would not have seen this as being necessary at all. Also, there is no mechanism used to evaluate the success of ICT, indicating that they are successful "when they are running".

Current Status

The design of the website remains unaltered. The business now has a Facebook presence which it updates on a monthly basis with images of the crops. There is little interaction on the page.

Sea Museum

Background

This family-driven organisation has two distinct business areas, one being a museum dedicated to a specific sea creature, the other relating to tours and expeditions. The long-term aim of the business as a whole is to carry out research into the life of these creatures and to track the effects that human-kind has upon them. The aim of the museum aspect of the business is to raise awareness of the issues relating to these particular sea creatures and is heavily subsidised by tours to see the creatures in the ocean. They have been in operation for more than 10 years and have identified the international market as their largest sector, with three-quarters of their customers being from overseas. The primary aim of the business is to keep growing the business; however, in the last two years, the amount of business they have attracted has not changed.

The Use of ICT

Technology plays a significant role within their organisation, the interviewee commenting that computers support the exhibitions and enable online bookings to both the museum and tours for museum visitors who wish to see the animals in their natural setting. Computers are also used for record-keeping, although they use extensive paperwork as well.

The business has been using computers since its inception, and currently uses four desktop computers (housed at the museum) and a laptop (which is used for the tours). Their website is interactive, with areas to view information about the museum and to book tours. The booking facility even shows how many places are left on each tour. Branching off from their website, they have also started a Facebook group. This was initiated by an employee who was an avid user and approved by the owner, who also uses Facebook.

The organisation considers its computers to be a vital and integral part of the business and feel that they could not survive without ICT.

Current Status

The main website primarily serves the tour/expeditions aspect of the business as well as having links to bookings, historical stories of the founders of the business and a gallery featuring an extensive range of photographs and videos. An information-only page details the opening times and location of the museum.

Bed and Breakfast (Extended Vignette)

Background

This rural B&B had been in operation for approximately eight years at the time of interview. It had two guest bedrooms with en-suite facilities and offered access to a guest lounge, kitchenette and dining room. The guest profile was 35% overseas, 55% from Australia outside the state and 10% within the state.

In regards to business direction, the owner indicated that whilst they ran the business to improve their lifestyle, they were still keen for it to be run on an efficient basis and for it to expand. It is perhaps not surprising that the business was regarded as an ICT leader as they were very meticulous in the conduct of other areas of the operation. They kept very detailed records about how customers find out about them. They were able to describe what types of customers they get and the reasons they visit the B&B. The owner also discussed the importance of more traditional forms of promotion in addition to using the Internet, such as using print media, being a member of local associations and having cooperations with tour businesses. The business was in a strong growth phase and links were being built with local associations and tour businesses, but it was felt that these connections would take some years to mature.

The Use of ICT

This business was regarded as an ICT leader due to the ICT expertise of the owner and the innovative manner in which it used ICT. Its governance process was judged as being adequate.

Four computers had been in use at one time, but these had been recently rationalised into two, with a laptop on the horizon later in the year. The main business areas that ICT were applied to were marketing/selling, customer services and finance/accounting. Not surprisingly (given his other responses) the owner identified marketing/selling as the area where ICT provided the best business value. At the time of the interview most contact with suppliers occurred via telephone, but communication with customers was split between the use of telephone and the Internet.

The owner suggested that 60% of his records were kept on computers at the time of interview. As suggested already, the owner viewed this as a vital part of knowing about the customers that the business attracted. Bookings received by telephone were initially logged on paper and then transferred to the computer database. Internet bookings, either from customers or other agents, were also entered into the database. The owner was very keen to use the Internet as a promotion tool, but at the same time suggested that print advertising was still important, suggesting that "print media now is not really the big thing, [but] you still have to have it, definitely, you still have to have it".

The owner was enthusiastic about a Tourism Commission software package that gave all SMEs access to Internet and statewide bookings.

The business had a website which it described as being "fully interactive". The original website was built by a vocational education student in 1999 and was presented as a relatively static website with links to a blog and YouTube presentations to allow potential guests to gain some impression of the local attractions and events. The owner had then expanded its functionality. He had also arranged for a 'blog' to be on the website for interaction with past and potential customers and used it to refer customers to YouTube videos of the local area. Having control over the website meant that the owner was able to update it and keep the information current. The owner commented that it had recently printed "1,000 or so" brochures and that they were now out of date because of changes in room availability or details of local events, but that it was able to keep the website "updated, in you know, 20 seconds" with the latest details.

As expected from the previous discussion, the business was considered to be ICT literate and felt that the levels of skill were higher than those of known competitors. The owner put this partly down to his analytical mind and his previous work in computers and communications. The business had invested in 'mail washer', software that was located on an external server so that it could download emails after they had been virus-checked rather than load them directly into the business computer. The owner considered he had the knowledge and expertise to deal with any practical issues raised by the technology relevant to the business and regarded the business as being "ahead of the game and quite happy being there". Guests could, on request, have access to emails, but this was not strongly encouraged due to the need to ensure the integrity of the system.

The owner suggested that he reviewed the need to upgrade his ICT on an annual basis. However, he did indicate that "I do keep an eye on you know, papers and newspapers, magazines, see what's out there, see what's current and that sort of thing . . .". This was part of an overall plan that could lead to an upgrade occurring towards the end of the financial year.

He was comfortable with backing-up procedures although he did not have a formal policy for managing this on a regular basis. The use of two computers gave him some sense of security on the basis that it was unlikely that both would fail at the same time. However, he also acknowledged that 18 months previously, in a very hot summer, a power transformer at the end of the street had overheated and shut down a number of times for three or four hours. He was aware that this sudden loss of power posed a threat to the computers and it was partly in response to this concern that consideration was being given to a laptop computer.

When asked about judging the success of their ICT the answer was a little vague. The owner indicated that his wife worked in the finance area and knew exactly how much everything cost in regards to a night's accommodation by spreading all costs (including ICT) over the year. In that way the overall return could be determined, but it may be difficult to extract the benefit of ICT specifically from that. This would not be the first business to have difficulty determining the benefits of ICT compared to knowing the costs.

At the time of the interview, the website provided images and details of the accommodation, special 'packages' on offer, tariffs, booking facilities (via a database), directions to the property, and links to local wineries, restaurants and attractions.

Current Status

At the time of writing the website design had been updated. Booking and payment occurred through a third-party website, but its appearance showed seamless integration into the business website. Additionally, there are now 'live' links to a calendar of events in the region that can be filtered by searches of festivals, music, art, wine, markets, tours, food and sport. There are still specific links to local wineries, restaurants and attractions.

The website indicates that free Wi-Fi is now offered at the B&B.

Since the initial interview, the business has embraced social media with links on the website to Facebook, Twitter, Flickr, Foursquare, YouTube and TripAdvisor. In addition there is also a link to the online communication tool, Skype.

The business's Facebook page is kept up to date on a regular basis and includes some comments and reviews by customers. In addition to basic details of the business and current events, there is also a direct link to the business's TripAdvisor page, which included traveller pictures and reviews. The business has also embedded its booking engine so that customers are able to book directly without having to be referred to the business website or a third-party website. Other key aspects of the website (such as special offers) are available.

The business Twitter page is mainly used to provide details of activities and events in the local area, mostly by 'retweeting' these from the source.

The Flickr page showed the images of the business property that were on their business website. The YouTube page was actually a 'channel' created by the owner. It contained a number of videos that did not appear to link directly to the business. The Foursquare page had had no content added in the previous two years. Apart from the Flickr page, it would seem that the most logical thing to do would be to remove the links to these websites.

A quick search of the Internet (Google) revealed that it was possible to book accommodation at the property via the following websites: Booking. com, Airbnb, Wotif, TripAdvisor, Lastminute and other local accommodation booking services.

Additionally, the business was listed on a number of local business directories.

All in all, it appears that the innovative practices and ICT skills of the business that lead to a high rating being given to the business in the areas of ICT Expertise and ICT use and innovation at the time of interview have resulted in a the business now extending its online operations with a sophisticated website and dynamic social media presence (when compared to similar businesses). The average ranking allocated for ICT governance is perhaps again reflected in the number of links to out-of-date social media websites that could be easily removed with little effort.

Picture Framing and Gallery

Background

This gallery and picture framing business is a rural business and has been operational for the past 11 years. The market they primarily serve is a very local one, with the occasional interstate transaction. They have expanded every year since establishment and, when the interview was conducted, were trying to recruit a third member of staff. The main focus for the owners is to run an efficient business with the aim of maintaining or enhancing a particular lifestyle.

The Use of ICT

The business has been using computers since they were established and are of the opinion that "you couldn't live without them". They have two PCs and a laptop, all running Windows XP, with one PC connected to the Internet. The computers were originally all networked but have not been reconnected since moving to new premises.

Record-keeping is undertaken on the computer, but they do also keep paper copies of all the quotes, receipts and job invoices, mainly for backup purposes. They are able to use the computer to automate picture framing using industry-standard software to control frame cutting.

They have set up their own website which currently only provides basic information. The interviewee was investigating the option of making it more interactive, but a shortage of time means that this has not yet been fully achieved. One interactive option they do have on their website is an 'added value' facility for the customer to see how their picture would look once framed.

They have not yet explored the use of social networking.

The ICT skill level of the owners could be considered as intermediate, as they know most of the computer terms listed. The owner recognises the importance of computers, noting that when they started the business 11 years ago it was rare to see them in small businesses, but they are now a common business tool.

When the owners have sought computer training courses, they have been dissatisfied with them, their main need being more one-on-one help with implementation of software and hardware.

The level of ICT governance in the business was assessed as high. They review their hardware and software needs every three months, and the owner has a weekly backup copy with him at all times.

Current Status

The website has now been redesigned but still only provides basic information about the services offered by the business. A Facebook presence had been created and was updated by the business every month or so, usually with images of new works of art. There was little interaction on the page.

Marine Life Nature Attraction

Background

This marine life natural history attraction has been in operation for a little over six years and moved to the current central metropolitan location about one year ago. The business employs two full-time and two part-time staff. The motivation for commencing the business was related to the owner's lifestyle interest, but developed into a clearer business operation once it was realised that interest in specific marine life was receiving increased attention in the media. Interest was initially local but gradually expanded to include national and international customers.

The Use of ICT

The business owns and operates a single personal computer that had recently had the operating system updated (Windows Vista from XP) with help from the business owner's daughter. The approach to data management is to initially record details on paper then to transfer the data onto the computer. A traditional non-electronic cash register is used for day-to-day business operations with collected financial totals being transferred at the end of the day to a spreadsheet. The spreadsheet is also used to record visitor demographics and inventory details. The owner strongly feels that a manual system was still required because power failure could have an adverse impact upon any ICT that was in use when dealing with visitors to the attraction venue.

The owner uses the spreadsheet to generate a monthly report that provides a detailed breakdown of sales by item, to help to track how well the various items of stock are selling and the profit levels for each item summary. This data forms the basis for future buying patterns. In a similar manner the owner analyses visitor demographics to determine where the advertising dollar is best spent. Furthermore, the owner of the business manages her own tax affairs because she feels that this helps her to keep an active understanding of business costs and profits.

The Internet is used extensively by the owner to identify potential new suppliers and products that she might be able to use. The Internet offers her the benefits of efficiency and breadth of search. The business has its own website, designed by the owner but implemented by an external consultant.

Various products related to the natural history attraction are offered via the website and online orders can be placed on the website or advised via email; however, no direct online payment method currently exists. In addition to marketing material, the website offers information relating to the marine life that forms the focus of the attraction and a discussion board is provided for hobbyists.

Data is backed up onto a flash disk every two days and to CD-ROM annually. A comprehensive paper trail is also maintained. The business's ICT requirements are formally reviewed roughly every two years, although the owner does monitor developments periodically to identify any technologies or ICT services that could be of benefit to the business.

The focus of this business upon a specific marine attraction leads the owner to feel that ICT would not confer any benefits to any potential competitors. The only significant threat that she sees for the business is that some potential competitors may be able to access government funding that would provide them with a stronger position.

Current Status

No details could be found about this business online at the time of writing.

Sculpture Park, Gallery, Design Service and Café

Background

This small (two full-time plus two part-time staff) business was originally established in 1982 as a gallery and working sculpture studio. The business designs and builds sculptures and has links to Japan and Spain where their sculptures are sold. They experienced limited local sales and in 2007 decided to expand the business and develop the premises as a café to allow them to sell wine as well, later adding a coffee machine and tapas. They also offer sculpture and painting classes, targeted mainly at corporate groups. They have attracted a local audience but are gradually drawing from wider state tourism.

The Use of ICT

Use of ICT in the business goes back to the early days of the Amstrad personal computer (late 1980s). One of the business owners was so appalled by the 'clunkiness' of the system that she bought an iMac as soon as it appeared (1998) and the business, as is typical with many arts-related users, has stayed with them ever since. They currently have two laptops and two desktop machines.

One of the chief benefits of ICT for the business is that they can design a piece of artwork in their studio, scan it and then send the image by email overseas and receive feedback the following day. This allows them to make any modifications and then start work on the actual sculpture. All designs and final sculptures are scanned or photographed and the images archived on the iMac for future reference. Skype is used to show designs to their contact in Madrid and there is some interest in the use of Facebook to reach a wider audience.

All records relating to the business are held on the computer, including designs, course bookings, finances for tax purposes and information relating to bookings and café supplies. Email is actively used to communicate with customers and suppliers. They have a website that provides details of their various activities and a gallery of sculpture and artwork images.

There is no formal recovery plan in the event of major failure but they do back up once per week. Their latest system provides automatic backup based on a user-defined schedule. They have had excellent support for the Mac in the first year as part of their purchase deal and, on the few occasions it has been needed, have found continued support to be good.

Current Status

The website for the business comprises a single page noting that the business is no longer in its original location and that a new website will be forthcoming.

Motel and Apartments

Background

This family-run rural motel and apartments business has been managed for 3–5 years by the current manager, who has taken over from his parents who had run the business for 27 years. Originally this was a lifestyle choice for the current manager, but since taking the business over from his parents he has set about expanding the business. The motel has 30 apartments of various sizes on the site and caters mainly for interstate visitors. The motel is located in a popular tourist area close to wineries and other attractions.

The Use of ICT

The ICT comprises three networked PCs plus one stand-alone laptop, and although the technology was only reviewed infrequently, in the past the business has instituted regular reviews and updates to the technology. When PCs are out of date they are rotated to a part of the business where they are not critical as new machines are brought into the high-risk or high-demand areas. Backup is carried out on alternate days using both external hard disks and flash drives. The manager learned about ICT through a combination of trial and error and support from friends and teenage sons. He considers himself to be a follower rather than a leader in the ICT realm.

The manager constantly peruses ICT-related magazines and industry reviews for new ideas that could be incorporated into the business. A cost-benefit analysis is carried out on any new ideas before any new technology is purchased but, if it appears to be suitable, expense is not a key concern. It was during this external scanning process that the manager came across the idea of opening guest rooms via the telephone system to cut down on lost door keys.

The reception has a touch-screen to allow guests to look for suitable meals, specials and local events and attractions. The screen also allows for guest self check-in which allows the manager more freedom to deal with any ongoing issues. Guests can see images of rooms and choose actual rooms from this terminal and this can also be carried out online.

The website provides details of local events and attractions, room availability and rates and offers booking facilities including selection of a specific room. Links do exist to state tourism systems, but a minimal number of rooms are advertised through this channel to avoid the risk of double bookings.

The use of ICT, specifically the online booking system and ability of customers to see rooms prior to arrival, has changed the customer base. Typical customers used to be younger customers booking cheapest rooms for the odd night. Now it is older ("baby boomer") customers who tend to choose more expensive rooms for five- or six-night bookings.

Current Status

Full online booking facilities are available and it is possible to view plans of the rooms. There is no Wi-Fi, but the rooms have Internet connection points. Links to local places and events are present and there is a guest feedback function.

Country Hairdressing

Background

This business is a growing rural hairdressing business that has been operating for the past six years; however, the current owner has only had the business for about five months and has inherited the current computer system. The main focus of the business is to offer their customers "a great service". This mantra appears to have been working well, as they are about to add another branch in a neighbouring town.

The Use of ICT

The business has been using the current computer system for the past three years. The former owner bought touch-screen computers and installed industry-based software to tailor services to the customer's needs.

The new owner has started preparations for a new website. It will begin as an 'information only' website and transition into an interactive website "down the track". The ICT skill level of the owners was assessed at the intermediate level.

The level of ICT governance in the business was assessed as high. The owner reviews the need for hardware and software requirements every year and they back up their data every day. Most of the record-keeping is computer-based, with the owner only printing documents for backup purposes. The advent of a new store means that they are currently reviewing their ICT situation.

This organisation has embraced technology and is using it to record information about their clients. However, as the business expands to add another location, it will be interesting to see if their current computer system can handle the adjustment.

Current Status

The website is still 'information only'. There is no evidence of the business having a social media presence.

Adventure Boat Rides

Background

This business has been in existence around for about three years and offers 'extreme' boat rides for the more adventurous tourist. The company is a small business (one person) and their primary market is the local one. The current strategy is to target business parties and celebrations rather than individuals. The business had a difficult first 18 months and is now starting to focus on running an efficient business with the aim of providing a better lifestyle for the owner.

Currently, the record-keeping is divided roughly 50-50 between computer and paper-based approaches, however there is an intention to move towards managing all record-keeping on a computer system. However, the owner feels that it will only be possible to manage around 85% of the records with a computer system and feels that some aspects, such as bookings, will still be carried out using paper-based approaches. His concern is that total reliance on a computer may be imprudent due to the risk of hardware or software failure, although he admits to being rather 'old school' in his view of computer systems in general.

The Use of ICT

Although this business has been using computers from the start, the owner admits to being somewhat naive when it comes to their use. His self-assessment of his knowledge of computers is low and that is why he relies upon third parties to manage his ICT for him.

He does use a computer to help him with his marketing. He screens calls and bookings and asks customers or potential customers how they found out about the business, the data then being used to help him consider his marketing strategy. One innovative use of computers that he has thought of is live-streaming of video from his tour boats to a shore-based shop to attract or inform new customers. He has not yet implemented this.

There is no formal measure for determining the value of his current or future ICT investment. The owner identified major hardware failure as his biggest concern when using computers and has lost his data before due to poor backing-up techniques. He commented that although he is always looking for technology that will benefit any aspect of the business, whether through specific technology or improved communication with clients, he has no specific plan for determining the strategic value of ICT for the business.

Current Status

It has not been possible to determine the current status of this business. It may no longer be in existence.

The ICT Operationals

Beach Hostel

Background

This business offers backpacking-style accommodation alongside one of Australia's most beautiful beaches. This organisation has recently changed ownership but has always been known as a hostel. A majority, around 90%, of guests are international tourists, with the other 10% coming from interstate. The current owner has only had the business for a little over 12 months and is currently in a maintenance phase in terms of ensuring that they continue to satisfy guests and maintain the status quo of the business. Within the next year they will look at ways in which they can expand the business.

The Use of ICT

Most of the record-keeping is computer-based activities including online banking, maintaining contacts for guest and suppliers and storing transaction information, although they still use paper receipts. These paper receipts are written out for all accommodation payments from their backpackers. They do not have bookings on their website, however, in common with most other similar accommodation businesses, they do use external websites and agencies for this. The interviewee commented that they are able to receive bookings from their website, but on review of their website there is no clear function to undertake this activity other than email reservation of rooms for backpackers.

Currently, they use the Office suite to help manage the business, for example, MS Excel for bookings, MS Outlook for contacts and MYOB (Mind Your Own Business) for transactions. The owner commented that larger hostels did use industry-specific software that provides integrated and interactive systems to manage their businesses but felt that they were not yet sufficiently large to pursue this path. This is, however, a possibility for the future.

They have five desktop computers supporting the business and have plans in place to buy four more machines (with Internet access) for the guests to use. The interviewee commented that providing PCs for guests to access the Internet is an increasingly popular trend.

The company did not have a Facebook account at the time but is aware that enabling guests to communicate with one another may have a beneficial impact on future bookings. He is watching carefully to see what path other competing hostels take and would seem to be willing to adopt ICT if it will offer him tangible business benefits.

The owner is enthusiastic about the potential of ICT, as indicated by his aspiration to have an integrated system for the business, but is also concerned that a major danger with ICT use is that of over-reliance upon technology. On the day of the interview the loss of the network severely impacted upon the business and this was a source of concern for the owner.

Current Status

The minimally interactive website shows a 24-hour Internet café on site. Bookings are not possible online, email and telephone contact details being provided.

Aromatherapy

Background

This micro business offers aromatherapy services and had commenced operation some three years before the time of interview. The business is located in the centre of a rural township and the main products sold are emu oil, soap and candles. The business also runs classes in making soap and candles. A significant proportion of the business's sales occur via their website.

The Use of ICT

The business has used ICT since its inception for basic word processing and some spreadsheet-based account-keeping tasks. They have also installed a bar coding system which they describe as a "huge undertaking", but they have reaped significant benefits in the form of improved operational efficiencies.

The owner described their business website as 'interactive'. They have to notify the website host to back up the site when they update it. This complexity has led them to consider a different approach to their website management.

The owner's ICT skill levels were assessed as being at a high level, especially in regards to familiarity with traditional and newer types of ICT terms.

The business backs up its database and other important files on a regular basis, reflecting an understanding of the importance of these electronic resources to business continuity.

Current Status

The domain name of the website has been altered to reflect the natural aromatherapy products being offered, with the old domain name being discontinued. The new website is interactive, with clients able to purchase aromatherapy products online. There is also a blog on the new website, although it is not interactive, the business posting notices such as when new courses were being offered. There were no comments from clients. The business is listed on various third-party natural therapy business directories. The business does not have a social media presence.

Weddings and Events Planning

Background

Based in a small rural town, this business plans and organises weddings, conferences and other events in and around the local area. Prior to operating this business, the owner had extensive experience in the travel sector. At the time of the interview with the owner, the business had been in operation for three years and had expanded in the two years prior to the interview. The main reason for running the business is to maintain lifestyle.

The Use of ICT

ICT has been used within the business since it commenced operations, making use of one PC and an Internet connection in the home. This was shared between business use and the children, which was seen as being a "bit of a problem".

The business has two separate websites for different aspects of the business, each being tailored to the target market. One site is used for private events (i.e., weddings) and is presented in 'soft' colours; the other site is for corporate customers and presented in a much sharper style.

The owner also discussed how she listed the business on government-sponsored websites that provided good support and allowed businesses to change their details themselves. At the time of interview, the owner expressed only a passing interest in a social media presence.

Whilst only being a micro business and with the owner's ICT skills assessed as being at the 'average' level, this business is unusually characterised by excellent ICT governance practices. It has a formal plan to assess the need to upgrade its ICT on a regular basis and a formal backup and recovery regimen. It assesses the performance of its ICT through measuring the number of enquiries and bookings for events.

Current Status

The private event website is very professionally presented (designed by a web design business) and is supported by a Facebook and Twitter presence, both of which are updated infrequently. The business was also listed on a number of local business directories. The separate website for corporate customers is no longer evident.

Country Club and Golf Course

Background

The golf course business surveyed here is part of a large 4½-star resort located an hour or so drive by car from the metropolis. This is one of more than five international 'championship' golf courses located in the region. The country club attracts state, interstate and international tourists visiting the region and has conference facilities in addition to the associated golf business. The main hotel business has been in existence for over 10 years, the golf-related business having been developed in the last five years. The golf business offers tuition, sale of golf clubs and equipment and hire of equipment for guests travelling without their own.

The Use of ICT

Internet business is steadily increasing, but the manager still feels that use of the telephone allows them to provide faster and more specific answers to any questions customers may have. A database of previous customers allows 'specials' to be sent to them via email. All golf carts have GPS tracking, which serves the purposes of asset management and of providing players with accurate indications of their location of the course.

The golf aspect of the business utilises three personal computers and one laptop, the main country club having a separate ICT provision comprising six networked workstations. The manager feels that he has good ICT skills but has also established links with local computer service providers that could be contacted if he is unable to deal with an issue. There is a formal contingency plan but this has never been tested. Backup of both the hotel and the golf business machines takes place once a day, backup copies of the hotel business being held off-site. Review of their ICT provision is on an 'as required' basis (i.e., irregular and unplanned), but there are plans to introduce a formal review on a six-monthly basis.

The key perceived value that the use of ICT provides is that of improved efficiency, this taking the form of efficient and timely communication with all parties associated with the business, improved reporting and staff scheduling without the need to employ extra staff. He recognises that ICT can also bring benefits for his competitors but is not currently sure what threats may emerge in the future. The business would consider any new technology if it brings business benefits for them, provided that it is not too expensive or complex. The manager felt that they have probably got the right skills at the moment but might have problems if new technologies were introduced to the existing workforce. Pressure of work in the business means that very little time is available for training staff.

Current Status

The current website serves both the country club and the golf course, and online reservations can be made. Free Wi-Fi is offered and the website features Facebook, Twitter, TripAdvisor and Instagram.

Booking Office

Background

This business has been in operation for over 10 years and employs less than five staff. Originally having a major focus on the provision of motor insurance, it has gradually moved more strongly into the tourism sector in the last five years and now serves as a booking office for the local region. The business provides tourists with information to help them find and plan holidays, comparing prices of various options that might interest them, and doing some of the booking for them. Customers are the central concern and the business seeks to provide them with an efficient and friendly experience and to produce satisfied customers who "feel that they have got more from us than they expected".

The Use of ICT

Most of the business is conducted over the counter of the shop, but Internet enquiries have increased steadily and now account for around 45% of the business. They have four Windows XP personal computers, two of which are networked. There is no formal contingency plan and in the event of an ICT problem they would revert to the use of telephones while they waited for a local ICT supplier to come and attend to the problems. Some training was provided when the original motoring association system was installed, but since that time self-learning seems to have been more typical. The members of staff do share their understandings and all felt that they were proficient in their use of ICT.

They do find considerable benefits in the use of ICT, essentially in allowing them to provide rapid and wide-ranging responses to customer enquiries. Enquiries may relate to local attractions, accommodation, events, maps and visitor information in general. The use of ICT allows them to access more information and more rapidly than was possible with paper brochures and to provide a more professional service. This improved speed and efficiency has been obtained without any increase in manpower. Although the staff very much appreciate the benefits of ICT in providing effective support for customers, there did appear to be some frustration with senior management who viewed the benefits of ICT more through a lens of cost saving rather than improved customer experience.

Staff commented that the negative side of increased use of email is that enquirers expect an almost instant response to their query. This demand for immediate answers also seemed to be appearing in their face-to-face communications, leading them to comment that customers seem to be far less patient than before.

Current Status

The current website provides a short video of the immediate surrounding area and links to current and forthcoming local events. There is an online facility for booking accommodation within the state and links are provided to art galleries, tours, golf and so on.

Tour Company (Extended Vignette)

Background

This business is a tours and event business which operates specialist walking and other tours in and around the centre of the city. The business grew in the previous three years from operating on a part-time basis (two days per week) as a home-based business to a full-time (six days per week) business that employs two part-time staff. The owner commented that growth is important as the tourism market has few repeat customers. The international market is dynamic and the business needs to tap into that client base. The owner made a specific point of emphasising that he concentrates upon both the event and tour aspect of the business. The key to this is operating a set of tours, but targeting these to operate around a set of specific events or dates throughout the year. Interestingly, the owner indicated that he had actually tried to diversify the business too much in his first year of operation, subsequently narrowing the focus of activities and concentrating upon running an efficient business within this focus whilst growing his clientele.

The Use of ICT

This business has made good use of the Internet through the use of a website and a social media presence. Their website is interactive and has a facility to book and pay for tours as well as a range of information pertaining to tourist destinations in the city. They preferred to operate and update their own website (rather than rely on a third party) as they have total control of the information that is placed on it. This business has seen a good return on their website investment, with 70% of their business being booked through the website. The Internet has allowed the business to grow quickly, being able to attract international customers before they reach Australia. The owner commented that "it is important to have a good website that can be linked to other professional sites" such as state government destination websites. Importantly, at the time of interview, the owner had recently begun using a 'BlackBerry-type' mobile device that allowed him to stay in touch with the business whilst being "on the move". The basic record-keeping of the business was also predominantly computer-based and operated a wireless network, which was not common at that time.

Marketing is the most important use of their ICT systems. The business needs to engage the customer before they reach the local area and the Web allows this to be achieved more effectively than other methods of business communication.

The business is also able to use computer applications to maintain scheduling and costing models of all the tours that they operate. This prevents overbooking of tours and identifies when a second tour should be organised to accommodate demand.

The online, real-time booking system on the website allows the owner to control the manner by which tours are organised and to determine when they are fully booked. Previously, the business used a third-party booking service that was cumbersome and prevented the process from running cohesively. The owner believes that the website booking system gives the company an edge over other tour businesses that do not have this facility directly on their website. Recently, the business found that many customers have started to make numerous enquiries (email and phone) about purchasing tour gift vouchers. The business has now set up a section of the website where the gift vouchers are offered, allowing enquiries to not only be reduced, but potentially making other customers aware of this type of gift voucher product/service.

The tour-booking system allows the business to control the scheduling of tours and to cost them effectively. It also prevents overbooking of tours and alerts them when they need to schedule extra tours to accommodate extra demand.

The business's presence on Facebook provides it with a public profile and highlights affiliate events and activities, things that may be appreciated by prospective clients. The use of TripAdvisor allows the business to respond to customer issues/statements and to determine how the services it offers are being assessed by customers.

Overall, the owner judged that the areas of the business that ICT benefited the most were marketing/selling, customer service and finance/accounting. Of these, marketing is the most important.

Whilst the use of ICT by the business was assessed as being quite advanced, the other important aspects of ICT use were not considered to be at that level, with ICT governance and ICT skills being assessed at average levels.

The owner appeared to be quite technologically capable and aware of the various computing solutions that could assist the business. He used the Web 2.0 environment successfully with well thought-out reasons as to how the business can use these social networking sites. He judged his own ICT skills to be intermediate, this being reflected in a sound knowledge of basic ICT terms but less knowledge of more advanced concepts. He recognised that his skills continually had to be updated to reflect "the changing face of technology and new devices".

In regards to ICT governance, reviews of the need to upgrade the business ICT were performed fairly regularly, but formal plans for ICT recovery should the business ICT fail were not in place. Backups tended to occur every two weeks or, more likely, when the owner remembered. This is somewhat unusual as the business had experienced a hard disk crash a few years earlier and lost nearly a third of its data. Additionally, there was no formal mechanism to judge the success of ICT use.

Current Status

At the time of writing, the business website had undergone a major redesign and looked much more professional, although the basic functionality remained similar.

There were links to dedicated Google +, Facebook, Twitter, YouTube, TripAdvisor and Instagram pages. Of these, the Facebook page remained the most active, with comments from the business, clients and other businesses in the area. The Google+ page was less active but was updated by the business on a reasonably regular basis. The business sent out 1–2 tweets per day on their Twitter site, having over 6,000 followers. YouTube was not updated as regularly, with the last video posted a year ago. The TripAdvisor page mainly showed reviews of the business (209 out of the 234 reviews rated the tours as 'excellent'), good enough that the business had been awarded a 'Certificate of Excellence' from TripAdvisor, given to those businesses that consistently earn 'great reviews'. The Instagram showed the pictures that were shown on some of the other sites (mainly Facebook and Twitter).

The business was listed on many travel and tourism directories.

Corporate Catering

Background

This small catering business is located on the outskirts of a major city and mainly services corporate customers in the city. At the time of interview, they had been in operation for eight years. The interviewee runs the business with the support of nine other employees. When asked about the main focus of the business, he replied that "my office staff would probably say that running an efficient business was the most important thing". The business had expanded in the two years prior to the interview.

The Use of ICT

The business has one PC, three laptop computers and a wireless Internet connection. ICT have been used within the business since its inception, but this use appeared to be very conservative due to the business experiencing significant computer problems (slow PC and two hard disk failures) in the recent past. As a result of their experiences, all four computers are now backed up and the laptops are taken home each night.

Another consequence of these computer failures is that they routinely print everything they receive including all their business-related emails. There appears to be a tension between feeling that a 'belt and braces' approach is needed to protect their data and a concern that they are wasting large amounts of paper. The business is seemingly a hostage to the previous poor ICT experiences which have shaped the way it uses valuable time on backing up files and data records.

The interviewee indicated that the business relies predominantly on email with minimal orders being placed using fax. The business operates a simple website with an online order form, but customers are actually encouraged to just send in orders using regular email.

The business does not have a social media presence.

Whilst the ICT skills of the interviewee were self-assessed as being at the lower level, he indicated that the business had an office manager who was quite experienced in the use of ICT. The interviewee expressed the view that he would adopt more ICT if there was a need and that it was necessary to update to new technology to maintain a competitive position.

Current Status

Today, the website remains a simple site, albeit with a more sophisticated online ordering form. The business also has an extended online presence *through third-party promotional sites such as the Yellow Pages and White Pages websites and various other business directories.*

Indigenous Art Gallery

Background

The gallery is run by the owner-manager as a solo business and focuses on selling aboriginal artwork from a small shopfront gallery that was established in the late 1990s. Although considering herself a solo operator, she also draws on family members to assist her in running the business should things become busy or if she needs to visit indigenous painters in outback Australia. Visiting tourists have been identified as a key market in the sale of unique aboriginal artwork, the other important market segment comprising expatriate Australians. The owner has a passion for promoting and selling indigenous art and has an endearing affection to communicate the intricacies of the artworks' information to others. Hence, the business strategy is not primarily one of growth, but rather to be an efficient operation in terms of sourcing and selling unique artwork products.

The Use of ICT

The business uses information technology in the key business areas dealing with record-keeping accounting practices, the MYOB package being the application of choice. The business's website, although basic in design, is an important channel that is purely informational in nature. The website has been deliberately designed to be simplistic and to provide the reader with an overview of the business offerings. The rationale behind designing the website this way is to try to initiate contact with new or prospective customers, allowing the business owner to follow up with further conversation and enquiry. All the artwork displayed on the website is presented so that customers know the price of paintings, a practice that is not always followed by her competitors.

The website also encourages people to sign up for the art gallery's e-newsletter, which is an important element in building a customer distribution list. The e-newsletter sign-up feature is seemingly premised on permission email marketing principles where people interested in the business's products deliberately choose to regularly receive information. The limited availability of a product such as indigenous artwork lends itself well to the direct marketing opportunities potentially provided via this approach.

The owner uses email as a significant channel for communication with painters in remote areas of Australia. Email exchanges with indigenous painters allow her to receive images of paintings that have been completed but are located in remote Australia. These images can be subsequently forwarded to prospective customers as a follow-up to their enquiries. The concept of the digital image of a painting collected at source in the outback of

Australia and then sent on to international customers via email underpins an important marketing strategy used by the business. Although this image-email approach is successful, the final stages of clinching a deal are generally achieved in a face-to-face environment in negotiating the final price of a painting. The owner indicated that she feels that there is no way that technology can replace this final stage.

The business typically backs up computer applications and data informally. The owner also indicates that time and skills are an issue when it comes to learning more about how to increase or better use computers. She acknowledges that she lacks confidence in using the technology due to its complexity. When the technology breaks down, a third party is contracted to visit the premises and undertake repairs.

Current Status

The business website has had a slight makeover with an updated design and online purchases of artworks and gift certificates added. The business now has an active presence on Facebook, the video websites Vimeo and YouTube (where they display artwork and post interviews with artists) and LinkedIn (with details of the owner).

Period Farm and Cottage

Background

This is a micro business that has been in operation for four years and combines a small hobby farm and period cottage (circa 1858) located near a rural town. The cottage contains two bedrooms and supplements the income gained from the hobby farm, which contains a collection of local and imported animals. The hosts live on the property in a separate house.

The Use of ICT

Since its establishment, the business has been using ICT for basic record-keeping and also uses Microsoft Publisher to prepare brochures and gift vouchers.

The business originally did not have an Internet connection, but once one became available they introduced an interactive website that prompted enquiries from overseas, although not many of these converted to actual business. They also offered accommodation via eBay, some via auction and some via fixed price.

The business does not have a social media presence.

The owners had a basic general ICT knowledge but were unfamiliar with many of the more recent ICT terms. "Work information" is stored on the home computer, which is not regularly backed up.

Current Status

The individual website has been removed and instead there are links to the business through many different other sites, such as local tourism and accommodation portals and directories. Thus, one type of online presence (a focussed website) has been replaced by a more 'scattered' online strategy. Interestingly, none of these provide a facility to book directly online; it is necessary to call the business to make a booking. This suggests that the early promise shown by online booking was not realised, but that there is still a benefit to be gained by being listed online. There was still no evidence of a social media presence.

Country Trips

Background

This is a small rural tourism business that has been in operation for 16 years. The business's main product is providing day trips for small groups of people to explore local scenic sights in a region which includes nearby wineries. The business's customers are mainly drawn from interstate and overseas. The business has three full-time employees (including the owner), but also nine tour drivers/hosts that work on a casual basis.

The Use of ICT

The business has used ICT from its inception for basic record-keeping purposes, for email and also to create tour-related brochures. The owner originally distributed brochures through hotels in the nearest metropolitan city area but now has an ICT-based approach, with most of the tour bookings being placed via the business's website. The owner identified that processing emails was a major time-consuming task as the business received up to 100 emails a day, some 90 or so being regarded as non-viable "garbage" and "were dumped".

The business has an interactive website which accepts online tour bookings. The site accepts credit card details to confirm and hold the booking, allowing people to pay either in cash or credit on the day of the tour. The owner indicated that it would be particularly useful to have an online, portable EFTPOS (electronic funds transfer at point of sale) machine to allow payment to occur on the tour vehicles.

The business has established a presence on Facebook where they post the latest news about the local region and where customers are encouraged to post comments about their tour experiences. The business has also a Twitter presence, but this does not appear to be as active as Facebook. The business also appears on a number of local and wine-dedicated online tourism directories.

The owners have a basic general ICT knowledge, including familiarity with some of the more recent ICT terms. They track where every enquiry comes from, whether via telephone, the website or email, providing some measure of the success of the different communication channels they use. The use of eBay allows them to see how many people have viewed their page. Accounting files are regularly backed up.

Current Status

The website is more professionally designed with similar functionality, a slightly expanded range of tours and the inclusion of an online newsletter. The booking process is similar, customers having access to an online booking form to book a tour, the booking being manually confirmed by the business within 48 hours. The business is still active on social media, predominantly on Facebook rather than Twitter. However, there is little interaction on these pages.

Spa and Coffee Shop

Background

This is a micro business that has been operating in a rural town for nearly five years. The business offers a day spa and coffee shop for local customers and tourists. At the time of the interview, due to some public works, access to the business via foot was extremely difficult, so 'walk in' traffic was virtually "non-existent". The owner commented that they needed to get the message out that the business is still operating.

The Use of ICT

The business has used ICT throughout its existence for record-keeping and basic word processing, as well as Microsoft Publisher and graphics software to produce advertising brochures. They would like to email clients with website links, but have found that anti-virus software "strips off" the actual links. ICT has changed the way they operate as they have had to put bar codes on items and install bar code scanners.

The business website could be described as marginally interactive. However, the owner suggested that whilst they receive lots of 'hits', the website has provided little business value.

The owners have a basic general ICT knowledge but were unfamiliar with many of the more recent ICT terms. The business has already had one hard disk failure where they were required to manually re-enter all of the accounting details into the system. Now the business has a network and their MYOB files are backed up. The owner was concerned that the business did not host its own website and had no backup if the hosts "fell over".

Current Status

The website has been replaced by a single web page listing 'natural therapies', which provides contact details for the business. There is a link on the page to the original business name, but this link is non-operational (that is, it did not link to the 'old' website). It appears that the business may have rebranded itself and the 'new' business name is listed on a number of business directories devoted to natural therapies. There is no evidence of a social networking presence for either the old or new business brands.

Mini Tours

Background

This eight-year-old company offers a number of air-conditioned tours to popular local tourist destinations within the state for parties up to 40 clients. The owner delivers some of the tours himself but also employs a number of drivers on a part-time basis and describes the size of the business as six full-time-equivalent staff. The business offers pick-up and return from accommodation and can provide bespoke tours in addition to five different prescribed tours. The business has been in operation for around five years and initially served the local tourism market (currently 5% of the business), but growth in recent years has been achieved in national (currently 35%) and international (currently 60%) markets.

The Use of ICT

The business has been using ICT for around four years and currently makes use of one PC and two laptops. The key areas where the business owner feels that ICT makes a significant contribution to the business include improved efficiencies and cost savings, opportunities to develop new services and improved communication with potential customers. Of these, it is the communication with customers that is felt to be the most significant. Although the website provides tour details and has online booking facilities, many potential customers do ask for clarification or variations to standard tours, and email (supported by mobile phones) provides a quick and easy way to address any such issues and to keep an audit trail. Links to other businesses provide a higher profile than a single website, though some care is needed to avoid any possibility of double-bookings when more than one booking channel is available.

All bookings are held on a database and spreadsheets are used for management of general financial aspects of the business as well as specifically tracking fuel expenses. Drivers' manifests are computer-generated and printed so that they can be passed to individual tour drivers. Use is also made of word processing and publishing packages to create and produce advertising materials, support material for the tours and so on.

Data is backed up once per week to flash disk and use is made of regularly updated virus software. Mobile phones are an essential part of the ICT provision and phones are all on contracts where replacements can be quickly obtained.

The owner indicated that he was not aware of any competitors using specific ICT that would pose a threat to him and suggested that the tourism market was sufficiently large for a number of similar businesses to operate without causing him problems.

Current Status

The current website provides contact details and a small number of images illustrating some of the tours offered along with details of the tours and online booking facilities. A page shows testimonials from previous customers and a link is provided to Facebook.

Motel

Background

This motel is located in the city centre and has been in operation for approximately five years. Their primary market is interstate tourists and their business focus is to run an efficient business.

The Use of ICT

Investment in ICT has taken second place to the development of an efficient business and 90% of the record-keeping is paper-based. They have one Mac computer and a basic website and this is viewed primarily as a tool to provide information. Access to a booking form is provided on the website, but this needs to be completed and emailed back to the business. There is a business belief that direct and personal contact with customers via telephone is the most important way to communicate. ICT is viewed by the owner as "mainly an extra way for people to find us and make bookings; that's pretty much it".

One benefit of the lack of reliance on ICT is that the business could still operate (for a while at least) if the computer system was to fail. The only backup approach used is to print out the email booking and write the bookings down in a book.

Some of the guests have asked for Internet access, but they currently do not provide this service. They are considering this for the future.

Current Status

At the time of writing, the website is no longer operational. The business relies on its listing on many accommodation websites for any online bookings.

Children's Entertainment

Background

This medium-sized business has been in operation for a number of years. They provide indoor and some outdoor on-site games, rides and entertainment for children. The games include dodgem cars, bumper boats, arcade games and so on. The majority of their clientele are local and the primary focus at the moment is to grow the business.

The Use of ICT

Computers are an integral part of this business, a total of 20 PCs being used for a variety of purposes. The marketing, accounting and record-keeping are computer-based and all of the games and rides are controlled by an integrated computer system. The centralised computer system uses proprietary software and manages all of the game machines and rides. A game card, charged with a certain monetary or time value, is used to activate the games. This card can be programmed to reflect different events; for example, if there is a children's party, the card can be programmed for a set block of hours for the party, giving access to any game that the card is validated for.

At the time of the interview, their website was only information-based. However, the owner did want to update the website to make it more interactive to allow online bookings.

This organisation does not have any formal recovery processes if the systems go down. The interviewee noted that if the computer system fails, the rides will not activate and there is no manual way to activate the rides. Given the importance of the central computer, they do have a company that comes in to maintain rides and to check that the computer is working properly.

Current Status

The main page has links to Facebook, Google+, Pinterest, YouTube and Instagram. There are several non-functional internal site links but, at the time of writing, the site appears to be undergoing some updating. A deposit for parties can be paid online, over the phone or in person.

Backpacker Company

Background

This small accommodation provider was established more than 10 years ago and is located close to city's central train station. It employs between six and 19 people at different times of the year. As a backpacker establishment it has 18 rooms usually available for rent, accommodating up to 80 people at any one time. The business's primary target audience is the international traveller who is budget conscious and seeking convenient accommodation when visiting the city. Backpacker travellers are an important component in Australian tourism, with many businesses catering to this particular segment. The geographical location of this backpacker operation is an area where many similar low-budget hostels and hotels are found; hence competition for travellers can be fierce at times. The manager of the business indicated that travellers' needs are the primary focus of the business rather than future growth.

The Use of ICT

The business makes good use of information technology across a range of operational areas that includes the control of room check-in and check-out, an online booking facility that is associated with the business's website and the automation of much of the business's administrative areas. It has two stand-alone PCs, both running Windows XP, and has used computers since the establishment of the business.

The use of the web-based room reservation systems is important for the business, assisting prospective customers to book rooms directly or via third-party businesses. At the time of interview, the website had been implemented for 12 months and was used as a primary information source for prospective travellers. The interviewee indicated that they viewed the website as providing strategic value from a marketing perspective in that it allowed them to control the promotion of the business and also capture direct bookings. Notably, the room bookings undertaken via the website provided travellers with a payment option, rather than through the typical exchange of emails between business and customer to confirm a booking. Arguably, the direct payment option allows the business to be more efficient in its accounting practices as well as assisting with earlier-than-usual cash flow after taking a deposit. Importantly, the direct bookings made through the business's website bypass the third-party services, saving on commissions paid to them. The business also operates an Internet café, providing a value-added service for travellers, and used a wireless approach to interconnecting all available computers.

One area where computers have not been able to assist the business is associated with tourist-related checks and authentication. In this instance, paper-based traveller records still need to be collected for various compliance and legal reasons. The business typically backs up data captured as part of the business operations about once a month so that reservations are not lost and they stated that this approach has proved to be reliable. The implied notion here is that the system is unlikely to fail and potentially the manager may have a lack of understanding of this issue. On a similar theme, the interviewee felt that more time for updating people's skills and getting training was needed to understand the use of computers, particularly the reservation system.

The adoption of the Facebook social media platform was initially used to stay in touch with previous travellers, however, more recently the social media presence is used to promote some of the relevant 'what's on' activities to do with the central city environment. The business uses email as the primary communication channel with existing and prospective travellers. However, email has also proven to be an important channel to communicate with some of the company's closely located competitors. In a show of reciprocity, many of the budget accommodation businesses in the city centre refer queries from prospective clients when their rooms are fully booked. Another example of this reciprocity is that email communication is used to exchange customer information with other backpacker businesses, allowing "dodgy people" (generally non-paying guests) to be identified as they move from one accommodation provider to another.

Current Status

The website has recently been significantly updated, with more interactivity having been added in the form of an interactive calendar with event listings and links to pertinent mobile apps that tourists can download and use when in the city.

Farmers Market

Background

This farmers market was established in 2001 in a small rural town with the aim of creating a venue for local producers to showcase and sell a wide range of fresh primary products to locals and visitors. The manager, a former Information Technology manager with a local council, is the sole full-time employee. His duties include advertising and promoting the market, allocating stall spaces on a week-by-week basis and monitoring both the quality and authenticity of stall-holders' produce as well as customer perceptions.

The Use of ICT

This micro business is managed by an individual with good ICT skills gained in former employment and the governance policies were well thought through. Pressure of work means that the execution of those policies is perhaps a little lax at times, but much of the data is also held in paper form and even with a severe computer problem it should be possible to maintain an effective business operation.

The ICT facilities of this organisation are based upon one laptop and one desktop machine with a local network between them and Internet access from both machines. Software includes the usual Microsoft Office, with word processing, databases and spreadsheets being actively used on a daily basis along with MYOB.

The manager was quite dismissive of social media, noting that ' . . . it's just another phase, the next one will come along in a month's time or two years time'. He noted that there had been a Friends Reunited 'bubble' and that although his partner used Facebook, he did not have the time to devote to investigating it.

His main interest in new ICT opportunities lies in the direction of space allocation software to help him allocate stall locations within the market. This allocation process occurs on a weekly basis and accommodates both new stalls and the changing needs of existing stall holders, while at the same time creating an interesting environment and 'flow' for the public visiting the market. No suitable software, at least at an affordable price, had been identified and the weekly allocation process therefore involved local knowledge in conjunction with a simple spreadsheet model that the manager was developing.

At the time of interview, the Web presence provided basic information about the market and there was no intention to attempt to build a more interactive website due to funding issues and to some concerns about the ability of their website developer to incorporate complex transactional features.

Current Status

The market has grown from 18 stalls at the time of the interview to more than 60 and the current website is rich with links to Facebook, Instagram, Google+ and Pinterest as well as offering a virtual tour of the market, links to the various stall-holder websites where details, including short videos, of individual stalls can be obtained, as well as media releases, market history and so on.

The ICT Laggards

Guided Tours

Background

This one-man business offers a number of regularly scheduled full-day, half-day and evening tours to attractions in and around the city and to local wine regions. A maximum of 11 clients are catered to on each tour and although a number of specific tours are offered, it is possible to charter the owner for bespoke tours. The business has been in operation for around six years and has expanded the number of tours offered and number of clients attracted during that time.

The Use of ICT

One personal computer is used by this business, mainly for email and the production of leaflets and brochures, with documents and other files being backed up to flash disk approximately every six months. He does have a Web presence that provides details of the various tours along with landline and mobile phone numbers and email address for bookings and general enquiries. The father of the business owner lends a hand from time to time, mainly by manning the business landline phone. A fax machine is still in use, mainly for receiving queries from other businesses.

He carries his paperwork with him while he is on the road with his tour groups and considers the mobile phone to be the most vital ICT available to him. His father answers the landline phone when the owner is out on tour but refers all queries and request for booking to his son via the mobile phone, ringing the client back once a booking can be confirmed.

Although the business owner recognises the potential benefits of ICT beyond the present website and brochure printing, he still manages his income and expenditure accounts, records relating to tours and vehicles and customer details in paper form. He currently finds his paper-based approach easier and quicker than using the computer. He has considered linking his website to the state-based tourism system but is concerned that this could lead to double-bookings with potential reputational damage if he had to cancel or rearrange booked tours.

His caution in the use of ICT is predicated on this concern to avoid double-bookings, but he does monitor the ICT scene by regularly visiting ICT shops to maintain awareness of what technologies are emerging that could potentially help to support his business. He feels that although his current ICT cover all of his current requirements, it is always good to look ahead for new possibilities. He looks particularly for those technologies that could offer improved efficiency, cost saving and revenue generation and improving communication.

Current Status

The current website allows clients to choose dates for 11 different full-day, half-day and evening tours and to book and pay securely online. One external link is provided to the Australian Visa Bureau and a mobile version of the bookings page is available.

Rural Market

Background

This market has been in operation for over a decade in a rural town and has doubled in size during that period (now standing at 250 stalls), mainly through the assistance of state government grants. The market is heavily involved in the community through the development of local infrastructure (such as a new barbecue area for the town) and free stalls are offered to local fundraisers as is the opportunity to run raffles to raise revenue.

The Use of ICT

ICT has been used by the business in the last five years and the usage is essentially for basic record-keeping and email, but of considerable value. Their biggest problem was handling receipts; they were trying to avoid having to do this twice (once on the day and then formally afterwards). In manual form this involved the use of six people collecting money and writing receipts for two hours each on market days.

The company has a brochureware website to provide basic information for customers, but one of the problems they identified is that it is expensive to change anything on the website. However, the owner pointed out that one of the great benefits was having a comprehensive list of stall-holders on the website with links directly to their specific business websites.

The owners have a basic general ICT knowledge but were unfamiliar with many of the more recent ICT terms.

Accounts for the business are kept by the treasurer, who backs up these files infrequently, perhaps on a monthly basis. This may be due to a lack of understanding about backup processes.

There is no formal process to determine if their use of ICT is successful, but their comments regarding update of the website indicated they were aware of what was not working for them.

Current Status

The website has been redesigned by a local website designer with a few new pages and some more pictures, but is still a brochureware website. There is no listing of stall-holders. The business is also listed on a number of 'market' portals and regional directories. The business has a Facebook page created for it, but there was no detail on the site other than the business name.

Beauty Salon

Background

This business had existed for around two years at the time of interview, serving mainly local clients but also benefiting from interstate and international tourism accommodation in the local area. The business offers a range of beauty services including facial and body treatments, manicures, pedicures and massage.

The Use of ICT

Telephone bookings are typically the first contact with clients and appointments are recorded in a paper diary before being copied onto the single laptop computer in the shop. Email is used infrequently. Contact with clients, after the initial phone enquiry, is primarily face-to-face in the shop although there are plans to email special offers to clients.

All details of supplies and services are stored on a simple database on a laptop computer and MYOB is used for financial management. Prior to the use of MYOB, the owner used Excel and had been on a formal course to learn how to use this package. She moved to MYOB because she finds it simple, easy to use and perfect for her needs. She regularly reviews stock movement on the database to help her manage changes in stock demand over time.

Help for setting up of the initial system was obtained through friends and family. There are no formal recovery or regular backup practices, the last backup being to a memory stick around six months prior to the interview. She was not aware of any other backup procedures and has a tendency to misplace the memory sticks. She commented that at the end of a busy day all she wanted to do was shut up the shop and go home rather than do backups.

The main value she obtains from the use of ICT is that she can print high-quality materials, especially gift vouchers, and thus offer a professional face to clients. A database is used to track the issue and fulfilment of the gift vouchers. She is also about to launch a loyalty card and this will also be printed in house and managed via the database. She has actively considered the purchase of salon-specific software but feels that they are too feature-rich and expensive at the current stage of the business development.

A website is currently under development and will take the form of an electronic catalogue. The only reason that she is going down this path is that her competitors have websites. There is no intention to have high levels of interactivity, it being seen more as an extended shopfront into another customer space. She can currently see no value to be obtained from the use of social media.

Current Status

No details could be found about this business online at the time of writing.

Australiana

Background

This business is located in the centre of the city and sells 'Australiana' (Australian-themed items) to tourists. The shop employs only three people and the manager has only worked there for five months. The business has been in operation for around four years, and the manager, who was the interviewee, is trying to grow the business. The business has expanded its operations in the previous two years.

The Use of ICT

The business is trying to keep their ICT use as simple as possible. They have two computers, one for the shop and for general printing and one at home to manage the accounts. They do not have a website, but the manager said they were "always thinking about it though" and that their customers have asked about an online store.

Although the manager considers herself an 'expert' with ICT, there are no formal plans for data recovery or any regular consideration of upgrading their computers. The only judgment of success of their computer systems is that it "saves time". Most of these interactions with customers are face-to-face rather than via any ICT. Although the telephone is still the primary communication method, they have been saving some time by emailing their orders to suppliers.

They do not have a website or any social media presence. Their current rationale for not using computers to a greater extent is that business is expanding and that they are sufficiently well established to not have to worry about competition.

Current Status

At the time of writing the business still does not have a website or any dedicated social media page. However, one thing that was found was a YouTube video about them (only a montage of photos accompanied by music), prepared by a company which makes these videos on a commercial basis. This video has only had very limited viewing.

City-Based Walking Tours

Background

The business was established around 2002 and specialises in providing walking tours of local indigenous sites. The business's primary product is relatively unique in that it focuses on showing people the significant aboriginal sites located around the city, providing pertinent background information and the cultural stories associated with each location. The business's primary market comprises people from around the state, but they also target local and international tourists. The business strategy is one of growth, with the manager indicating that "bigger is better for aboriginal people", which possibly reflects personal sentiments of trying to promote an area of indigenous culture under-represented in mainstream tourism. The manager indicated that the business has been expanding well.

The Use of ICT

This business is not a particularly 'technology aware' company with the main use of their ICT being applied to record-keeping and administration activities. The company has only one desktop computer which is located and used at an office in the city centre. The computer and the systems associated with the business are administered by an externally hired third party who is responsible for dealing with network issues, backing up of data and replacement/upgrading of hardware and software. The manager of the business said that he has a 'better than novice' level of computer proficiency but did feel that he should know more.

This business has a website that provides information about the walking tours offered. Feedback from his customers suggests that they would like an online facility to book tours and use some form of electronic payment. This is one of the ICT challenges the manager is currently grappling with.

The manager has not explored the world of social media and, in the foreseeable future, does not intend to.

Current Status

The business website is now located within the website of the parklands where the business is located. It has links to a YouTube video and the website allows for online bookings for the walking tours to be made. There is no evidence of the business having a social media presence.

Rural Riding Academy

Background

The Rural Riding Academy offers horse riding courses and horse trail rides and attracts customers from the local area and from the city. This is a micro business with four employees, comprising husband-and-wife owners and two employees. Both owners and employees assist in offering the training courses and supervising trail rides. The business has been in operation for 35 years, with the lifestyle associated with the business being the most important focus. The business had recently expanded unexpectedly due to increased interest in horse riding that coincided with the release of a television series called *Saddle Club*.

The Use of ICT

The business has only been using computers for five years. Initial use of ICT was limited and associated with undertaking basic accounting tasks through the Quicken software application. The business has had a website offering basic information about the horse riding courses and horse trail rides, but this has been discontinued. Although the website allowed people to directly book online only "one in 200" customers actually booked via their website. They openly encouraged clients to contact them by telephone as they always carry their phones with them and still have basic listings on Google+, Yellow Pages and many online business directories such as True Local.

The business had no social media presence.

The ICT skill level of the owners could be considered basic. Their understanding of basic ICT terms and familiarity with newer ICT terms reflected their general lack of interest in the use of ICT. One of the owners had been on a training course, but the content was focused on an entirely different operating system to the one that was used by the business; hence it was of little use.

The level of ICT governance in the business could be regarded as adequate. Although there were no immediate plans to upgrade their ICT systems, the business does have a data recovery plan that involves regular backups and storage of important data files by a third party (their accountant). The fact that their PC was used by their children for homework and games was not ideal. They did not formally evaluate the success of their ICT use, but they did recognise that there had been an increase in the number of emails that they have received in recent times.

Current Status

At the time of writing the business still did not have a website or a presence on social media. It had maintained its listings on third-party business directories.

Personalised Tours

Background

This four-year-old micro business provides transport for corporate functions, special occasions and winery tours that are tailored to the needs of individual clients or very small groups. Prior to the winery tours, the business's solo owner and manager determines the wine tastes of the client, the tour being then tailored to those specific requirements. The tour includes transport services to and from the airport as well as exclusive personal services of the owner. The owner was previously self-employed in the marketing sector and has a clear vision of his business focus, which is one of adapting the business to fit with his lifestyle.

The Use of ICT

The owner views his personal computer, laptop, PDA and mobile phone to be essential tools for running his business. He is also acutely aware that loss of data could severely impact upon his business and he therefore also uses a physical paper diary to record key client details including contact numbers, dates booked for tours and so on. He observed that technology is moving on at a rapid pace and that any ICT-related investment he made was only in reliable and proven technology. Fuel was his greatest operating cost and he would rather spend money on buying and storing extra fuel when it was cheap rather than purchase the latest ICT that may not offer such tangible financial benefits for the business.

He has a Web presence and around 35% of his bookings are received via email. The website could be considered as being quite sparse, but his philosophy is that a multi-page or overly complex site tends to tax the attention span of people. The site features a short promotional video, basic tour details, contact details and links to relevant external sites. Despite contact with the local state tourism organisation, he had received very few bookings from them and had reduced his reliance on external advertisers. He has future plans to offer tour packages on his website and to provide facilities for payment. He highlighted how the surcharge associated with credit cards when making a booking added too much extra price to his tours and that PayPal is a useful alternative transaction facility.

A considerable number of bookings are received as a result of personal referrals from previous clients and he feels that he should be able to capitalise on the enthusiasm expressed by them. He suggested that what was needed was a website that would, on a single page, list all providers of similar tours along with a facility for clients of those tours to leave personal feedback. This, he felt, would allow potential clients to make a more informed decision about the quality and service offered by the various businesses. Paradoxically he felt that putting some of the glowing testimonials he had received onto a website could be regarded as rather brash.

Current Status

At the time of writing this business was still listed in some tourism documentation on the Web, but it was not possible to connect to his website. It has not been possible to determine the current status of this business. It may no longer be in existence.

Airport Passenger Transport

Background

This business has been in existence for around eight years and provides transport services for customers to and from the local airport and train station. The owner employs six part-time drivers and has a similar business in another state. ICT has only been a feature of the business for the last two years and was initially adopted with a view to providing extra value for customers by improving communications as well as offering efficiencies for the business itself. Although the owner recognised the potential that ICT could offer, he still currently relies more upon paperwork and heavy use of mobile phones to manage the business.

The Use of ICT

The business uses two PCs at the base but the major ICT, in the view of the owner, is in the form of the mobile phones that allow communication between drivers and the base. At the moment the PC is seen as a useful tool for taking email bookings, keeping tax and accounting information on MYOB, and word processing and desktop publishing for information sheets and brochures. Brochures are prepared in-house using desktop publishing, after which draft printed copies are sent out to a commercial printer. Expertise in installing the computers came from the daughter of the business owner and friends are also consulted when required. The owner feels that he does not have sufficient 'free' time to investigate new ICT products and has the general view that ICT is too complex, too expensive and offers limited benefits for the business. He does not feel that ICT has changed the way that the business operates.

There is no formal review process for evaluating the benefits of ICT or for considering new ICT and there is no backup or recovery plan. The PC has been reliable but they have had three printer failures in the last six months. This has been particularly annoying because the ability to quickly produce printed information sheets and brochures is seen as a significant benefit of ICT.

The website is a small part of a broader transport organisation and offers basic details of prices along with contact numbers and email address.

Current Status

The current website offers online or phone booking for transport between airport and provides an option for obtaining an online quote. There is also a link to a 'sister' business that appears to target a more corporate market, offering uniformed chauffeur transport to and from the airport as well as day or half-day tours of local wine regions.

Aboriginal Artwork

Background

This two-person business is based in the city centre and has focused on selling indigenous artwork for over 14 years. The predominant objectives motivating this small business, other than providing artwork products, is to run as efficiently as possible within the highly competitive business sector it operates in. The owner expressed a concern that the Australian government was not regulating the influx of cheap copies of Australian indigenous artwork from other countries in the region. The business's primary sales are centred on the international market, with the owner suggesting that Australians tend not want to purchase the artwork being produced. The level of business has not really changed in the last two years.

The Use of ICT

The business does not use any computers in their day-to-day activities, all their business activities relying purely upon well-run and effectively organised paper-based data collection. The business redirects all paper receipts to their accountant every month for their record-keeping.

Even though most of their clients are international, a situation where a website may have been advantageous, most of their sales are to people "dropping in" or calling from overseas. When asked about this lack of ICT, the owner indicated that "when my boy takes this shop over, he will introduce computers". This reference to generational change is a commonly encountered issue associated with the non-adoption of technology in the small business sector. They do appear on third-party websites where telephone and email addresses appear.

Current Status

The business now has a Facebook group, but only a handful of fans were active on this social media site. Although no website was established, the business had taken the opportunity to actually register an appropriate domain name. Collectively these small technological changes were presumed to be indicators of family members having an influence on introducing new ways and technological applications into the business environment.

Guided Golf Tours (Extended Vignette)

Background

This sole owner works in collaboration with a 33-room hotel (partly owned by him) to offer golfing packages that range from one day to one week. His extensive knowledge of all local golf courses allows him to align the specific playing characteristics of the various courses to the abilities and aspirations of the clients. He has been in the accommodation business for more than 10 years and has organised the golfing tour business for approximately two years. Most of the clients are from within Australia, but he has a growing international market. He can see the international aspect as being a key part of the business into the future.

The Use of ICT

The owner regards himself as being "computer illiterate" but notes that he is not hostile to new technologies, and in fact he regards them as an absolutely necessity. He was aware of the basic ICT terms but only some of the advanced ones. He felt that if he were younger he would probably be keen to do a course but has never had time to get around to doing it. One bonus of having the hotel business is that there is an individual in the hotel (the bottle shop/off-licence manager) who manages his computing needs for him. That person seems to be able solve most of the computer problems that are encountered. His real passion has always been in starting and growing businesses and dealing with customers. He does not possess a computer at home.

He sees the mobile phone as the most essential technology for his business and on a day-to-day basis he carries "a hell of a lot" of mobile phones and a paper diary. He spends considerable time talking with potential clients to build a golfing tour package that will suit their specific needs. He carries around extensive paper records that he uses to support this. The details of clients, tour dates and places are transferred to the hotel computer system at a later date by the hotel computer staff. He has considered a PDA but is still unsure that it would offer benefits beyond his well tried and tested paper system.

The tour business leverages its ICT off the accommodation business, which has five PCs. Only two of these are linked in a network. He described the main use of ICT for the tours business as communication. At the time of the interview he had not explored using social networking websites for the business. He did not see use of ICT by competitors as a threat. He indicated that in the end the customers kept returning to the area due the "secret of the place" and the packages that he puts together for them, rather than anything that ICT can provide. His business records are currently split between manual and computerised records as already described, but he could see that the Internet was gradually usurping phone and fax.

He does have a Web presence for the hotel and the tour business leverages off this—with a page devoted to the golf tours. He has an email address, accessed through the main hotel site. He described his website as an 'electronic brochure', which is linked to local tourism associations. This allows him to advertise his services, show example tours and place "hot deals" that are updated on a regular basis. When hotel accommodation space is lightly utilised he can offer special package deals for rooms and the guided tour. He does use email to communicate with customers and emails them newsletters. He commented that this was much easier than addressing 200 envelopes. Email allows him to help clients to tailor their tours.

He appreciates the potential value of ICT and felt that cost would not be a barrier to adoption, provided that it could be demonstrated that it either brought in extra customers or improved efficiency. He recognised that the dynamic nature of ICT would require regular upgrading, but again with a strict cost-benefit view.

He had little idea when asked about how often they considered the need to upgrade or renew ICT. He did indicate that he knew ICT people "in the town" and they assist them to "keep a pretty good eye on it". He equated upgrading their ICT to upgrading furniture or carpet on an ongoing basis, which is an interesting analogy. Although they had no specific plans in regards to ICT, he did talk about the support that they get from the local ICT business and suggested that they tended to be "efficient, well reasonably efficient anyway". This suggests a somewhat reactive strategy to potential ICT problems.

The owner of the business was somewhat vague when asked how he judged the success (or otherwise) of ICT. He did indicate that even if he didn't like them that they are the way of the future and "you can't run this business without them". He has no formal measures for judging the success of ICT. Whilst none of these were necessarily in place, he did indicate that they kept an eye on the costs of maintaining and purchasing equipment in general and that you needed to do this for taxation purposes (in regards to depreciation). This really reinforced the view that this business treated its ICT as a necessity (cost) rather than a strategic investment.

"I think that you can spend an absolute fortune and have the best, but if it doesn't bring one more customer through, then you may have to do something that doesn't bring a customer but improves the efficiency of the operation anyway; so it's going to happen, you're going to have to keep upgrading".

Overall this business was listed as an *ICT laggard* because it did not use ICT in any innovative way, lacked dedicated ICT backup and evaluation, and the skills of the owner were minimal (although these had been somewhat improved indirectly by having access to a staff member of the accommodation business with some ICT expertise and the ability to access some support from the local ICT business).

Current Status

The accommodation web page had undergone an overhaul with a more professional look and an interactive page to book accommodation. The golf tour page was still a link off the accommodation website and booking for this still occurred via telephone or email. The accommodation website also had a Facebook link which was updated with the latest news on a regular basis, although the last comments by visitors were from a year earlier. The golf tours were not advertised on this website.

The hotel was listed on some of the major accommodation portals (TripAdvisor, Wotif, Hotels.com) and some local directories. Strangely, none of these actually specifically mention the fact that you can also book golf tour packages in conjunction with the hotel. The closest is a local business directory, which lists the following in relation to the hotel—its beaches, the tours, the local wildlife and other local attractions.

It seems that the golf tour aspect of the business has missed out on an opportunity to leverage the various sites that the accommodation business is listed on to further promote its offerings. There was no indication that this business had made any significant inroads into ICT use since the time of the interview.

References

Banks, D. A., Monday, A., Burgess, S., & Sellitto, C. (2010). Focusing on SMTEs: Using audience response technology to refine a research project. *Journal of Issues in Informing Science and Information Technology, 7*, 311–320.

Buhalis, D., & Law, R. (2008). Progress in information technology and tourism management: 20 years on and 10 years after the Internet—the state of e-tourism research. *Tourism Management, 29*(4), 609–623.

Burgess, S., Sellitto, C., Banks, D., & Monday, A. (2009). *The use of information and communications technologies in SMTEs: The effect of varying levels of expertise.* 4th International Scientific Conference "Planning for the Future—Learning from the Past: Contemporary Developments in Tourism, Travel & Hospitality", Rhodes Island, Greece.

Cragg, P., Caldeira, M., & Ward, J. (2011). Organizational information systems competences in small and medium-sized enterprises. *Information & Management, 48*(8), 353–363.

Getz, D., & Carlsen, J. (2005). Family business in tourism: State of the art. *Annals of Tourism Research, 32*(1), 237–258.

Grol-Prokopczyk, H., Freese, J., & Hauser, R. (2011). Using anchoring vignettes to assess group differences in general self-rated health. *Journal of Health and Social Behaviour, 52*(2), 246–261.

Jackson, J., & Murphy, P. (2006). Clusters in regional tourism an Australian case. *Annals of Tourism Research, 33*(4), 1018–1035.

Liu, Z. (2000). *Internet tourism marketing: Potential and constraints.* Fourth International Conference, "Tourism in Southeast Asia & Indo-China: Development, Marketing and Sustainability", Chiang Mai, Thailand.

McDonagh, P., & Prothero, A. (2000). Euroclicking and the Irish SME: Prepared for E-commerce and the single currency? *Irish Marketing Review, 13*(1), 21–33.

Morrison, A., & King, B. (2002). Small tourism business and E-commerce: Victorian tourism online. *Tourism and Hospitality Research, 4*(2), 104–115.

Peltier, J., Schibrowsky, J., & Zhao, Y. (2009). Understanding the antecedents to the adoption of CRM technology by small retailers: Entrepreneurs vs. owner-managers. *International Small Business Journal, 27*(3), 307–336.

Rogers, E. M. (2003). *Diffusion of innovations* (5th ed.). New York: The Free Press.

Schauder, D., Johanson, G., Denison, T., & Stillman, L. (2005). *Draft information economy strategy for Australian civil society.* Melbourne, Australia: Centre for Community Networking Research, Monash University.

Sellitto, C., Banks, D., Monday, A., & Burgess, S. (2009). A study of Australian small to medium tourism enterprises (SMTEs) and their ICT adoption. *The International Journal of Knowledge, Culture and Change Management, 9*(6), 1–14.

Velupillai, V. (2004). *Hicksian visions and vignettes on (non-linear) trade cycle theories.* Trento, Italy: University of Trento.

4 Small Australian Tourism Businesses and LIAISE

Introduction

In the previous chapter each individual ICT business 'story' was presented through the use of a concise vignette. The vignettes formed the basis for categorising the individual businesses on the basis of how they were deemed to reflect lower, middle or upper characteristics in regards to several ICT domains. These domains reflected ICT use and innovation, the ICT skills available and evidence of the business having ICT governance practices. Furthermore, these features were used to collectively group businesses into the adopter categories that were deemed to be the ICT Leaders, ICT Operationals or ICT Laggards.

Also described in the previous chapter was the rationale for deriving the ICT business domains from the LIAISE framework. It was argued that ICT use and innovation was aligned with LIAISE's Information Content and Communication (I) area; ICT skills and requirements had a strong affiliation with Literacy (L), which reflected a business's understanding of ICT capabilities; and ICT governance aligned with Evaluation (E), which was informed by the manner in which a business identified, measured and valued ICT. In this chapter the data underpinning the vignettes and derived from the individual businesses is used to present an analytical perspective to the study, shedding further understanding on some of the overarching aspects of ICT adoption. The findings are presented using the areas of the LIAISE framework. The chapter also includes a summary commentary on the findings based around the three adopter groups.

The Small Business Features

A number of different types of businesses participated in the study. The sample included accommodation providers, businesses associated with organising and running events, tour businesses and what were denoted as tourism attractions businesses. The attraction and tour businesses made up more than 60% of the sample. Seven out of the 10 small businesses had only one to five employees. This is consistent with the literature that indicates that the majority of tourism businesses tend to be small family-run enterprises (Getz & Carlsen, 2005; Sellitto, Banks, Monday, & Burgess, 2009). Furthermore, given the relatively high number of businesses that had only 1–5 employees (a defining element of very small businesses), the study could be also viewed as one that captures aspects of how a small business concerns itself with ICT use and adoption. There was a reasonably equal split between businesses located in metropolitan and rural areas, although there were substantially more metropolitan tour businesses. Most of the businesses that participated in the study had been in operation for three or more years. More detail of the demographics of the focus, size and location of study's small businesses are provided in a preceding chapter of the book.

The literature suggests that the strategic focus adopted by a small business will invariably influence the manner in which it uses ICT. Participating businesses were asked to nominate their *primary* business focus from a list provided that included:

- *Growth*—those businesses looking to grow their business in future
- *Efficiency*—those businesses currently happy with the size of their operations but looking for ways to run more efficiently and keep costs down
- *Lifestyle*—those businesses that were predominantly operating to maintain a particular lifestyle for business owners
- *Other*—those businesses not falling into any of the above areas

There were a variety of responses from participants. Just over one-third of businesses (33%) classified themselves as having business growth as their primary business focus. A similar number (31%) selected lifestyle, and a slightly smaller proportion (25%) selected business efficiency as their main focus. A small number of businesses (11%) could not select a single business focus from those that were listed.

The ICT practices of the businesses are described in the following sections in relation to the various sectors of the LIAISE framework that could be seen to be under the control of the business. Furthermore, the analysis presented draws on the years of experience amongst the authors in the small business and ICT research area. As previously indicated, the infrastructure category of the LIAISE framework is not discussed because it is outside the control of the small business entities.

Literacy—Reflecting a Business's ICT Skills

This section focuses on the skills needed to use ICT effectively. The authors classified businesses into different levels of ICT expertise in an endeavour to identify what were termed 'naïve' and 'good practice' users. This classification of tourism businesses used a three-level system that was based on their perceived practical understanding and familiarity of ICT as well as the total number of years of using ICT. The determination of business expertise when it came to ICT included the:

- Familiarity and understanding of basic ICT applications
- Familiarity with basic ICT-related terms (list provided)
- Familiarity and understanding of more advanced ICT (list provided)

Based on the responses to this set of questions, the participating businesses were grouped into a spectrum of lower, middle and upper levels of ICT expertise. The businesses that had a lower classification represented the naïve ICT small business users, whilst the upper classified businesses were ones that were more expert in their use and understanding of ICT, reflecting what the researchers viewed as good practices. Businesses rated as middle in terms of ICT skills were deemed to be the businesses building their expertise beyond the naïve stage. Table 4.1 shows the classification of ICT expertise by area.

The analysis showed that one in two businesses were classified as being at the *middle* ICT expertise level, with a third of the businesses classified in the upper level. This meant that only one in six businesses was classified at the lower ICT expertise level. The authors were expecting a greater proportion of businesses at this lower level due to the widely reported notion that small businesses lack understanding and/or competency when it comes to information technology (Beckinsale, Levy, & Powell, 2006; Burgess, 2002; Cragg, Caldeira, & Ward, 2011; Eikebrokk & Olsen, 2007). This may be explained by small businesses generally having a greater level of familiarity with ICT, especially in the tourism area.

Some businesses that were classified with a lower level of ICT skills did not seem to comprehend or be aware that their ICT skills were lacking or deficient. For instance, one metropolitan tour business that only knew half of the basic ICT terms commented, "I know enough of them". A rural

Table 4.1 ICT Expertise Level of Participating Businesses

ICT Expertise Classification	Location		Total (N)	Overall %
	Metro	Rural		
Upper (Good practice users)	8	5	13	32
Middle (Users building expertise)	9	12	21	51
Lower (Naïve users)	4	3	7	17
Total	21	20	41	100

attraction business indicated that "we don't use computers and we really don't want to use them". However, that particular business actually did use computers, having a misconception of what they perceived as being a computer device. Another group of businesses that were relatively business-aware and creative acknowledged their lack of ICT skills. For instance, a family-run attraction business was aware of their ICT skills limitations and was waiting for their children to get to a stage where they would take the initiative to introduce computers. A metropolitan tour business that only used computers for communication purposes found it was ". . . more convenient just to grab my folder and write it [a tour booking] down . . . I find bookwork easier and quicker, just convenience I suppose".

Another aspect of Literacy relates to having data or systems recovery plans in place should the business's ICT fail. Having a data recovery plan for a major ICT disaster has been noted to be a relatively low priority feature for many small businesses (Cragg et al., 2011). Arguably, the inclusion of an ICT recovery plan by a small business manager reflects an understanding of the consequences of losing some or all of their ICT functions and information capabilities, with the resultant negative impact on the business. Around three in four businesses that participated in the study indicated that they had disaster recovery plans in place, in anticipation that something could go amiss with their ICT. This anticipatory planning was highest in the businesses classed in the upper level of ICT skills, with eight out of 10 of these businesses having a plan in place. The businesses classified at the *lower* level of ICT skills performed poorly here, with around four in 10 of these businesses not having a recovery plan in place. In fact, one business that thought its ICT practices were good did not appreciate it was carrying out an ineffective backup of its systems.

Indeed, for many businesses, a previous unfortunate experience seemed to be a catalyst for introducing a recovery plan. For instance, a rural attraction business "lost everything" when their house was struck by lightning. A rural tour business that "had one crash" now backs up its important files every month. Another metropolitan attraction business also backs up once per month on an external hard drive, whilst a rural-located business suggested that it was difficult to know what to do when actually performing a backup of their data. There were a few examples of more sophisticated backup procedures. For instance, one attraction business stored disk copies of files at different data integrity stages and stored them at a secondary location to where the business operated. An accommodation business used a traditional paper records approach for every electronic transaction that occurred as well as backing up their database onto disk every night.

Businesses classified at the lower end of ICT skills often used just basic technologies for a number of reasons. Notably, the degree of ICT-related skill levels possessed by a small business has been previously identified as influencing not only adoption levels, but also the diverse types of complex ICT applications that might be used (Lockett, Brown, & Kaewkitipong, 2006).

For instance, a naïve-rated metropolitan attraction business suggested that their business did not need new technologies and that they found them to be too complex. A rural tour business commented that technology moved too quickly and that it was difficult to determine what comprised a good investment. Interestingly, a complication for a rural attraction business was that their business computer was shared with their young school-age children for homework and games. This raised a number of issues, predominantly around potential security problems and deciding who had priority of access. A tour business that only used computers for communications felt that his competitors might have an advantage by using computers in more advanced ways, making it easier for their customers to book itineraries.

Numerous businesses mentioned that having the necessary time to develop their ICT skills was a problem, a commonly encountered situation reported in the literature (Barba-Sánchez, Martínez-Ruiz, & Jimenez-Zarco, 2007; Beckinsale et al., 2006; Cragg et al., 2011).

In summary, although the literature suggests that small businesses struggle with ICT literacy (Sellitto et al., 2009), there was generally a higher level of ICT competence in the businesses that were interviewed than was expected by the authors. There was, however, still evidence that levels of ICT-related literacy of some businesses could be improved. Although it seems reasonable to assume that the ICT practices such as a regular review of existing ICT and existence of an ICT disaster recovery plans would be improved with this higher level of competence, it is not guaranteed.

Support—Augmenting the Business's ICT Skills

The LIAISE Support area is closely aligned with allowing an organisation to improve or augment ICT Literacy from external sources, which is particularly important when trying to build business ICT capacity. In the context of previously derived business domains, Support is grouped as a sub-area under Literacy even though it appears as a distinct entity in the original LIAISE framework. This subordinate grouping does not diminish the importance of the LIAISE Support element, but highlights the overarching area of Literacy.

As suggested previously, research that has examined the adoption and use of information technology in the small business sphere has identified that one of the barriers encountered is associated with ICT skills acquisition and training (Burgess, 2002; Sellitto et al., 2009). From the LIAISE framework viewpoint, these skills are acquired (via various forms of support services) to ensure that the business has the adequate Literacy to access ICT effectively when existing skill levels within the business are inadequate. The study explored the issue of whether businesses perceived they had appropriate skills that allowed them to address their ICT requirements. Moreover, given the resource and financial limitations associated with running a small business (Eikebrokk & Olsen, 2007), the research identified the primary information and training sources that were used by businesses to improve their ICT skill base. This typically sheds light on the Support aspect of the LIAISE framework where external resources are used when trying to build business ICT capacity and which augments people's ICT Literacy. Most businesses sourced their ICT skills through a range of areas, the most popular being consultants, 'other' sources (previous work experience, product manuals and suppliers, other businesses/competitors and associations and the Internet), friends, training courses and family. Indeed, some businesses classified in the upper level of ICT skills recognised that it was important to access specialised computing support when certain circumstances presented. For instance, the manager of a metropolitan-based attraction business indicated that it was looking for consultancy services to assist with a database application. A few of these businesses discussed attending training courses, however a common issue was the time needed to do this.

A business classified as having lower ICT skills commonly sourced ICT support from family members but found that the situation changed dramatically when the family IT support became unavailable due to people moving to another township or locality. The business also had friends who assisted with specific technical issues; however part of the problem was not knowing where to source suitable support, the owner indicating that "it would be nice to be able to just telephone someone and have a solution provided". A rural tour business offered the view that the level of ICT expertise within the business had improved when the business hired an employee that also happened to be ICT-proficient, reflecting the notion of an employee acting in the tacit role of a computer champion. These observations fit with previous literature (Burgess & Sellitto, 2005) that documents the behaviour of the resource-poor small businesses as tending to adopt informal approaches to sourcing required skills through family, friends or a knowledgeable employee.

It was anticipated, based on the literature review, that 'informal' means of sourcing ICT skills (in the form of family and friends) would be an important sources in this study. These types of sources can provide inexpensive, but not necessarily appropriate ICT advice. Indeed, the use of family and friends were the most commonly used source of ICT expertise in those businesses that were classified by the researchers as being at the lower end of ICT skills. Interestingly, some of these businesses also relied on the use of consultants and training courses to gain new ICT skills. A number of businesses commented that whilst consultants had the technical expertise, they were not always able to offer advice that was relevant to their particular business, nor were they able to communicate in lay terms. A theme that also emerged was the time taken to resolve problems when they did occur. For instance, the network of a metropolitan accommodation business "went down" on the day of the interview with the manager indicating ". . . we can't receive emails, we can't go and update the website and things like that—so that's a big problem!"

Another interesting aspect of this study is that businesses that were identified in the lower range of ICT skills actually identified more sources of ICT skills on average than the other levels. This was definitely an unexpected finding and contrasts with previous investigations (Burgess, Sellitto, & Karanasios, 2009; Denison, 2008; Karanasios, Sellitto, Burgess, Johanson, Schauder, & Denison, 2006) that suggested that small businesses were more likely to adopt informal means to source required ICT expertise, rather than through structured programs such as those offered by consultants. It is possible that those businesses with the higher levels of ICT skills are more confident of their own skills and are also more likely to only access more formal sources of skills when external expertise was required. A number of businesses in this group had gained skills in dealing with ICT in previous employment before becoming small business entities.

Access—Reflecting Available ICT Infrastructure

From the point of view of this study, Access to ICT is viewed as being something that occurs at a point in time (that is, a business either has access to ICT or it does not). This function is clearly closely aligned with available Infrastructure, as well as facets of Literacy and Support. Thus, it was not expected that there would be many comments here as the majority of the businesses that were interviewed were using ICT in some form. However, a number of business that operated away from their main premises (which, in some instances, was their home), reported that it was a significant disadvantage that they were unable to access their computers whilst away, particularly to record bookings or orders. One metropolitan attraction business actually had their computer set up at home and could not enter information at their work premises, requiring the entry of daily data on their return home at the end of the day. Similarly, a rural tour business took bookings by mobile telephone when on the road, recording these on paper for later translation to a computer back at their home base. Another tour business made extensive use of multiple mobile phones to manage the business while on the road. A tourism business practicing winery tourism was able to remotely control various aspects of his business, providing significant benefits and advantages in efficiency. Although few in number, these are important examples of the use of mobile devices for information access and reflect the increasing adoption of 'anywhere and anytime' communication technology by small businesses (Cragg et al., 2011).

Information and Content—Reflecting ICT Use and Innovation

In the LIAISE framework, information and content was related to how ICT is being employed within the business and in particular its innovative applications. The matrix of ICT applications for added-value benefits identifies a range of areas in which businesses can use ICT applications to improve business operations. These improvements also reflect how ICT might be used to derive added-value benefits for the business in different areas. Table 4.2 documents an abridged version of the elements that compose the matrix and is presented to remind the reader of the presentation structure of the study's findings under the information and content area.

The most common and expected uses of ICT from the literature (record-keeping and accounting) were prominent in the responses of the majority of businesses. Such ICT use represented off-the-shelf applications as noted in the early work on this theme by McDonagh and Prothero (2000). However, there were some more creative ICT applications from businesses classified at the upper and middle ICT skill levels. A number of these businesses were deriving a significant proportion of their sales from their online presence and their websites. One metropolitan tour business used PayPal to offer gift vouchers to prospective or existing clients. This was successful for the business because not all vouchers were redeemed and, even when they were claimed, it meant that the business did not have to deal with cash-based transactions during the physical running of tours. A number of businesses implemented online bookings and payments services, some used ICT for successful marketing and promotion and others used the Internet for business-related research. For instance, one winery-tourism business with upper-level ICT skills used the Internet to research developments associated with new grape varieties, as well as to search for new employees that had appropriate vineyard skills. These businesses also appeared to be more likely to adopt specific ICT applications that were not part of the traditional 'grouping' of small business ICT applications, which contrasts with Schubert and Leimstoll's (2007) suggestion that small businesses are not generally overt users of atypical or complex ICT applications. Notably a business rated at the lower level of ICT skills classifications still mainly operated with paper-based accounts which were then manually converted to an electronic form using the Quicken

Table 4.2 Matrix of ICT Applications for Added Value (abridged)

Areas in which ICT applications can be used to improve business operations						
Improved Information Search	Improved Recording & Monitoring	Effective and Improved Communications	Improved Decision Support	Improved Relationships	Improved Work Practices	The Big Picture
Areas in which ICT applications can be used to derive added-value benefits						
Generic Added Value	Product Related	Price Related	Delivery and/or Distribution Related		Other	

accounts package prior to being sent to their accountant. However, this business did have a website and received the occasional online booking ("one in 200"). Another rural tour business classified at the lower level of ICT skills commented that its competitive advantage came from its unique business offerings reflecting products and services, and not from how it might use ICT.

General Use of ICT

The study's participants were requested to identify the most prominent use of ICT within their businesses. Many businesses listed the uses of ICT that had been previously encountered in the literature referring to:

- Record-keeping/ accounting/ banking/spreadsheet
- Word processing/ producing reports
- Taking online orders or payments
- Communications, such as email.
- Marketing/ promotions

As suggested in the literature, small businesses have used ICT for many years for cost savings and efficiency improvements, so it was expected ICT applications relating to accounting and word processing would be prominent for most participants. This would be expected amongst conservative small business types as well as those that might have had innovative ICT applications that may have been core to their business operations. However, some other ICT applications were also prominent in the list, including orders and bookings (mostly taken over the Internet), communications and email (internal and external to the business) and the use of marketing/ promotional ICT applications that allowed a business to engage customers.

In relation to the different types of ICT applications (see Matrix of ICT Applications for Added Value, Table 2.1 in Chapter 2), the businesses' experiences with ICT tended to fit into the categories of improving record-keeping and improved communications. Most of the benefits of these would be classified as 'general', except perhaps for online ordering or payment, which might be seen as streamlining the delivery and distribution process, which is arguably an adding-value activity practiced by the business.

When considering the most prominent use of ICT within their businesses, some small tourism businesses identified specific ICT applications or initiatives which they regarded as being particularly important or well suited to their business. This is consistent with Rogers' (2003) notion that an innovation can just be an application of a technology that is perceived to be new or novel for a particular business entity. These ICT initiatives are now described and discussed with regards to the matrix summarised in Table 4.2. Note that a number of the ICT applications could be classified as providing more than one added-value benefit, so the benefit considered most appropriate was selected (and 'general' was selected where this was not possible).

Information Search

There were a few examples that fell under this grouping. The ability to search for new, timely and specific information by a small business owner was identified by the researchers as an important example of the ICT added-value activity. In addition to using the Internet to search for new grape varieties (mentioned earlier), a rural attraction business (a farm that grew and cultivated berries) used a traditional Internet browser to conduct research into new growing techniques that were directly relevant to their core business. The identification of specific information was an enabler that allowed the small business to redevelop some of their core products (berry varieties). In regards to the added value of this ICT application, the significant benefit of using an information search was that it allowed the business to improve its product.

Effective and Improved Communications

Almost 40% of businesses mentioned that ICT were used for some form of communication (mainly email) when they discussed their general use of ICT. Six businesses went on to discuss specific approaches and applications in which they employed ICT for communication purposes. Four of the businesses identified particular Web 2.0 features to specifically improve their offerings. These involved using social networking tools such as Facebook, online discussion tools and blogs to mainly receive feedback about products and in one case (a tour business) to identify potential tour areas. These applications all provided product-related benefits.

An accommodation business used SMS messaging to keep in touch with customers to inform them of tourism events in the regions in which it operated. This provided an added-value feature to the business's customers by keeping them up to date and appropriately informed. This example would also fit into Gilmore, Carson, O'Donnell, and Cummins's (1999) 'other' category of added value as the benefits did not directly relate to product, price or delivery.

One tour business mentioned the use of a mobile device to add flexibility to their practices by allowing them to "manage from afar". This provides value to the business which cannot easily be translated to benefits to the customers.

Improved Recording and Monitoring

Five businesses identified specific uses of ICT that could be categorised as improving operational areas associated with recording or monitoring processes.

A metropolitan tour business utilised its website to offer travel gift vouchers to customers through the ancillary use of the third-party payment service,

PayPal. This aided with the removal of the traditional cumbersome mechanism of pre-paying and using the slow postal system to deliver purchased vouchers to customers. By using a third-party service, the small business overcame the costly overheads associated with running and maintaining the facility themselves. Another tour business was in the process of establishing electronic loyalty cards in conjunction with other local businesses. Both of these applications of ICT provided customers with an increased choice of product or rewards offerings and can be categorised as 'other' added value examples.

Two accommodation businesses used their website to promote available rooms, allowing prospective customers to view rooms online and book them directly if interested. A tour business also mentioned that they had an online booking service. These facilities sped up the 'supply chain' for customers as the response was found to be immediate, so it could be argued that the added value achieved was in the delivery/distribution area.

Another accommodation provider used satellite technology (GPS or global positioning system) for asset management, specifically to track the location of hotel accessories or equipment that were loaned or hired to travellers and visitors. A quite innovative use of ICT was identified by an attraction business (a berry farm) that used sophisticated hardware and software to monitor crops on a remotely located growing site. When the temperature dropped below a certain level, threatening crop viability, the owner was sent a signal message via phone allowing them to undertake action to avoid potential disaster. These applications provided benefits to the businesses that were not directly received by the customers.

Improved Work Practices

A number of ICT applications were identified that improved working practices. One business area where improvements occurred was marketing and promotion. For instance, one tour business used the social media video network YouTube to screen promotional videos about its tours and services. An accommodation business that did not have a restaurant was considering linking their website to those of local cafés and restaurants so that their latest menus were available to their guests online. A nature park attraction business installed webcams in their café (also owned by the business) showing live images of the unique and unusual animals located in the adjacent nature park. At the time of the interview they were awaiting a broadband connection so that the images could be directly streamed to their website. These applications would be classified as providing general benefits for the business (through increased custom) as opposed to specific added value for customers.

A number of other working practices were identified. For instance, an event business was using software to allow it to manage the operating and exhibition space they required on a weekly basis. A gallery used special frame-cutting software and associated hardware to automatically position, secure and cut the frame. The gallery was able to use the software to generate an image of how a painting would look before the frame was actually cut. This allowed the customer to 'view' the product before committing to a purchase and thus provided an 'other' value-added benefit for them. An attraction business used SMS messages to assist them in managing their staff rosters, resulting in operational efficiencies and improved timely communication. A rural attraction business used online research to find new employees when required. Another unique use of ICT was an accommodation business that collaborated with competitors via email to identify non-paying customers. These applications provided added-value benefits to the business and were not directly received by the customer.

Improved Relationships

A number of different ICT applications were identified by the small businesses as being particularly relevant to improving relationships with their customers or suppliers. Most of these related to improving relationships with customers.

Two businesses were found to provide customers with free and complimentary access to Internet browsing and email via free Wi-Fi access whilst visiting their business premises. Such complimentary ICT access was in addition to the services and products that the customers usually experienced. An accommodation business operated an Internet café as a supplement to their existing business and an attraction business was investigating whether to establish a centrally located "hot spot" to provide email and Internet access to its customers. These extra ICT services provide added-value attributes for the customer but are not directly related to the businesses' primary offerings. Such offerings can be considered to be intrinsic to establishing and developing the business-client relationship.

Examples of customer relationship development were documented amongst several attraction businesses, and included:

- A business that used industry-based software to store customer data and subsequently recall preferences when they next visited. This is a product-related benefit to the customer as it affects their experience at their next visit, as they do not have to repeat their requirements. Additionally, businesses may be able to tailor product offers or specials that are specific to customers' individual characteristics.
- A business that used ICT to provide customers with access to photo-printing to capture a timely record of their adventure activity. This is a product-related benefit.
- A business that used the social media Facebook site in a relatively unique way, not necessarily for them to communicate with customers

but more to link their followers, who have common interests, via their Facebook presence. This provided added value for the followers but did not directly relate to the business's primary offerings.

In regards to relationships with suppliers, an attraction business had linked with the databases of some of their suppliers online. This provides generic added value for the business. Arguably, the overall low use of ICT for this activity is a concern given the important nature of suppliers in the product/ service chain.

Summary of the ICT Applications and Added-Value Benefits

Table 4.3 provides a summary of the different types of ICT applications identified in the study and the types of added-value benefits that were generated. This summary presentation is based on the matrix of ICT applications for added value previously introduced. It is interesting to note that most of the benefits fell into several categories, ones that provided generic value-added benefits for the business, ones that related to the business's product offering or ones that provided some other type of added value reward for the customer. It could be argued that a number of the applications that provided generic added value would eventually relate in lower prices as it assists the business to become a 'low-cost producer' (as per Porter and Millar's (1985) generic strategies). The use of ICT for asset management, off-site monitoring, space management, roster management, identifying non-paying customers and linking to supplier databases could all potentially result in lower costs, and thus prices. It is more appropriate to list these as 'generic' benefits as they are not realised directly.

In total, 15 of the 41 interviewees identified these specific applications of ICT. It was found that no ICT use or initiatives were identified to support value-added benefits in the 'improved decision support' and 'pricing' categories. Furthermore, there were also no 'improving the big picture' ICT initiatives mentioned by any of the participants that were deemed to fall into this group. This latter finding was perhaps expected as most of the businesses were micro businesses, where the typical small business approach is one of operating and surviving from day to day, rather than having long-term aims.

Table 4.4 compares the businesses in the study across different primary business foci with the proportion that specifically identified ICT initiatives. It was expected that a higher proportion of growth businesses would identify added-value ICT initiatives or benefits (when compared with their representation in the study) and this was the case. However, the results were not conclusive. The proportion of other businesses with different primary business foci was still relatively close to their level of representation. The sample of businesses is not large enough to make any strong conclusion here.

Table 4.3 Small Tourism Business ICT Applications and Value-Added Benefits

Type of ICT Application	Generic Added Value	Added-Value Benefits		
		Product	Delivery/ Distribution	Other
Improved information search		Online search to improve product-growing techniques and search for grape varieties		
Improved communications	Mobile device used to 'manage from afar'	Social media to improve business offerings		SMS to inform customers of local events
Improved recording and monitoring	GPS for asset management Automatic off-site monitoring		Online booking/ payment	Online gift vouchers Loyalty cards
Improved work practices	YouTube and own website to promote offerings Specific software for location-space management Frame-cutting software and hardware SMS to manage rosters Email to identify non-paying customers			Special software so clients are able to see a final product before it is made up
Improved relationships	Specifically linked to the business's supplier databases	Instant printing of photos of adventure activities Database for retaining customer preferences		Provision of Internet to supplement offerings Facebook to encourage customers to communicate with one another

Table 4.4 Innovative Uses of ICT Classified by Primary Business Focus

Primary Business Focus	% Businesses	% Businesses Where ICT Added-Value Benefits Were Identified
Growth	33	34
Efficiency	25	28
Lifestyle	31	24
Multiple	11	14

Table 4.5 Variety and Geographical Location of Participating Businesses

Type of Business	% Businesses	% Businesses Where ICT Added-Value Benefits Were identified
Attraction	37	53
Tour	24	20
Accommodation	17	20
Event	10	7
Other	12	-

Table 4.5 shows the proportion of business types against the proportion that identified added-value ICT applications. Attraction businesses were very well represented. In future studies it may be interesting to examine if there is a reason for this or if it is just an aberration of this study. The results of the study support the notion that ICT are still used by Australian small businesses to improve business efficiencies or other processes internal to the business's operation. However, there appear to be many more examples than expected of the use of ICT for other purposes, such as improved communications with customers and the use of ICT to form alliances of different types or to just co-operating with other small businesses, be they in competition or in the form of co-opetition. The authors contend that this is due to three factors: the suitability of the small business sector selected for the study (tourism) to use ICT applications, the recent popularity of Internet applications, and the relatively higher ICT skill level of the small businesses that adopted these innovative solutions.

Furthermore, the study identified a number of added-value benefits that ICT applications provided to the businesses. What was interesting was that the identified group of added-value benefits was not limited to small businesses that had a focus on expansion and growth, with a reasonable proportion of efficiency and lifestyle businesses introducing ICT initiatives that could be classified as being innovative.

Evaluation—Reflecting ICT Governance

In the LIAISE framework, evaluation was concerned with how the performance of ICT is measured within the business. It was previously argued that ICT governance was closely aligned with LIAISE's Evaluation (E) area that was informed by the manner in which a small business identified and subsequently measured ICT adoption. Hence, this section reports the range of perceived benefits identified as a result of businesses using their adopted ICT. The ICT benefits derived by small businesses are argued as equating to a governance attribute that can reflect ICT business performance. Indeed, the notion of ICT benefits as a direct governance attribute is a practical one that can be clearly identified and articulated by owners in describing the utility of ICT in running their operations. In particular, participants were asked to identify the business benefits they derived from using ICT from the following:

- Enhancing operational efficiencies leading to cost saving
- Increasing or generating extra revenue
- Providing extra value for customers
- Improving communication and decision-making
- Strategic positioning
- Developing new services/products.

Not surprisingly, increased efficiency and improved communications were identified by most businesses as the benefits they received from ICT use, a finding that is reported amongst the small business and ICT literature (Burgess, 2002; Cragg et al., 2011). A number of businesses also mentioned increased revenue, extra value for customers and improved decision-making as business benefits. This suggests that many of the participating tourism businesses are aware that ICT can be used for more than just improving operational efficiencies, highlighting the capabilities of small business that are associated with aspects of ICT business strategy as noted by Cragg et al. (2011). This observation also lends support to these businesses exhibiting competencies that allow them to leverage ICT-related practices (Eikebrokk & Olsen, 2007).

Consistent with the other results in this study, those businesses at the lower skill classification were less likely to identify benefits outside of the expected responses, such as the use of ICT for strategic positioning and for new product/service development. A typical response of businesses at this level was that they carried out no evaluation of ICT performance at all, although some did suggest that they were happy if they kept the costs of running their computers to a reasonable level. However, some other findings of interest did emerge. Those businesses that did judge the performance of their ICT as being successful predominantly did so using perceived measures of efficiency, usefulness and the notion that they actually work. This is in striking contrast with more difficult evaluative measures of ICT performance reflected in benefits associated with indicators of increases in market share. This finding tends to reflect a reactive, rather than a proactive approach to measuring ICT implementation (Burgess, 2002; Lin, Lin, & Tsao, 2005). Some of the businesses classified with having an upper level of skills segregated their online sales from other sales to evaluate their performance. Given the emphasis on ICT use for automating business processes identified in the literature, this result is not surprising. Note also that only a small number of businesses (one in six) indicated that they used more than one method of judging ICT success and that one in 10 participants identified instinct or gut feeling as a way to judge the successful performance of their ICT usage.

The Value of the LIAISE Framework in the Small Business Environment

The LIAISE framework was proposed as being well suited and adaptable to the study's small business environment, providing a structured manner in which to investigate, analyse and document findings. Arguably, this approach could effectively be used for similar studies.

LIAISE was originally developed for non-profit and community-based sectors and addresses some of the fundamental requirements of ICT adoption such as ICT understanding and Literacy, highlighting the relative importance of ICT Access, Support and Evaluation to a group or entity. The authors noted the close analogies between small businesses and non-profits when it comes to ICT adoption, which allowed the LIAISE framework to be critically argued as a suitable vehicle to use in this research.

Indeed, this use of LIAISE to underpin the study is an important contribution to the domain that deals with small business and information and communication technology. By reformulating the LIAISE framework to understand the small business factors that guide adoption and subsequent use of ICT, the authors have demonstrated a framework that is flexible to accommodate the particularities commonly encountered in the small business environment. Furthermore, this reformulation of the LIAISE framework included modifications presented in the previous chapter where the authors argued the close alignment of LIAISE's Information Content and Communication (I) area with the innovative uses of ICT, Literacy (L) with ICT skills and Evaluation (E) with ICT governance. These three newly proposed focus points (ICT skills, governance and innovation) were deemed to be reflective of important ICT applications in the small business domain. The framework's emphasis on ICT Literacy as an antecedent to accessing and using ICT effectively provides solid foundations for investigating small business from a holistic perspective.

The reformulation of the LIAISE framework also utilised the matrix of ICT applications that reflected added-value benefits. The matrix allowed known operational areas to be juxtaposed with ICT benefits that aligned with added-value features in regards to business performance. Indeed, the tenets of the matrix were used under the Evaluation (E) area of the LIAISE framework to document added-value benefits derived by small businesses when using ICT.

Clearly, the LIAISE framework can provide a useful and structured tool for investigating, classifying and reporting ICT use by small business entities. The LIAISE framework used in this study has been reformulated by deconstructing the multiple areas of the original framework into smaller, intuitive and workable groupings, which are aligned with the commonly encountered ICT issues associated with small business.

The Leaders, the Operationals and the Laggards

In the previous chapter the rationale for grouping small businesses into lower, middle and upper categories allowed three classes of small business adopters to be proposed: The Leaders, The Operationals and The Laggards.

It would be appropriate to comment on these three types of adopters in regards to some common ICT similarities within each adopter group. The Leaders were not so much first or early adopters, but those businesses that used ICT at a level that would allow them to gain some form of advantage. These leaders typically had high scores in at least two of the three domains of ICT skills possession, ICT governance and innovative ICT use. In terms of the case studies only two businesses, the Market Tours and Recreation and Nature Park businesses, rated at the highest level for each ICT domain. Typically, the Leaders used their ICT in an innovative manner, with only three businesses in this group being rated at the middle level. Some innovative ICT uses included the leverage of applications to undertake scheduling and costing of tour operations to determine the viable number of tourists needed for the tour to be profitable; adopting several social media platforms such as Twitter, Facebook and Instagram to interact with a diverse number of people; and using remote webcams to allow people to view wildlife from afar, limiting the impact of visitors on the natural environment of the park's wildlife. Notably, the ICT skills domain was the main area in which many businesses in this adopter category did not rate at a high level. Most Leaders had a relatively high rating in regards to ICT governance, reflecting an understanding of the importance of business data as a core resource, a resource that needed to be appropriately stored and correctly maintained.

The Operationals were deemed to be small businesses that were rated at a lower level of ICT adoption when compared to the Leaders group across the three ICT domains. Many businesses in this group had adopted ICT for achieving business operational efficiencies typically encountered in the small business environment. Notably, only two businesses in this group scored a high rating in terms of innovative ICT use. Amongst the Operationals numerous businesses were found to rate at lower levels for ICT skills and

ICT governance. The important ICT application points amongst the Operationals included the use of basic word processing and account-keeping, enabling real-time bookings of the services they offered, implementing a bar coding system so as to manage inventory, asset management, scheduling and costing of business tours, timely communication with business partners and employees and improved reporting practices.

The Laggards are typically the non-adopters or the last to use new innovations (Rogers, 2003). In this study the Laggards were scored at a low level across the three ICT domains compared to their counterparts in the study. Indeed, the ICT innovation domain was found to be particularly challenging for these businesses. Notably, some of the issues encountered in this group relate to owners and managers having an inflexible attitude when it came to changing business-related tasks associated with ICT. The researchers observed that many of the small businesses that were rated as ICT Laggards were typically entrepreneurial and creative in running other aspects of their businesses. However, ICT was not being appropriately utilised, which was mainly due to the lack of ICT knowledge and skills available to them.

Conclusion

In this chapter, small business responses were classified according to the LIAISE framework, which was an informative exercise as it assisted in identifying areas where small businesses could potentially improve their ICT performance. The research involved a large, qualitative study using in-depth semi-structured interviews with 41 small tourism businesses. The authors expect that the matrix that has been developed for this study will be of significant value in other studies of ICT use by small business, or even applied to the medium business sector. However, it is not possible to claim a generalisation of the findings to other small businesses. Clearly, tourism entities are unique in that their information requirements align particularly well with adoption and use of ICT. The nature of the industry means that the authors certainly recommend caution in applying the results of the study to small businesses in general, especially in relation to interpreting the innovative uses of ICT that were identified in the study. As mentioned earlier, the authors believe that the matrix they have developed can be applied in other contexts.

In relation to the results of this study, the authors were surprised at the greater-than-expected levels of knowledge and sophistication shown by some businesses in their uses of ICT, especially those businesses classified as having upper- and middle-level ICT skills. On reflection, the authors feel that this might be due to the nature of the sector examined, tourism being a competitive and information-intensive industry that is well suited to computer-based applications. Arguably, the chapter's proposed LIAISE framework may be even better suited to evaluate the use of ICT in *general* small businesses, which are more likely to fall prey to some of the barriers to ICT use mentioned in the literature discussed.

References

Barba-Sánchez, V., Martínez-Ruiz, M. P., & Jimenez-Zarco, A. I. (2007). Drivers, benefits and challenges of ICT adoption by small and medium sized enterprises (SMEs): A literature review. *Problems and Perspectives in Management, 5*(1), 104–115.

Beckinsale, M., Levy, M., & Powell, P. (2006). Exploring internet adoption drivers in SMEs. *Electronic Markets, 16*(4), 361–370.

Burgess, S. (2002). Information technology in small business: Issues and challenges. In S. Burgess (Ed.), *Information technology in small business: challenges and solutions* (pp. 1–17). Hershey, PA: Idea Group Publishing.

Burgess, S., & Sellitto, C. (2005). Knowledge acquisition in small businesses. In T. van Weert, & A. Tatnall (Eds.), *Information and communications technologies and real-life learning: New education for the knowledge society* (pp. 47–54). New York: Springer.

Burgess, S., Sellitto, C., & Karanasios, S. (2009). *Effective web presence solutions for small businesses: Strategies for successful implementation.* Hershey, PA: Information Science Reference.

Cragg, P., Caldeira, M., & Ward, J. (2011). Organizational information systems competences in small and medium-sized enterprises. *Information & Management, 48*(8), 353–363.

Denison, T. (2008). *Barriers to the effective use of web technologies by community sector organisations.* CIRN 2008 Community Informatics Conference: ICT for Social Inclusion: What is the Reality, Prato, Italy.

Eikebrokk, T., & Olsen, D. (2007). An empirical investigation of competency factors affecting e-business success in European SMEs. *Information & Management, 44*(4), 364–383.

Getz, D., & Carlsen, J. (2005). Family business in tourism: State of the art. *Annals of Tourism Research, 32*(1), 237–258.

Gilmore, A., Carson, D., O'Donnell, A., & Cummins, D. (1999). Added value: A qualitative assessment of SME marketing. *Irish Marketing Review, 12*(1), 27–35.

Karanasios, S., Sellitto, C., Burgess, S., Johanson, G., Schauder, D., & Denison, T. (2006). *The role of the internet in building capacity: Small businesses and community based organisations in Australia.* 7th Working for E-Business Conference, Victoria University, Melbourne, Australia, Melbourne, Australia.

Lin, K., Lin, C., & Tsao, H. (2005). IS/IT investment evaluation and benefit realization practices in Taiwanese SMEs. *Journal of Information Science and Technology, 2*(4), 44–71.

Lockett, N., Brown, D. H., & Kaewkitipong, L. (2006). The use of hosted enterprise applications by SMEs: A dual market and user perspective. *Electronic Markets, 16*(1), 85–96.

McDonagh, P., & Prothero, A. (2000). Euroclicking and the Irish SME: Prepared for E-commerce and the single currency? *Irish Marketing Review, 13*(1), 21–33.

Porter, M. E., & Millar, V. E. (1985). How information gives you competitive advantage. *Harvard Business Review, 63*(4), 149–174.

Rogers, E. M. (2003). *Diffusion of innovations* (5th ed.). New York: The Free Press.

Schubert, P., & Leimstoll, U. (2007). Importance and use of information technology in small and medium-sized companies. *Electronic Markets, 17*(1), 38–55.

Sellitto, C., Banks, D., Monday, A., & Burgess, S. (2009). A study of Australian small to medium tourism enterprises (SMTEs) and their ICT adoption. *The International Journal of Knowledge, Culture and Change Management, 9*(6), 1–14.

Part III

A Study of English Coastal Small Businesses

5 The UK Small Coastal Business Vignettes

Introduction

The previous chapters presented the results of a study that examined a set of Australian small businesses in regards to their ICT adoption and subsequent use. The LIAISE framework was used as the basis for the study, which focused on a set of tourism businesses situated in urban and metropolitan areas located across two Australian states.

Clearly the notion of future research recommendations from the previous use of the LIAISE framework would logically reflect an extension of the Australian-based study. Such an extension might be to replicate investigations, not only in specific small businesses sectors, but also within the general small business environment in other parts of the world. Notably, the reformulated LIAISE is easily adaptable as the basis of an evaluation framework that allows researchers to evaluate both ICT adoption and implementation. In this section we document the second component of the research, which focused on a diverse number of small business located in the UK. The UK was selected as a comparison country as matter of convenience, as one of the researchers now resides in the small coastal town in England, which allowed him to access and engage with the small business entities.

General Background

The aim for this aspect of the study was to provide a broader representation of small businesses in general than just the tourism businesses examined in the Australian leg of the study. Table 5.1 shows the types of small businesses studied in the UK stage.

The number of people employed by the businesses that participated in the study is summarised in Table 5.2. Some 70% of business had only 1–5 employees, which is consistent with the notion that businesses engaged in tourism-affiliated industries are predominantly micro businesses.

As with the Australian aspect of the study, most of the UK businesses (79%) had been in operation for three or more years. Another similarity was that most of the businesses (84%) indicated that they had been using ICT for as long as they had been in operation. Again, all the businesses that

Table 5.1 The Different Types of Participating Businesses (UK)

Type of Business	Total	Overall Percentage
Attraction (leisure/café/gallery)	4	21.0
Accommodation	1	5.3
Retail	8	42.2
Construction/maintenance	4	21.0
Manufacturing	2	10.5
Total	19	100.0

Table 5.2 Size of Participating Businesses

Number of employees	Total	Overall Percentage
1–5 (Micro businesses)	13	68.4
6–19 (Other small businesses)	6	31.6
Total	19	100.0

had been in existence for five years or less indicated that they had been using ICT for the life of the business.

Having set the scene for small tourism businesses and provided some of the background of the participants in this first data collection phase, the rest of this chapter tells the individual stories of the participating businesses in regards to how they used ICT in their operations.

The UK Business Cases

As in the chapter that reported the findings associated with the Australian-based businesses, a black-grey-white visual moniker is used to group each of the UK small businesses into respective ICT domains and then their adopter category. Table 5.3 summarises the grouping of businesses into adopter categories. We reiterate that the ICT domains are aligned with the various components of the LIAISE framework. The use of black shading is affiliated with an upper ICT rating; the grey colour reflects a middle level and white a lower one. As indicated previously, an upper black rating was equivalent to 2 points, a middle grey rating 1 point and a lower white rating scored 0 points. Based on the numerical scoring of each UK firm across the three ICT domains, they were subsequently categorised as a particular type of adopter: the Laggards (score: 0–2), the Operationals (score: 3–4) and the Leaders (score: 5–6).

The remainder of this chapter includes each individual business's ICT 'story' as reflected through the use of a vignette beginning with the Leaders. As previously argued, the Leaders are the businesses that have adopted ICT that allow them to gain some form of business competitive advantage, the Operationals are businesses using ICT for the typically standard business operations, the Laggards are the slow or non-adopters of ICT.

Table 5.3 Adopter Categories and the ICT Domains

Adopter Category	Business Name (code)	ICT Skills	ICT Governance	ICT Use and Innovation
ICT Leaders	Double Glazer	Upper	Upper	Middle
	Kitchen Design and Installation	Upper	Middle	Upper
	Online Clothing Retailer	Upper	Middle	Upper
	Adventure Park	Upper	Middle	Upper
	Seaside Galley	Middle	Upper	Upper
	Building and Handyman Services	Upper	Middle	Middle
	Printer and Gallery	Middle	Middle	Upper
	DVD Rental	Middle	Middle	Middle
ICT Operationals	Beach Footwear and Seaside Lifestyle Retailer	Middle	Middle	Middle
	Florist	Middle	Middle	Middle
	Farmhouse Café and Restaurant	Middle	Middle	Middle
	Café and Gallery	Upper	Middle	Lower
	Curtain Maker and Retailer	Middle	Upper	Lower
	Books and Antique Guns Retailer	Lower	Upper	Middle
ICT Laggards	Tea House and B&B	Lower	Middle	Middle
	Glass Engraver	Lower	Middle	Middle
	Carpet Retailer and Fitter	Middle	Middle	Lower
	Plumber	Lower	Lower	Lower
	Antiques and Militaria Retailer	Lower	Lower	Lower

As with the earlier (Australian) data collection, there is one slightly 'extended' vignette provided for each adopter category. Additionally, each vignette contains a 'current status' section which represents an update of the business at the time of writing (2015) and provides an idea of the progress of their business plans a few years down the track.

The ICT Leaders

Double Glazer (Extended Vignette)

Background

This family business specialises in providing a range of styles and finishes on glass windows and doors. Additionally, the business specialises in building conservatories and other similar house additions.

The micro business operates as a husband-and-wife team, also employing two apprentices. The interview was conducted with the wife, who is also responsible for running the office. For over a decade the business had operated as a home-based business, but just over a year ago had moved into a shopfront. However, any major construction works are still carried out at home.

The business mainly operates with a local clientele, but they also service the local county area. At the time of the interview they were in the process of expanding the business and had just taken on a new employee.

The Use of ICT

As well as managing the office, the interviewee was also responsible for the use of ICT in the business. Record-keeping for the business was split 50/50 between paper-based and computer-based records. The business had been using computers since it commenced. Initially this was for accounting purposes, but now this had expanded into maintaining the website, the use of cameras and sending and receiving emails. The business had two PCs and one Apple Macintosh laptop (which also ran MS Windows). These were connected by a wireless network in the office. The business had an ADSL (asymmetric digital subscriber line) link to the Internet. The laptop appeared to be the primary machine for operating the business.

The business had a website that was mainly information-based and the interviewee was interested in developing it further. She suggested that although the next logical step for many businesses would be electronic bookings, the 'custom-made' aspect of their business meant that they "probably won't go down this path". As a manufacturer they would find it difficult to sell products online and, now that they have a dedicated person in the office, most people just telephone them in regards to work.

The website provided lots of information about the business and the services that they offered. They had a page of the website devoted to 'customer feedback'. This contained selected quotes that had been chosen by the business, as well as a series of audio files that contained recorded recommendations from customers. One interesting aspect of the website is that the business claims that 80% of its customers come via personal recommendations.

The business did use a professional drawing program (which was used by architects, designers and builders) to assist them with their work.

All employees of the business had smartphones and these were used to synchronise their calendars to ensure that all of their appointments were met.

The business had a social networking presence (Facebook) and there was a link to this on the business website. However, the interviewee suggested that at the time they only had 11 'likes' and that they had enough work without going down the social networking path. Interestingly, the business also flirted with a Twitter account, but indicated that it was not being used.

Although this business was classified as an ICT leader, it was not because of its level of ICT use and innovation, which was considered to be fairly standard for small businesses. Its ICT use did appear to be suited to the type of operation the business carried out (apart from the dead link on the website). In fact, when asked if they could provide any innovative examples of how they used ICT, the interviewee replied "nope".

The business shone in regards to its level of ICT skills. The interviewee was familiar with both simple and advanced ICT terms and described herself as an ICT expert. She felt that she had the necessary ICT skills for use in the business now and into the future. If she ever needed to access further skills she would do this via the local Apple reseller, external consultants or training courses as necessary.

The business was also rated well in regards to ICT governance. They review their need to upgrade their ICT on an ongoing basis. In fact, the interviewee wondered whether the business was being exploited, as every time there was a software update "you need to update the hardware". This (the cost of updating) was described as something that might inhibit their uptake of new technologies into the future.

The business backs up their files on the Cloud and also through the 'time machine' feature on the Macintosh. Additionally, they use a number of measures to formally judge the success of their online presence, such as the number of 'clicks' on their website and on the Yellow Pages directory. Also, they monitor "the level of output" from their computers. Informally, they receive "good comments" from their customers about how professional their website looks. The interviewee identified marketing/selling, customer service and finance/accounting as the areas of the business that benefit most from the use of ICT. They are also interested in setting up ICT links to their suppliers.

It has already been indicated that the business is listed on the Yellow Pages. They are also located on a number of general business and local business directories. Most of these provide simple text descriptions on the business offerings, with location maps, links to the website, address and/or a telephone number. Some sites also have photographs of sample work and provide the opportunity for customers to leave reviews.

Current Status

At the time of writing, the website had been redesigned but no new functionality had been added. The Facebook page had been removed (although the link to the 'dead' page was still on the website). The Twitter account is still accessible (with only a few 'tweets' by the business from years earlier being the only contribution). This lack of social media presence is perhaps not surprising given the attitude of the owner at the time of the interview.

Kitchen Design and Installation

Background

This business is based in a small English town and has been running for about 25 years with two branches, one in the town centre and the other, where the interview was conducted, on the outskirts. The business mainly serves the local area but on occasion has taken opportunities to consult and sell kitchens for new houses in Europe. The owner commented that despite the downturn in the local and national economy his business has remained reasonably level. He attributes this to the fact that the main clients are typically well-paid professionals that have not been substantially affected by the economic downturn.

The Use of ICT

The owner of the business has been using computers, usually Macs, since the mid-1980s. He currently has three Macs (two at the main store and one at the satellite store), which are all networked to one another through the iCloud. Using the iCloud allows access to key files when he is out of the office. He estimates that about half of his record-keeping is paper-based (for example invoices, kitchen layouts, etc.) and he keeps a paper folder for each of his clients. He said that although he could digitise them, there is no problem with keeping them in paper form in a folder.

He implements good practice with regards to backing up, utilising the Mac Time Machine facility that provide copies from an hour ago, a day ago and a month ago. He assesses his ICT expertise as somewhere between intermediate and expert.

The owner is conscious of the way in which competitors use ICT, particularly in the innovative approach used by competitors to generate a virtual walk-through of the new kitchen for the client. Although he can see clear benefits in this, he has yet to introduce such a system. He commented the cost was the biggest barrier to ICT investment but still remains on the lookout for innovative technologies for his business.

The owner is not interested in investing in the world of social media, commenting that "it scares me that it might make the business vulnerable to other people's comments". However, he does 'google' his business from time to time to see if people are talking about the business and, if so, what comments they are making.

Current Status

The town-based part of the business has now moved out to the outskirts site to provide a combined kitchen and bedroom design and installation service. The website is very crisp with sections for bedroom, kitchen, home office and decorations/furnishings. Each aspect of the business is detailed and accompanied by extensive photograph galleries. A 'news' section of the site contains a link to Twitter.

Online Clothing Retailer

Background

This business is unique in this book as it is solely an online store using eBay as the shopfront. This online clothing store has been in operation for around four years. It has been based in an office for the last six months, but prior to that, it was run from the owner's home. The primary market for this business is worldwide, and the owner states that her business has expanded in the last three years. She stated that she has made the leap from online hobby shop enthusiast to having this as her sole income.

The Use of ICT

Most of her record-keeping is performed using a laptop computer running Windows XP computers. The online store takes full advantage of eBay as its shopfront. The owner has a long term vision of creating her own website with e-commerce facilities but one of the barriers holding her back is the potential cost of building and maintaining such a website. At the moment, she does not have to worry about this while using eBay. In addition to stock control, email activities and eBay communications, all financial information is held on the laptop.

Because of the nature of having an online store, social media would be expected to play a large part in business operations. However, the owner has only used social media in a fairly limited manner. Although she does have a Facebook page for her business, and she appreciates the business potential, she does not have the sufficient time to spend exploring them.

The owner has also used training courses to increase her knowledge of ICT and how they can benefit her business. However, after attending a couple of courses (including the European Computer Driving License course), she found them much too general and said it was hard to implement what she had learnt. Technical support comes mainly from family and friends. She does back up her data on a weekly basis to an external hard disk.

This owner aims to run a tight ship and argues that using eBay to sell her products is a great way to start if you are unwilling, or unable, to maintain a website and online storefront yourself. The key concern is that of maintaining a strong business reputation rather than concerns about ICT itself.

Current Status

This business was an online business. eBay has said that this shopfront does not exist anymore, and her Facebook page said there was a big sale of all the old stock. The last entry on this page was in March 2013. The owner has advised us that she has ceased to function due to significant difficulties with her suppliers.

Adventure Park

Background

This business is a military-themed adventure park that is set on a warehouse site and offers physical games that emulate war-style battles, paintballs or laser tags. The organisation has been in operation for around three and a half years and primarily serves children and teenagers during the school holidays. The main focus of the business is to provide the best quality of service.

The Use of ICT

They have been using computers in their business since they opened. Currently, their record-keeping methods vary from paper-based (about a third), computer-based (again a third), and online (the remaining third). The interviewee commented that they had to use all three methods as "Different things have different methods. Deliveries are paper invoices, bookings can be done online".

They have had to meet the challenges of upholding the highest health and safety standards (paintball guns are very dangerous) on a very large site whilst looking after children. Their quite innovative solution has been to use one desktop computer connected to a private scalable wireless network throughout the premises, allowing them to connect all their CCTV cameras to the wireless network and record the video on a central computer. They are also able to connect to portable laptop and transaction machines. Communication with employees is via their personal mobile phones. They felt that this seemed the most straightforward solution, as they have such a large playing field, and their staff are rarely in their communal staff room.

The interviewee viewed social media as being vitally important to the business. The organisation has Facebook and Twitter accounts, but they view TripAdvisor as being the most important. They found out by accident that they were on TripAdvisor, but since then they target only "really happy customers to review us". When asked if they have had any negative comments, he said "yes, and we address them as we are in the tourist industry, and TripAdvisor is really important".

In regards to maintenance of the computer equipment, they review their computer needs every two to three years. The business backs up their computer to an external hard drive every night.

One thing they feel may restrict their adoption of new technology would be the manager's lack of time. The interviewee felt, however, that he was quite competent with ICT and would also ask his friends and external consultants for their opinions as well.

Current Status

The website is active, detailing their various military-style adventure features and having Twitter and Facebook links.

Seaside Gallery

Background

This business is an art gallery that displays and sells art from local and national artists. The company was only seven months old at the time of the interview. The business is part of a franchise model, where each gallery has its own region and is told which painting to sell.

Half of their business is scattered throughout the world, with most of their orders coming from their website. The other half is made up of local traders. Their goal is to grow the business, and in their seven months, this has happened. The business keeps around 80% of their records on computer. This generally involves transferring paper invoices and transactions into MYOB, and then giving a copy of the data to their accountant on a CD.

The Use of ICT

The business has been using computers since it started and has one desktop computer in the gallery. Their website only provides information about the gallery at the moment, but there is an online form for people to send requests and queries about possible purchase of pieces of artwork. He noted that he needs reliable broadband Internet as the business handles large picture files.

The owner classed himself as inexperienced with ICT and indicated that new technology makes him feel "stressed out". This reluctance to use complex technology extends to the point where he does not have a smartphone, just a mobile phone with basic features which he only uses for calls and texts. The business does, however, have a formal backup process, the owner backing up the daily transactions onto a hard drive every day.

The business has started using a number of Web 2.0 applications to help continue the growth of their business. One of the major tools they use is Facebook, which they use to promote their business to a global market. The interviewee described his attitude to social media and Web 2.0 applications as being more proactive. He used to class himself as 'reactive', but is "learning to embrace it and have it as part of the business now" and has hired a consultant to analyse his client and Web 2.0 interactions.

The owner judges the success of his ICT by seeing "if they turn on". He is unsure if he has the necessary ICT skills for the future, but he hopes he will get support from the central headquarters. However, as they are a franchise, they do not have the authority to dictate what ICT they can use.

Current Status

This business is no longer in operation. From the records kept by the UK government, it dissolved after five years.

The ICT Operationals

Building and Handyman Services

Background

This small general building and handyman business has been operational for over six years and services the local area. The sole proprietor thinks that the level of business has contracted in the previous two years and suggests that this is due to the downturn in the economy. His focus at the moment is to run a "good and efficient business", as he is happy with his lifestyle (which includes minimal debts and a home loan with a low balance).

The Use of ICT

The owner has been using computers for as long as he has had the business and uses computers for typical business functions such as record-keeping and administration. However, for his larger jobs he uses SketchUp, the free drawing and 3D modelling package. He finds the program easy to use and can transfer the files directly to clients or to other builders who use the program.

He would describe his attitude to social media as dismissive. However, he did set up an account with a website that allowed customers to "rate my work". In the beginning he asked people to comment, but it "fizzled out, and I haven't touched it in ages". He does have a website which he manages and updates using Microsoft FrontPage. He also has a separate business selling health supplements and has another website for this.

This organisation upgrades its computers on an infrequent basis, the owner commenting that once it stops working he will fix it, or buy a new one. He usually backs up his data once per week but does sometimes forget as it is a manual process.

Current Status

It has not been possible to determine the current status of this business.

Printer and Gallery

Background

This printing and gallery business has 'bucked the trend' of a recent economic downturn in the UK and expanded in the last three years. The proprietor bought the business from his father-in-law three years ago. His business has a gallery on the ground floor and a factory/printing area on the second.

The Use of ICT

This business uses their computers in three ways. Firstly, they are used for the standard business applications: record-keeping, accounts and email. Secondly they are used to operate the digital print machinery of the business. Lastly, they are used to maintain the business website.

The website is quite innovative and was developed by an external consultant. It allows local artists to upload high definition images of their art work, nominate a price for it, and receive payment every time the image is purchased on the website. When a customer purchases an image it is printed in the shop and mailed to the customer (or they can collect if they are local). Cost of printing is deducted from the artists' agreed price. The owners hopes to build a community with local artists, with the website providing an avenue for them to sell their work.

This website is beginning to generate revenue, with 15% of the business revenue being sourced in this manner. The owner views the revenue generated from his website as "icing on the cake" and still relies primarily on foot traffic visiting his shop. This view might change if he promotes his website better and starts to generate more revenue from it.

The owner has not really explored social networking and describes his business stance on it as 'reactive'. He does not actively search for his business online but feels that he should be doing more in this area.

The owner's ICT skills were assessed as being at the intermediate level and he indicated that a barrier to using new technologies was expense. He is trying to run his business without borrowing money and acknowledges that some technologies will have to wait.

Current Status

The website had changed little from the time of interview. It is listed in a number of local business directories. A basic Facebook presence had been set up for the business but there is no evidence of social networking activity such as comments posted by the business or its customers.

DVD Rental

Background

This sole owner-operator DVD rental business has been in operation since the mid-1980s and was purchased by the current owner in 1999. His market is essentially within a few miles of the shop in an area of fairly dense housing. The primary focus of the business is to maintain his lifestyle, but this has proved to be increasingly difficult as the business has entered a phase of contraction and he is "down to surviving".

The Use of ICT

He has one main computer for the business running Windows XP and finances are managed through an Excel spreadsheet. Day-to-day management of the rental library is through bespoke software developed in the 1990s and widely available to video/DVD stores at that time.

The business does not have a website but has investigated social media and has a Facebook page. He uses it to communicate information to customers, generally relating to new movies and 'specials'. He has also signed up to as many third-party directories as possible so that people can find him.

The owner thinks about upgrading his computers frequently. However, although he does have ICT expertise gained when he owned a computer repair business before he bought the DVD rental shop, he does not have sufficient finance to develop or expand the business further. He commented that if the main (computer) booking system "died", he would move to a paper-based system.

As noted above, the business is not thriving and he has added an Internet café (with five old computers running Linux) and started selling DVD and VHS videos on eBay to help increase his revenue. He also uses eBay to sell items from Africa (where his wife originates from) to help supplement his income.

Accounting data is backed-up onto a flash drive, but the main record system is not backed up, other than in the form of printouts. He commented that should the main booking system fail completely, he would move to a fully paper-based system.

Current Status

The business is no longer in operation.

Beach Footwear and Seaside Lifestyle Retailer

Background

This seafront shop sells beach footwear, clothing and seaside-themed homeware. Their primary market is mainly seasonal, targeting holidaymakers and tourists. This business has been in operation for two years and has two owners and three part-time staff. The primary focus of the business is to maintain the owners' lifestyle.

The Use of ICT

The business has been using computers since it first opened. Currently, they have two networked Windows 7 desktop computers (one acting as a Point of Sale terminal) and a stand-alone laptop with Internet access via Wi-Fi. About half of its record-keeping is undertaken on a computer, and around 40% is online, this being generally through their online store.

They identify themselves as having an intermediate understanding of ICT and they make use of external consultants. The professionally presented website was designed and implemented by a consultant and features an online store which accepts a wide range of payment options, including PayPal and Amazon.

The business feels that the key benefit from their computer system is that of improved decision-making about stockholding and sales as a result of access to back-end website data and their inventory system. Other benefits include customer service opportunities and ease of financial/accounting processes. They do employ a number of formal measures to analyse their systems, including data relating to online sales, hit rates and Google analytics.

The business is making limited use of social media in the form of a Facebook page. The owners also use Facebook but keep their personal and business social networking presence separate. Although the primary market for the business is tourists, they have not really investigated TripAdvisor. The interviewee commented that although they use TripAdvisor all the time for their own holidays, they had never thought of using it for their business.

They do not have any formal methods to assess the business value of their ICT nor do they have any formal technology upgrade reviews.

Current Status

The website has a newsletter link and a testimonials page. There is also a link to a new store that has recently opened in a nearby seaside town. The payment gateways, SagePay and RapidSSL, offer stronger security for online payments. The online shop appears to offer a way to extend their trading through the year rather than relying on tourist footfall.

Florist

Background

This sole owner-operator of a florist has been in business for 22 years, selling and delivering fresh flowers and bouquets for all occasions. The local town is the primary market although she does receive the occasional order from within the United Kingdom. The primary goal of the owner is to run an efficient business in order to maintain or improve her lifestyle. In the past two years her level of business has not significantly changed.

The Use of ICT

The owner describes herself as having a very basic, self-taught understanding in the practical use of computers. Her record-keeping is 80% paper-based, the other 20% is online mainly in the form of ordering flowers via her wholesaler. She still provides her accountant with paper documents. She has been using computers in her business for the last five years, mainly to order flowers from the wholesaler.

The owner has explored social media for her business, but only on a very limited basis. In the future she would like to have a Facebook shop, but thinks she needs more 'friends'. Her business is listed on QYPE (an online business directory), but has seen very little benefit from this.

She backs up her data to an external hard drive 'every now and then' and feels that she will only need to review her ICT every five years or so.

Current Status

The business now has a professionally designed website with fully interactive online store and galleries showing images of the various types of flower arrangements that she has available. Telephone contact is still encouraged so that details of wedding or funeral flowers and their presentation can be discussed personally.

Farmhouse Café and Restaurant

Background

This business is the café and restaurant component of a larger tourist attraction on the outskirts of a UK coastal town. The visitor attraction has a farm shop, bakery, honey bee exhibition, a camping and caravan site and a collection of craft workshops. Visitors to these various attractions typically eat and drink in the on-site café or have a meal in the restaurant. The café and restaurant has been operating for around for two years and can draw on 10 full-time staff members. The primary market served is divided between local and county visitors and the main focus of the business is efficiency.

The Use of ICT

Most of the record-keeping is managed on a computer. Most of their invoices arrive in paper form and this is manually entered into the computer. The business has been using computers since it opened two years ago and has two Windows desktop computers. They have a website which at the moment is information only, with no current plans to make it interactive. The primary reasons for using ICT are to reduce paperwork and to improve communication.

The owner has not yet investigated social media for the business, nor has he attempted to view any references to the café online. However he knows the attraction is mentioned on social media and most people view the café and the attraction as the same business.

As far as maintenance of his computers is concerned, he backs up the accounts onto an external hard drive and leaves it on-site. They have only had the current desktop computers for two years and do not see a need to upgrade them yet. He feels that he currently has the necessary skills to manage and use ICT in the business but recognises that in the near future they will need to turn to external consultants for advice regarding expansion or changes.

Current Status

The business has a website that is essentially information only. The number of craft shops on-site appears to have expanded. It is possible to download PDF files with details of menus for the tearoom as well as for special events such as weddings, Easter, Mother's Day and so on. The only way to contact the business appears to be via telephone.

Café and Gallery (Extended Vignette)

Background

This café and gallery selling contemporary art and ceramics is located in a suburb of a UK coastal town. At the time of the interview, they had been in operation for 18 months. The business is run by the two owners and two part-time employees, with additional staff at very busy times. The primary market of the business is mainly local customers, although the business does have a clientele that includes national and international customers. The turnover of the business had increased since its commencement.

The Use of ICT

ICT have been used within the business since it commenced, but not to any great extent. The reason given for this is that the business did not have "loads of other staff". It was predominantly a cash business and "at the end of the day you know what you've done". The business operates with one PC and one laptop that are not linked, although both have wireless access to the Internet (via ADSL). At the time of the interview, the business did not have a website but had set up a domain name and was still deciding whether or not to set up a website.

However, the business did have an active Facebook site which seemed to take on the role of information provision in place of a website, with basic business information and many pictures of artwork. The page is updated regularly with images of artwork and has a review feature which is used fairly regularly by customers to provide reviews of, and comments on, the artwork. The Facebook site advertises the artwork rather than the café side of the business, with the interviewee stating that "their Facebook site is a conduit for artists to discuss their own works and the works of others".

The interviewee had "a vague feeling" that the business was being mentioned on other social networking sites but did not consider there was anything negative being said about them: "I think you would wait and react when you hear about it—no news is good news!"

At the time of the interview, the business also had a dedicated email address and was "set up on Google Maps". The business did not use mobile devices for business purposes beyond normal telephone use as their operations were based at the gallery/café.

Interestingly, the interviewee's co-owner had worked with computers for nearly 20 years in a previous job and had set up the Facebook site, however, it appeared that ICT was generally on the periphery of the business. Apart from Facebook, the other main use of ICT was browsing the Internet to look at artists' websites to source new artworks.

In general, the business used ICT to improve the efficiency of their operations, save costs, as well as improve their decision-making and communication. The interviewee suggested that they did not use ICT in a more innovative way because that was the nature of the business. This was certainly the impression that was gathered by the interviewer. It seemed that this was a very innovative business, but that they did not need innovative uses of ICT for this to be the case.

Although the Use and Innovation of ICT was categorised at the lower level, overall the business was assessed as being an ICT Operational due to its high level of ICT Expertise and adequate ICT Governance practices.

In regards to ICT expertise, the background of the husband has already been mentioned, but the interviewee also indicated that she considered her ICT expertise to be in the intermediate/ expert range and was familiar with most of the ICT terms that were mentioned. It was certainly felt that they possessed the necessary skills for ICT use then and into the future. The interviewee suggested that they might consider using ICT consultants in the future if they decided to set up a website. Other sources of ICT expertise were family (her daughter was also familiar with ICT) and friends. One of the interviewee's real concerns in relation to ICT use was that they were not user-friendly: "They are not in the place you need them to be".

Evaluation of the success of ICT really boiled down to how the business assesses the Facebook site, and this occurs via online feedback from customers. There were no formal measures used to judge the success of their ICT use.

As there were no computerised accounts, the business backed up their files infrequently. When asked what they would do if their ICT failed, the response came that they would "just go out and buy a new machine". There did not appear to be any great concern about the potential loss of data associated with ICT failure as the interviewee indicated that there was no "really critical business data stored away".

There was no regular plan devised to determine when ICT should be upgraded. The interviewee suggested that upgrades occurred when her daughter (who ran an online business) advised her that they needed to be updated.

Current Status

At the time of writing the business also had a TripAdvisor posting under the local restaurants category. This page listed basic details about the business and allowed customers to post reviews about the business. They were also listed on a number of local, regional and business directories, as well as specialised websites (such as websites separately devoted to galleries and cafés). These websites generally provided basic details of the business, location maps, images and, in some instances, customer reviews. The business was also written up favourably in articles written for online newspapers.

Curtain Maker and Retailer

Background

This small business is a retail shop that specializes in standard and custom-made curtains and soft furnishings. Customers are generally drawn from the local area. This business has had challenges in the last several years due to the decline in the local and national economy.

The Use of ICT

The business has moved in the direction of using computers to support their business operations mainly in regards to accounting. All invoices, bills and even their Internet orders are in paper form, which are subsequently entered manually into the computer and, in turn, forwarded to the business's accountant.

The owner commented she finds it easier to sell standard curtain items than custom-made or specifically designed ones. She has tried to implement a custom made-to-order section on the business's online store but has encountered numerous issues due to people not measuring their windows correctly. With the downturn in the economy she has had to make some cutbacks, and one of these was to replace her usual IT person with a university student to maintain her systems.

She is not concerned about her competitors using ICT although she recognises that many of them use their computers in a far more advanced manner than she does. She is particularly aware that some competitors use simulations of how a customer's room might look when new curtains are added.

The owner has not investigated social media, the main reason being that she does not understand how it works. The primary driver for using ICT in her business is to provide extra value for her customers, improve her decision-making and develop new services and products. Although she assesses her ICT expertise at the novice level, she is acutely aware of the benefit that can be obtained from ICT and therefore explores all potential training avenues to access these skills.

Current Status

This business's physical storefront no longer exists. The owner has semi-retired but is still making and selling soft furnishings, on a much smaller scale, from her home.

Books and Antique Guns Retailer

Background

This sole owner-operated business is seven years old and buys and sells antiques, collectables and shooting-related items. The business shares a shop with three other businesses and the primary market he serves is national. The primary focus of the business is to maintain his lifestyle, however the downturn in the UK economy has had some impact upon his aspirations. He sells from the shop, but there is little local interest in antique guns or associated paraphernalia so most sales take place at trade fairs. The online side of the business appears to offer an avenue for growth.

The Use of ICT

He sources much of his stock from contacts he has built up over the years and most of his sales are through the website.

All of his record-keeping is undertaken on his computer. He uses one Widows 7 laptop, which he has migrated to from a desktop computer. He rates himself as 'inexperienced' in his practical understanding of ICT and uses an external consultant to develop his website with a shopfront. Online sales account for around 35% of his revenue and appear to be growing.

The owner has not investigated social media for his business although the website has an inactive 'Follow me' link that was intended to connect to Twitter. The owner has signed his business up to a couple of third-party directories, but this has not yet proved to be of any benefit.

He will look into upgrading the computer equipment in three to four years time, or when he feels his computer is running slowly. He does back up his data onto an external hard drive once a month.

Current Status

The website is attractive and has links to a blog which shares information about antique weapons and highlights items wanted and for sale. There is a short biography of the owner and details of forthcoming antiques arms fairs and game fairs that he will be attending. There is also a gallery of images showing items for sale with price details.

The ICT Laggards

Tea House and B&B

Background

This home-based family business operates as a tea house and bed and breakfast. This business has been in operation for the past seven years, staffed by three people, although casual staff are employed in the summer. The main focus of the business owners is to maintain their current lifestyle and run an efficient business. In the past two years, the amount of business has not changed, and their guests travel from all parts to visit them, as they are set in a historical building.

The Use of ICT

The company prefers to limit their use of ICT, one of the business owners being an ex-banker who "is happy to keep it all paper-based". They use MS Word to back up some of the important paper documents, although this is limited to copying and storing invoices, confirming numbers and guest details. They have two standalone PCs, both having access to the Internet.

They have a website, but it is only there to provide the guests with some introductory information about the location, including pictures and directions. The interviewee said they like to talk to the guests beforehand on the telephone to "see what kind of people they are". They are not currently signed up to any review-style website, although they commented that they may consider TripAdvisor, but this was not a high priority.

This business, in common with many family businesses, appears to be on the edge of a generational transition. The current owners assessed their ICT expertise at novice level, but believed that their son will have enough ICT skills to continue the business. When the son was asked about this, he said he would like to modernise the computer system they have and save time on the administration.

Current Status

The business now regularly appears on TripAdvisor UK, with a number of excellent reviews.

Glass Engraver

Background

This family-owned and operated glass engraving business has been in operation for over 20 years. The business sells a variety of glass products (wine and whisky glasses, Christmas snow globes, etc.) that can be engraved on-site to customer requirements. Currently only the manager is full time with six part-time staff members, including three of her daughters. A High Street shop serves her local market, but she also has worldwide sales via an eBay store. Over the past two years, her business overall has expanded, but only due to the introduction of sales of electronic cigarettes. Sales of glass products have been falling and without the e-cigarette sales, accounting for around 80% of her revenue, the business would have contracted.

The Use of ICT

Most of her record-keeping is through the computer. The organisation has one desktop computer and two laptops, all running Windows XP. They are not networked, but all of them have access to the Internet. The computers may be networked sometime in the future, although the plans are currently rather vague.

The business has a website which is connected to her eBay store. The owner updates the website herself and would like to see the site substantially updated when finances permit it. One problem with eBay sales is that glass is heavy and fragile, leading to high postage costs and the need to deal with breakages in transit.

She has a Facebook page and would like to grow that more if she can find the time.

At the time of the interview, the owner was backing up her data onto an external hard drive. However, she had just signed up to a Cloud service to do it automatically, although she is still in the process of setting up. Her own knowledge of ICT is limited and she relies upon help from one of her daughters.

Current Status

The shop website is active as is the eBay site. The range of products sold appears to have expanded to include greetings cards, ceramic objects and more Christmas decorations, all personalised to customer requirements. There is no evidence of e-cigarette sales.

Carpet Retailer and Fitter

Background

This family-owned business has been operating in the town for more than 65 years and has been in its present location for the previous 34 years. The business mainly serves the local area. The business has contracted to some extent in the last three years due to a weaker local economy.

The Use of ICT

This organisation only uses their computer system for operational needs. They have three networked computers (all running Windows XP) connected to a server. However, the internal network is not connected to the Internet. They have a non-networked 'stand-alone' computer in the reception area that is connected to the Internet for staff use. The business does not have laptops or tablets for mobile use as the owner is "happy to do stuff when I get back to the office".

There is no regular pattern for replacing their hardware, replacement taking place when a computer starts to "feel a little slow". There is a backup procedure where the bookkeeper will back up the accounts everyday onto a USB drive and then lock it in a fireproof box.

The owner has not really explored social networking or generating a Web presence. The interviewee described his attitude to social networking websites as "dismissive" and will not actively search for his business online, but added that "but now you mention it, I might start to". The company's website is for information provision only. The interviewee added that due to the nature of the product, it is "too hard to sell them online".

Although his ICT skills were assessed as being at the intermediate level, he indicated that new technologies were too complex and having to learn them is a barrier. The use of ICT by the business can be regarded as being fairly conservative, mainly being used for record-keeping and information provision online.

Current Status

The website has received an overhaul producing a neater layout and including testimonials from customers. An online form for contacting the business directly, previously hidden way in a secondary page, has been moved to the home page. There is still no indication of a social networking presence.

Plumber (Extended Vignette)

Background

This small plumbing business provides plumbing services within a small English coastal town. The business owner has been a plumber for 26 years. The business is a classic home-based enterprise with the owner working from home and typically travelling to private homes and business premises offering plumbing services. The business record-keeping and office administration is undertaken by his wife. The business has not experienced any significant changes in the amount of work being booked over the last two years. The owner indicated that he was happy that he had not tried to expand the business when the economy was performing better as he had been busy enough in recent times.

The Use of ICT

The owner has used computers in his business for more than 10 years. Prior to using the technology, all of the paperwork, including accounting and billing was office-based. Nowadays, the owner indicates that "it all goes into the computer (through his wife), and it handles it all". He estimated that 80% of the business records were computer-based with the remainder being paper-based. He possesses two computers, a laptop and a PC, but the laptop was only for "social use".

At home, the owner has an ADSL Internet connection which is used for business and social purposes. The business does not have a website, although he has considered the possibility of having a site to promote his business, although this is still in its initial stages of planning. Nevertheless, the owner's son, who is a plumbing apprentice, wants to start using the Internet to build up the business. This has started to play a very small role in his business, with his wife organising some jobs through her personal Facebook account, so he "doesn't know how it all works". Other than this small foray into social media, the owner does not know if his business has been reviewed or listed on any other websites. He commented that "I think I'll go and have a look (to see if people are reviewing the business online) when I get home".

Although the use of ICT in the business is limited, the owner indicated a number of areas that had benefited from its use, particularly improved decision-making (using spreadsheets to calculate quotes), improved communication (email allowed him to communicate with a client who was deaf), generating extra revenue (through Facebook) and providing extra value for customers (as he was able to search for cheaper materials to use online).

The business was assessed as being an ICT laggard because it had basic ICT use and innovation, but also rated poorly in regards to ICT skills and ICT governance. There were signs of an awareness of this and a willingness to address these shortcomings.

Whilst the owner assessed his ICT expertise at novice level, he is continually improving across all facets of computer use. He explained that when he had to renew his certificate for gas fitting, it used to take a week to get the results. Now, he undertakes the exam online and it takes an hour to get the results. The owner recognised that he had a lack of ICT skills for current and future use, but did state his wife had those skills for the business to operate their computers now.

The owner possesses a smartphone but didn't realise this until the interviewer pointed it out as he just used it for phone calls and text messages. However, he is interested in setting up email access on it.

The business rated poorly in regards to ICT governance. They do not have an active policy to review their need to upgrade their ICT. Basically they replace things "when something breaks". This was despite the business having had an alarming experience with hardware failure and no backup of his records. Both of his computers failed at the same time and he had to pay someone to recover the data. He now regularly backs up data and records once per week.

The business's ICT is judged as being "successful when they don't break down". No formal measures are used to judge the success of ICT operations.

Current Status

At the time of writing no online references to the business could be found, however, the business is still fully operational.

Antiques and Militaria Retailer

Background

This sole owner-operator sells small antiques and militaria. The organisation has been in the same location for the past 15 years after relocating from the main part of town to a shop close to one of the largest hotels in the town. The primary market for the business is generally tourists, and more specifically the older tourists, and business has operated in essentially the same way for the last 30 years. The business does not have a website. The main focus of this business is to maintain a lifestyle, with the owner noting that he is "ticking along and surviving until retirement". The amount of business he conducts has not changed in the last three years.

The Use of ICT

This business does not use computers, the owner preparing his reports and paperwork for his accountant in a traditional paper-based way. The owner has been using computers in his personal life for a number of years but has not introduced them to the business because "I've been in this industry for 35 years and have lots of contacts". This extensive and long-standing personal network means that he can sell to the public and trade with similar businesses without recourse to ICT. The business does not have a website, the owner noting that he is too busy running the store, and even if he did consider ICT, he would not know where to start. The business does not use social media, although when asked if he knew what people may be saying about the business he commented, "I will have to look and check it out later!"

Although his ICT skills were assessed as being above basic level, the owner indicated that he was very resistant to technology in general and to the use of it in his business. The only time he used the Internet in a business-related way was to see where auctions were being held and to view his competitor's website for price comparisons. He mentioned that he felt that the only reason his competitors had websites was to reach a larger or international market and that this was a market he felt he did not need at this time.

This business has a steady market of older tourists and a lean administration which has been built over 35 years. He felt that his business will not change or incorporate much technology until he sells it or retires.

Current Status

The owner has now retired and the business no longer exists.

6 Small UK Coastal Businesses and LIAISE

Introduction

The previous chapter documented the individual ICT 'stories' of businesses located in a coastal town in the UK. The UK set of vignettes supplement the Australian-based businesses reported in the first sections of the book and, collectively, the vignettes provide significant insight into the ICT adoption by a broad group of small businesses across two countries. In this chapter the data associated with the UK-based businesses is discussed to present an overview for this group in regards to their ICT adoption. The discussion is presented using the LIAISE framework where a business's ICT capabilities are examined in regards to their ICT Literacy (L), how their ICT governance aligns with Evaluation (E) and ICT use, and the way Information Content and Communication (I) is used. The chapter also includes a summary commentary on the findings based around the three adopter categories deemed as the ICT Leaders, the ICT Operationals and the ICT Laggards.

The Small Business Features

A range of small UK businesses agreed to take part in the study. The participants included retail businesses that had a diverse product offering, trade businesses that reflect sectors of the construction industry, food services providers and small businesses that were involved with art and recreational activities. The group of retail small businesses made up the majority of the sample (47.4%) followed by construction (21.1%) businesses. Thirteen of the 19 participating businesses had between 1–5 employees (micro businesses). Of the retail businesses investigated, just over half of them had contracted economically in terms of their business turnover, whilst nine businesses had increased and/or expanded their financial turnover. Most of the businesses that participated in the study had been in operation for three or more years, with over 50% having been established more than 10 years. Given the relatively high number of micro businesses in the study, the findings presented can be viewed as typically reflecting the behaviour and concerns of these types of small businesses in regards to ICT use and adoption.

As previously indicated, the literature suggests that the manner in which a business will use ICT is dictated by the strategy it considers and subsequently adopts (Burgess, Sellitto, & Karanasios, 2009). The small businesses who participated in the study were asked to nominate their primary business strategy or focus from a list provided that included:

- *Growth*—those businesses looking to grow their business in future
- *Efficiency*—those businesses currently happy with the size of their operations but looking for ways to run more efficiently and keep costs down
- *Lifestyle*—those businesses that were predominantly operating to maintain a particular lifestyle for business owners
- *Other*—those businesses not falling into any of the above areas

The responses from participants covered all possible strategic considerations offered; however, the majority (52.6%) indicated that their primary business focus was aligned with having a particular lifestyle. The next primary business focus nominated by businesses was efficiency (26.3%), whilst some 16% selected growth. Only one business could not select a single business focus from those listed.

The following sections describe the ICT practices of the businesses that participated in the study using the different areas of the LIAISE framework. The analysis draws on the collective experience of the researchers in the investigation of small business adoption of ICT to interpret, shape and present the findings. Because the Infrastructure category of the LIAISE framework was outside the control of the small business entities, it is not included as part of the findings.

Literacy—Reflecting a Business's ICT Skills

This section focuses upon ICT literacy. All the businesses were classified at the levels of their ICT expertise so as to identify and document the 'naïve' and 'good practice' businesses. The classification into ICT expertise was based on three areas which included a business's perceived understanding of practical ICT issues, their general familiarity with ICT and the total number of years they had used ICT. Business expertise in regards to ICT was guided by the following areas to determine expertise:

- Familiarity and understanding of basic ICT applications
- Familiarity with basic ICT-related terms (list provided)
- Familiarity and understanding of more advanced ICT (list provided)

Subsequently, the participating businesses were grouped as having a lower, middle or upper level of ICT expertise. Businesses with a lower classification level represented the naïve ICT small business users. The more expert businesses were those that recorded an upper classification level and arguably had a better understanding, familiarity and use of ICT. This expert group were deemed by the researchers to have enacted good ICT practice. Any business that was classified in the middle group was beyond the naïve stage and deemed as further developing and building their ICT skills and expertise. Table 6.1 summarises the businesses in regards to their classification of ICT expertise.

The majority of businesses occupied the middle ICT expertise level, whilst almost a third of the businesses were considered to be at the upper level of expertise. One in four businesses was designated as having a lower expertise level in regards to understanding, familiarity and use of ICT. As with the Australian businesses, the UK-based businesses had a surprisingly small number of businesses that can be classified as naïve ICT users. The lack of basic ICT skills has been shown to be a key issue in the UK that prevents small businesses from expanding and being successful (Diallo, Patel, & Wrelton, 2013). Indeed, this aligns with the observation that some small businesses have a lack of understanding of ICT which directly impacts on their competency to apply ICT applications (Beckinsale, Levy, & Powell, 2006; Burgess, 2002; Cragg, Caldeira, & Ward, 2011; Eikebrokk & Olsen, 2007). An interesting finding is that three of the four construction businesses have a seemingly greater level of familiarity with ICT than the other businesses investigated. This is unexpected, given that the sector is usually at the lower end of ICT users (Burgess et al., 2009). Across the 19 businesses that participated in the study, a total of 49 computers were being used for business-related activities, with 40 of the 49 computers being recorded against the upper and middle groups.

Many of the businesses classified with lower levels of ICT expertise were not aware that their ICT skills were at the lower end of the scale, which could suggest that their need for ICT was limited or that they did not

Table 6.1 ICT Expertise Level of Participating Businesses

ICT Expertise Classification	Total	Type of Small Business				
		Retail	Construction	Attractions	Manufacturing	Accommodation
Upper (Good practice)	6	2	3	1	–	–
Middle (Building expertise)	8	5	–	2	1	–
Lower (Naïve users)	5	2	1	–	1	1
Total	19					

perceive a need to know the technical details of its use. Two of these businesses had not established a website and several of the businesses could not identify the type of Internet connection they used. When the businesses that were assessed as having lower levels of ICT expertise used multiple computers in their operations, not one networked these machines. Whilst it is not always necessary to network computers, it could be expected that at least some of these businesses would have benefited from access to shared data or at least shared access to a printer. All members of this group were identified as being inexperienced in their understanding of the new types of ICT that regularly became available in the marketplace. Amongst the naïve users, several reasons for this lack of ICT expertise were identified as relating to generational issues. For instance, the accommodation business owner was well aware of its lack of ICT skills and was waiting for his son to take over what was ostensibly a paper-based business. The owners acknowledged that when the son took over the management of the business, it would be a more ICT-aware operation.

LIAISE Literacy can also be associated with having some form of data recovery plan enacted should the business's ICT fail. According to Cragg et al. (2011), some small businesses tend to overlook data recovery planning, considering it a low priority. Some 90% of businesses in the UK study had an ICT data recovery plan in place, suggesting that they had an understanding of the importance of their business data and the consequences of losing such data. Interestingly, four of the five small businesses that were rated as naïve users of ICT had gone to the effort of putting an ICT recovery plan in place. This contrasts with the Australian-based businesses documented earlier in the book, where having a recovery plan was predominantly practiced by businesses that had a higher level of ICT skills. It was noted that the approaches to implementing data recovery plans varied across the businesses. Some businesses undertook a systematic and planned backup of business data each day, whilst others used a longer time frame. The actual data backup practice in some instances involved the simple use of a USB device or a larger portable hard drive. In this scenario, both types of devices could be potentially kept off-site, adding an extra level of security to the business's data recovery plans. One retail business had their data backup automated through the use of a Cloud solution. This particular retailer automatically backed up their data every hour with the subsequent end-of-day copy to the Cloud. A business that used eBay as a sales platform had a semi-formal or hybrid approach to data backup, indicating that much of the business's data was automatically stored by eBay, with the local non-online data being backed up once per month. Some businesses, in common with the Australian businesses, indicated that although they had a recovery plan in place, they were not disciplined in their approach to backing up data, conceding that sometimes this activity was overlooked or forgotten.

The businesses that were classed as having lower levels of ICT expertise all remarked that they did not believe they had the necessary skills to run their current business ICT effectively, or to their potential. They also indicated that their ICT skills in the future were also likely to be deficient. This tends to reinforce the notion that variable ICT-related skill levels will impact on not only ICT adoption levels but also on the complex business tasks needed in undertaking various applications (Lockett, Brown, & Kaewkitipong, 2006). One of the naïve-rated businesses suggested that because they "did not grow up" in the computer era, there was a significant issue in gaining the appropriate skills. Implicit here is the relative complexity of ICT to the business. A common thread amongst several of the business owners in this naïve user group was their reliance on close family members, for instance, a son or daughter who was commonly called on to supplement skills needed to operate their computers. Furthermore, this group also mentioned that having the necessary time to develop their ICT skills and the expense of ICT training were a problem, reflecting one of commonly encountered reasons for poor ICT use in small businesses (Barba-Sánchez, Martínez-Ruiz, & Jimenez-Zarco, 2007; Beckinsale et al., 2006; Cragg et al., 2011).

It is suggested that small businesses tend to face challenges with ICT literacy (Sellitto, Banks, Monday, & Burgess, 2009). However, the findings from the investigation of this particular UK-based group of small businesses suggest that the ICT skills and competency was far higher than might have been expected, particularly amongst the upper- and middle-level-rated businesses.

Support—Augmenting the Business's ICT Skills

The Support construct of the LIAISE framework is closely aligned with ICT Literacy, explaining the importance of external resources in augmenting or building organisational ICT capacity. Support, although a distinct framework entity, is declared as a sub-area of LIAISE Literacy in order to highlight the pervasive aspects of Literacy.

When examining small business adoption of ICT, the generally accepted notion is that acquiring appropriate ICT skills and requisite training can be a significant barrier (Burgess, 2002; Sellitto et al., 2009). The LIAISE framework postulates that such ICT skills can be sourced through a number of ancillary business services, ensuring that businesses are able to possesses the appropriate ICT Literacy should their existing skills have intrinsic gaps, be absent or rudimentary. The resource limitations commonly encountered amongst small businesses (Eikebrokk & Olsen, 2007) hinders their ability to seek skills and training so as to improve their business acumen. Improving a business's ICT skills is one of those areas that also relates to what has been termed resource poverty, where purchasing a piece of technology might be viewed as both a first and final step for some (Burgess et al., 2009). The researchers explored the various primary information and training sources that could be used by businesses to improve their ICT skill base. The identification of these sources to improve the ability of businesses to better use ICT aligns closely with the LIAISE Support category. Indeed, the use of externally sourced resources can be viewed as having a capacity-building function that might extend and underpin the business's ICT Literacy.

A wide variety of areas were used by businesses to source ICT skills that they felt were not readily available or which were deficient in their business operating environment. Table 6.2 summarises the sourcing of ICT skills by businesses when considered from an ICT expertise perspective.

Consultants and friends were one of the main external sources used by small businesses to access ICT expertise. Consultants were a primary source of ICT knowledge support for middle-level businesses that were seemingly building their expertise in regards to how and why they might use business-related ICT. Fewer consultants were used by businesses in the upper level and naïve ICT users groups. The businesses classed with an upper level of ICT expertise were the only group that attended professional courses in order to support and build their ICT capacity. This may reflect initiatives that allowed them to gain knowledge of ICT through formal educational programs, such knowledge acquisition being viewed as a knowledge investment rather than a business ICT expense. Consultants tended to be used by numerous businesses for website support, which may have involved aspects of website design, development and maintenance. Some business owners were acutely aware of the importance of the website in certain business functions and indicated that through the use of consultants they had learnt new approaches to using a website. In one particular business, the consultants were an important component associated with providing support and maintenance for their operational computers, a task which was undertaken through remote access. Some of the other sources used by businesses included university students that were brought in to assist the businesses with ICT, self-teaching instruction manuals and an employee with an interest in championing computer use.

Across all the businesses, informal use of family members and friends collectively formed the greatest resource for accessing ICT skills. The family

Table 6.2 Sourcing ICT Skills and Business Classification of ICT Expertise

ICT Expertise Classification	Family	Friends	Consultants	Courses	Other
Upper (Good practice users)	–	3	2	2	1
Middle (Building expertise)	1	2	4	–	2
Lower (Naïve users)	4	2	1	–	1
Total	5	7	7	2	4

members were invariably either a son or daughter that possessed skills or expertise that their parents did not have. This tends to reflect one of the important cross-generational attributes that can be tapped into by businesses to alleviate the constantly changing ICT challenges small businesses encounter. Such family members can be highly skilled and sympathetic to challenging ICT issues in their family's business. This issue of how resource-poor businesses adopt informal approaches to gaining ICT skills through either family, friends or even a knowledgeable employee has been previously noted in the literature (Sellitto et al., 2009). The ever-increasing use of educated, younger and highly ICT skilled family members as a normal consequence of the digital age cannot be overlooked as a reliable, important and an inexpensive resource. Indeed, this might actually be an important skills acquisition phase for small businesses, particularly those having lower levels of ICT skills. Amongst the businesses investigated, the naïve businesses were the ones most commonly using family to source ICT expertise. Arguably, for those with higher levels of ICT skills, a more intense approach, through structured learning courses or one-on-one with consultants, may have been more conducive to further enhancing ICT expertise. This finding is counter to some of the previous literature (Burgess et al., 2009; Denison, 2008; Karanasios, Sellitto, Burgess, Johanson, Schauder, & Denison, 2006) that asserts that accessing ICT expertise through structured or formal methods is not commonly practiced by small businesses.

Access—Reflecting Available ICT Infrastructure

Access to ICT occurs at a particular point in time and is reliant on the information and communications infrastructure that is in place. Physical infrastructure in many instances will reflect government-controlled telecommunication services which are provided through private or public operations. ICT infrastructure may represent physical cabling conduits or the availability of the wireless mobile communication spectrum. Hence, this element of the LIAISE framework is heavily reliant on the capacity of available Infrastructure, as well as facets of Literacy and Support. All but one of the businesses participating in the study were using ICT in some form, many having access to a network that allowed ICT-based practices to be undertaken through wireless devices. The use of mobile devices, particularly in the construction sector, allowed some businesses to operate certain aspects of their business away from their main premises. The rising use of mobile devices for information access and/or communication reflects an opportunity for all businesses to achieve greater flexibility in running their operations. Indeed, wireless infrastructure that supports mobile devices, as well as traditional infrastructure, can potentially enable Cloud-based services that herald opportunities for businesses to increase efficiency, engage in remote working and enhance collaboration activities (Cragg et al., 2011; Deloitte, 2014).

Information and Content—Reflecting ICT Use and Innovation

Information and content within the context of the LIAISE framework was deemed to be aligned with how small businesses used ICT within the business environment. This is particularly relevant to the use of ICT by businesses in an innovative manner or through innovative applications. The matrix of ICT applications was previously introduced and described the added-value areas that ICT can be used by a business to enhance their operations. Table 6.3 summarises the components of the matrix and is re-presented for the reader so as to be able to more readily consider UK findings.

As with the Australian-based group of businesses, a common and expected use of ICT was associated with record-keeping and accounting (McDonagh & Prothero, 2000). Small businesses have traditionally used ICT to achieve cost savings and efficiency improvements particularly in regards to various accounting practices (Burgess et al., 2009). With the UK study being undertaken several years later than the Australian component of the research, several businesses were found to be utilising Cloud services that they viewed as an ICT application. In recent times, small businesses adopting Cloud services have been identified as positioning themselves ahead of their competitors, Cloud services being an ICT that allows them to grow quickly (Deloitte, 2014). Such Cloud services were predominately associated with record-keeping practices and using virtual storage to back up important resources. A number of businesses viewed Web presence as an important aspect of their ICT use, allowing them to derive an important element of their revenue through online sales. These businesses had in place interactive websites that automated online purchasing through a web store or web shop, with one particular business having their online store directly linked to their inventory system. Other businesses had adopted ICT that was directly adapted to supporting sales in their industry sector. For instance, a business had industrial-size electronic printing in place as a primary aspect of running their business efficiently and effectively. Schubert and Leimstoll

Table 6.3 Matrix of ICT Applications for Added Value (abridged)

Areas in which ICT applications can be used to improve business operations						
Improved Information Search	Improved Recording & Monitoring	Effective and Improved Communications	Improved Decision Support	Improved Relationships	Improved Work Practices	The Big Picture

Areas in which ICT applications can be used to derive added-value benefits				
Generic Added Value	Product Related	Price Related	Delivery and/or Distribution Related	Other

(2007) indicate that small businesses per se do not overtly use non-standard or complex ICT applications; however findings from this study suggest that in some instances there are notable exceptions to this assertion. When in place, the use of such ICT can be valuable for the adopting businesses. Given this observation of complex or atypical ICT sometimes being used, two businesses still used a paper-based system as their only form of documentation, with the majority having a mix of computer and paper.

In examining responses from businesses, it was found that some of the ways they used ICT in the small business environment were specific to their business or were part of an initiative to further enhance some aspect of their operations. As noted with the Australian-based businesses, this ICT adoption behaviour fits with innovation diffusion observations (Rogers, 2003), where an innovation can just be an application of a technology that is perceived to be new or novel for a particular business entity. These specific ICT applications and initiatives are now described and discussed with regards to the matrix summarised in Table 6.3. Where the use of ICT was deemed to provide more than one added-value benefit, the more appropriate grouping was selected.

Information Search

Access to online information using a range of different platforms has become an activity that might be expected amongst small businesses (Burgess et al., 2009). Arguably, the practice in accessing information that is current, timely and purposefully relevant allows businesses to undertake comparison pricing, competitor evaluation and the sourcing of cost-effective business items and decision-support activities. Such information search activities can also be viewed as value-adding, allowing the business to achieve cost savings that may be associated with efficiency or, on the other hand, improved customer satisfaction that may result in future loyalty and increased sales. Some businesses nominated information search activities as providing them with added-value benefits. An art gallery business was particularly interested in being able to identify and purchase new artistic works so that these could be added to their portfolio of offerings. They used a number of online resources that allowed the owners to aggregate information about artists and their works so that they might be directly evaluated, negotiated and subsequently purchased. The information search activity for this particular business allowed them to source products that might be otherwise difficult to find through their normal distribution channels. Another example of information search activity was evident in the construction sector. One construction business used online information searches to directly benefit the client through lower pricing. The business routinely identified and sourced lower-priced building products online, assisting them to provide more consistently affordable pre-contract quotes which were more favourable than their competitors and resulted in more business. One of the attractions businesses, specialising in antiques, used the online medium to research and identify stock that might be attractive to their clients and profitable for the business. Clearly, the ability to search for new, timely and specific information by these small business owners is distinctive and can be viewed as an important example of how even simple information search activities can have an added value proposition.

Effective and Improved Communications

Some 60% of the businesses indicated that ICT were used in their business for communication purposes, which was acknowledged as being a business benefit. Eleven of the businesses had some form of social media presence which contributed to several aspects of their operations. The main social networking practice involved having a Facebook site, with several businesses mentioning Facebook alerts as an important communication forum. A video store owner indicated that Facebook allowed him to "get information out to customers" and that the business posted regular morning messages that seemingly "keeps people interested".

Mobile phone devices were an important communication tool, with one business heralding his not-so-modern BlackBerry as being vital to the business. Indeed, one construction business highlighted the importance of smartphone functionality, giving the example of all employees using smartphones to synchronise appointment books and calendars so that meetings were not missed. Implicit here is the issue of how small businesses are following a common example utilised by larger businesses, where there is an expectation that people use/bring their own device (BYOD) into the workplace. The concept of BYOD was not explored in this study, however small businesses could potentially reduce (or share) ICT expenses through adopting a BYOD policy. Another construction business used the mobile phone in an asynchronous mode as this offered him the most convenience when he was working from a ladder or was located in some other problematic space that did not permit him to take direct voice calls. Collectively, these types of ICT applications tended to provide benefits that allowed businesses to better manage their day-to day operations, with the social media communication activities aligned with marketing activities.

Improved Recording and Monitoring

Thirteen of the 19 businesses nominated improved record-keeping as an important and valuable benefit associated with ICT applications. Implicit in businesses' responses was the alignment of record-keeping with the ability to monitor many of their financial or accounting operations. There was also variability in ICT use for record-keeping and monitoring purposes which reflected several different approaches to the replacement of paper-based business activities and the importance of digitally recording certain business transactions. One retailer specialising in flooring and carpeting, although only using computers for 50% of their record-keeping activities, commented that operations had become easier for the business, with improvements in operational speed since the adoption of computers. The business had tasked a specific employee to collect, collate and enter the paper-based data into a computer for easier access and subsequent use. Another retail business used computers for all their record-keeping activities. However, the accounting documents (invoices, orders, bills, etc.) were all manually entered onto a computer rather than electronically captured and stored. Internet orders were printed out and subsequently re-entered. A manufacturing business streamlined their record-keeping in order to make sure that the company could directly interact with their accountant at particular times of the year or when required. The business's website allowed for an automatic electronic capture of documents. A Web presence for certain businesses meant having an interactive website that seamlessly captured digital orders and provided them with electronic business records. In effect, this capture of data through online processes bypassed the traditional paper-printing phase of ordering and sales and can be viewed as a value-adding aspect of adopting ICT for record-keeping. One small business used eBay as a third-party provider to electronically document and record their business activities.

Improved Work Practices

Businesses were asked to identify the areas in which ICT provided value in operational practices. The marketing and sales area was a prominent area of function in which several businesses were using ICT to garner valuable benefits, particularly in regards to customer engagement. Across a number of small businesses, the website featured as an ICT that had added value, with one business indicating that "the rest of the areas are just core business tools . . . value is the website for customers". This particular curtain retailer noted even greater value provided by her competitors on their websites as they offered potential customers the opportunity to simulate how curtains would look in situ. The added-value aspect of this ICT application was one of allowing potential customers to visualise the curtains in a typical room setting, which would assist with their decision to purchase. Another retail business was implementing online product catalogues in an effort to further engage the customer base with a greater variety of offerings. This particular retailer recognised the importance of their website as a central avenue that allowed them to sell a larger number of products and was actively promoting the site for this purpose. Furthermore, the business also utilised database technology to segment customers, allowing them to more closely monitor and stay in touch with their larger clients. This use of ICT was a good reflection of how technology can assist with typical customer relationship management capabilities.

For an attractions business, ICT was a significant value-adding feature allowing them to efficiently manage their incoming supply of goods. The business was part of an art supplies franchise that needed to routinely source art products through its head office. The ability to access and use the central ordering system maintained by the head office allowed them to place orders and source art supplies seamlessly.

Another retailer using eBay as their online sales outlet embodied a holistic philosophy to managing their operations. Although working from home, the business distinguished itself on eBay from other traders by using the platform exclusively, compared to competitors that used the online site ancillary to their physical retail presence. The eBay site for the business was their primary virtual platform that facilitated Web presence. This allowed the business to fully integrate operational areas such as marketing, sales and supply chain management functions, resulting in important efficiency benefits. Arguably, the platform provided the small business the working environment (platform and software) to allow them to better integrate their operations, an issue recently noted by Deloitte (2014) as enabling small businesses to rapidly grow.

Improved Relationships

ICT applications can be used by businesses in their endeavours to engage with suppliers and clients to subsequently improve business relationships. Given the time lapse between the UK and Australian studies, the researchers identified that social media was an increasingly prominent business tool for building relationships with customers. In all instances, the businesses alluded to their customers as a primary focus of their social media use. Social media was explained in terms of available platforms (Facebook, Twitter and so forth) by the researchers in order to allow businesses to understand the tenets of what was meant by social media presence. Implicit in responses was the alignment of social media to businesses building relationships with potential clients and the potential of any online content originating from them. Ten businesses (56%) indicated that social media had had no real impact on how they operated. However, eight businesses (44%) identified that social media had had either a marginal or significant impact on operations. The researchers investigated the issue of social media adoption to determine if businesses:

- Had explored the notion of the social media from a business perspective
- Had subsequently implemented some form of social media presence
- Knew of any third-party platforms that had included information about their business or products and
- Had a particular attitude to social media (reactive, proactive or dismissive).

Table 6.4 provides a summary of responses based on the perceived impact that social media had on their operations.

Out of 19 businesses interviewed, 18 responded to this question. Of the businesses that had not considered or explored social media, many were either not aware of how it might be of use, or in some instances had identified negative aspects. For instance, one attractions business did not wish to get involved with the medium due to a perception that people outside the business would be able to steal details and information associated with the military antique products he offered. Another business indicated that they were quite concerned that it might make the business "vulnerable to other people's comments". Several businesses identified that resources were limited and prevented them from implementing this newly emerging innovation (Burgess et al., 2009), with time and understanding being typically mentioned as obstacles. Others that had explored social media concluded that it was not for them, with one construction business suggesting that the medium did not seem to be of value to the building sector. However, several of the other construction businesses did have a Facebook presence with mixed results. One used it primarily to upload images of their recent projects in order to promote the business but had only received limited feedback. Another construction business had been able to gain several jobs through their Facebook presence. This was primarily due to the builder's partner having good social media skills and being able to source and sign up new work.

A limited number of businesses in the study were quite involved with the use of social media. One of the more innovative small businesses with a social media presence was an attractions business that had a Facebook page as well as using Yelp (previously QYPE) to post business promotions.

Table 6.4 Perceived Impact of Social Media on Business Operations

Impact of ICT (social media)	Had explored a social media presence	Actually had a social media presence	Identified third-party sites with posts about the business	Attitude to social media
No Impact (N=10)	7	5	3	Dismissive—6 Reactive—2 Proactive—2
Marginal Impact (N=4)	2	2	1	Reactive—1 Unsure—2 Proactive—1
Significant Impact (N=4)	3	3	3	Proactive—3 Dismissive—1
Overall	15	10	7	Dismissive—7 Reactive—3 Unsure—2 Proactive—6

The operators of the businesses are proactive in monitoring and maintaining their social media presence, allowing them to benefit mainly through marketing activities.

One online retailer that sold all their offerings through eBay had explored both Facebook and Second Life as platforms. Second Life was dismissed as a non-viable option for the business. However, Facebook had been fruitful in generating new business, mainly as an informal relationship-building channel which helped to promote the business. The owner also noted that certain conversations or postings that occurred on Facebook had mentioned the business in a positive manner. These types of social media post provide extra unsolicited exposure for a pure online retailer that does not use other promotional avenues. The business, although wanting to be proactive in the social media space, identified that finding the time to be able to understand the medium was a limitation. One art gallery business noted that the collaborative nature of social media not only allowed them to capture customer feedback but also acted as a conduit for the artists who 'followed' them to discuss their works with others.

A theme park business that used social media as an important channel for promoting tourism was particularly astute, having both Twitter and Facebook presence. The business noted the significant promotional aspect of online comments mainly through being listed on a third-party tourism site (TripAdvisor). The owners found that it was important to be alert and proactive in making sure that any negative comments are addressed with appropriate and timely responses. In a similar manner comments posted by satisfied clients offered the opportunity to engage in relationship building through the use of targeted offers. Another business that had a proactive attitude when it came to social media was considering adding a Facebook store to their social media presence allowing them to have additional sales opportunities to complement their eBay activities.

Many of the social media experiences noted amongst businesses with a proactive attitude to using social media provide reasonably good added-value examples. The continuing evolution of social media tools and the advent of new platforms make examples of this particular class of ICT important to identify.

Summary of the ICT Applications and Added-Value Benefits

After investigating ICT adoption, the researchers noted that certain applications provided added-value benefits for some small businesses and were worthy of further consideration. The matrix previously proposed and used in the analysis of the Australian-based businesses has been used as the basis of Table 6.5 and summarises the ICT applications adopted by small UK businesses.

The added-value benefits identified are presented across several categories, reflecting how they might provide generic added value to the business, whether

Table 6.5 UK Small Business ICT Applications and Value-Added Benefits

Type of ICT Application	Generic Added Value	Added-Value Benefits		
		Product	Delivery/Distribution	Other
Improved Information Search		Sourcing products specific/unique to the niche offering of the business		Wholesaler dis-intermediation—sourcing components to provide lower pricing in quotes
Improved Communications	Asynchronous mobile phone text communication as a means of managing work interruptions			Mobile devices applications (apps) interlinked to synchronise employee appointment and meeting activities (customer service focus), Social media as an enabler of real-time communication with customers
Improved Recording and Monitoring	Capture of digital records to seamlessly transfer data for financial accounting purposes			
Improved Work Practices	eBay site as a primary virtual platform for facilitating Web presence, thus integrating operations such as marketing, sales and supply chain functions		Access to a centralised head office database enabling streamlined inventory control and ordering	Free mobile Wi-Fi service included with booking arrangements (distinctive offering in a remote seaside town), Customer database used for specific customer segmentation/activities
Improved Relationships	Using third-party social media sites, such as TripAdvisor to identify positive client experiences through comments (further offers), Negative comments addressed with appropriate responses	Social media used as a conduit for discussion of topics and products relevant to the business		Using different social media platforms (Facebook and Yelp) to promote the business

they focus on product offerings or if they provide a means to add value to customer activities. As previously indicated, generic added value offers businesses the potential to eventually reduce their running costs. For instance, the complete and seamless digital capture of the business's financial data for accounting purposes will, over time, translate into cost savings. It was found that no specific ICT use or initiatives were identified that directly supported value-added benefits in area of 'improved decision support'. Similarly, 'improving the big picture' with ICT initiatives was not evident amongst participants, even those that indicated that growth was their main business driver.

Thirteen of the 19 businesses identified various applications of ICT that were deemed to have some value-added benefit that the business was able to directly exploit. All businesses classified with upper levels of ICT skills were leveraging at least one ICT application in order to gain value-added benefits. One of the upper-level businesses did provide at least two clearly notable examples of how they used ICT for value-added purposes, both associated with customer activity (product simulation on their website and using their database for identifying and segmenting customers). A number of businesses classified with lower levels of ICT skills also provided relevant and clear examples of how ICT applications provided the business with value-added capability. For example, one business sourced products that directly impacted on their customer pricing or offering in order to differentiate itself amongst similar businesses in the coastal township. These businesses had a specific focus on using ICT applications to add value to benefit existing or prospective customers. Table 6.6 shows the business types against the added value afforded by the use of ICT applications.

All of the businesses that were part of the construction sector were seen to be using ICT for some value-added activity that offered them significant business benefits. Given that construction activities such as building and plumbing are often low-level users of ICT, this is an interesting finding. There was no evidence that any of the small businesses in this part of the study were using ICT for 'improving the big picture', which may reflect the typical small business environment where businesses will concentrate on using ICT to focus on short-term functions and operations rather than those that may be some time off.

Table 6.6 Variety and Identified Value-Added ICT of Participating UK Businesses

Type of Business	Businesses (%)	Businesses Where ICT Added-Value Benefits Identified (%)
Construction/maintenance	21.0	100
Attraction (leisure/café/ gallery)	21.0	75
Retail	42.2	50
Manufacturing	10.5	50

Evaluation—Reflecting ICT Governance

ICT governance was proposed as embodying elements associated with the Evaluation (E) stage in the LIAISE framework. Hence, ICT governance was viewed as directly reflecting the way in which small businesses identified and subsequently measured ICT adoption. Furthermore, the perceived benefits derived from ICT adoption by small businesses were previously argued as being closely aligned with governance. The rationale for equating ICT benefits with governance is a practical one, allowing the study's participants to clearly describe the usefulness (and benefits) of ICT in their operations. Participants in the study identified business benefits they derived from using ICT in the following operational areas:

- Cost Savings, through enhancing operational efficiencies
- Increased Revenue
- Enabling offerings that provided extra value for customers
- Improving communication (internal and external to the business)
- Enhanced decision-making
- Allowing the business to be more strategic in the way it worked (strategic positioning)
- Developing new services/products

As previously reported in the literature (Burgess et al., 2009; Cragg et al., 2011), the benefits of using ICT to increase operational efficiencies, enhance revenue streams and improve communications were prominent in business responses. Table 6.7 provides a summary of the perceived business benefits that ICT adoption provided small businesses based on lower, middle or

Table 6.7 Perceived ICT Benefits Based on ICT Skills Groups

Level	Efficiency	Revenue	Communi-cation	Decisions	New Product Service	Customer Value	Strategic
Upper (Good practice users) N=6	4	4	4	4	2	1	0
Middle (Building expertise) N=8	6	5	7	4	3	4	2
Lower (Naïve users) N=5	3	3	1	1	0	2	0
Total (all businesses)	13	12	12	9	5	7	2

upper level of ICT expertise. The one business reporting benefits amongst this group was a construction business, which placed particular importance on using their Internet-enabled mobile device as a work tool.

It was encouraging to note that almost 50% of businesses identified improved decision-making as a perceived business benefit of ICT use. This was interesting as it was noted earlier that no businesses had specifically introduced applications to solely influence decision-making. This suggests that small businesses are using computer applications for data collection, storage and documentation purposes, but that these can be used to possibly aggregate and interpret data into some actionable form which can be subsequently used to support decision-making. For instance, one construction business indicated that using a simple spreadsheet allowed him to subsequently quote jobs, the real-time update of certain spreadsheet cells providing a notional guide to profitability. A retailer also alluded to the use of the spreadsheet application as an ICT tool that assisted decision-making, allowing her to simulate particular business scenarios which subsequently informed business decisions. When small businesses move beyond a basic use of ICT to be more efficient in their business operations, they are said to embody certain competencies that allow them to leverage ICT-related practices (Eikebrokk & Olsen, 2007). Burgess et al. (2009) and Cragg et al. (2011) allude to small businesses moving beyond the use of ICT to improve operational efficiencies and communications, noting that when they do this they become more capable of leveraging their ICT for high-level business activities associated with business strategy, adding value to their products and customer service, acting in unison (complementing) other businesses or in creating new products.

The businesses deemed to be those possessing middle ICT skills levels were strongly represented in areas one would expect ICT to affect high-level business activities such as strategy, adding value for customers and creating new products or services. Two businesses in this group saw ICT as assisting them with achieving their business strategy. One business, a printing manufacturer, nominated their newly established website as a means to increase revenue through sales. The manufacturer, although not fully exploiting this Web presence, identified increased revenue generation through site advertising, the business receiving a fee each time purchases occurred.

The study noted that businesses classed as being in the naïve ICT skills class did not use ICT for strategic purposes or innovatively to generate new products. Arguably, to be able to undertake such relatively higher-level ICT activities tends to be commensurate with having a certain level of ICT skills needing a particular understanding and appreciation of ICT. However, two of the five businesses in this naïve class did indicate that ICT allowed them to achieve customer added-value activities. For instance, a construction business used different Internet search engines to manually collect and compare pricing information, allowing the company to subsequently source cheaper component products online. This effectively removed the wholesaler from the supply chain (disintermediation) and allowed the business to pass these savings on to clients.

Another element of ICT governance which is associated with the Evaluation (E) stage in the LIAISE framework is how an organisation might view ICT performance. Traditionally it has been argued that small businesses have been unaware of, or have consciously ignored, the evaluation of ICT's contribution to their business operations (Burgess, 2002). However, this was not the case with this particular group of businesses, with only one business indicating that they did not evaluate ICT performance. (This same business also had no data recovery plan in place and infrequently updated their ICT.) Contrary to earlier literature, the majority of other businesses did have some evaluation method to judge the performance of their ICT with just over half of the businesses using the perceived measures of efficiency, usefulness and the more general notion that the ICT actually 'worked'.

Eight out of the 19 businesses declared that they had no formal evaluation process in place to determine ICT performance. However, a number of these indicated that they did use volume statistics or metrics that informally determined certain aspects of their ICT performance. These metrics were mainly related to website activity or social media presence and involved data collected through the use of Google Analytics, website hits, Facebook 'likes' and even metrics from third-party websites such as Yellow Pages. Clearly many small businesses in his study are proactive in their endeavours to undertake some form of performance evaluation of their ICT use, be it through judgement measures (efficiency, etc.), informal online metrics (Google Analytics, etc.) or more precise measures such as website sales. This is a significant shift from the reactive nature of small businesses in evaluating their ICT adoption, implementation and subsequent use (Burgess, 2002; Lin, Lin, & Tsao, 2005).

The Leaders, the Operationals and the Laggards in Regards to ICT Adoption

The grouping of small businesses based on their ICT expertise reflected what we deemed to be naïve ICT businesses (lower), those developing and building their ICT skills and expertise (middle) and expert businesses that had a better understanding, familiarity and use of ICT (upper). Each expertise area or domain was aligned with capabilities reflecting ICT skills, use and governance. Based on these three ICT expertise domains, small businesses were subsequently classed into one of three adopter categories: the Leaders, the Operationals and the Laggards.

The Leaders as previously described are not so much first or early adopters, but businesses that leverage their ICT for advantage beyond what might be normally expected amongst small businesses. Leaders typically scored high in at least two of the three domains that identified with the possession of ICT skills, the practice of ICT governance and whether ICT was used in an innovative manner. No small business was found to be rated at the highest level across all three domains. Notably, amongst the Leaders, ICT governance was found to be most challenging.

Typically, the Leaders were identified as being suitably skilled in their use of ICT and computer applications. Indeed, of the six businesses identified in the study as having upper-level ICT skills, four were categorised as being Leaders. The interesting issue in regards to Leaders was that as a group they tended to use consultants and attended educational training courses in order to attain appropriate ICT skills. When it came to acquiring ICT skills, some of the leaders made effective use of the Internet, indicating that these channels were used to enable ICT skills acquisition and development. Another business also found that engagement with their industry allowed them to address their ICT skills needs, presumably through information exchanges with other businesses.

The Leaders, as might be expected, also used their ICT for innovative business activities and were noted for the way that they applied ICT to a range of business functions. For instance, one business leveraged their ICT applications to access a centralised ordering system to streamline inventory and orders; a retailer positioned themselves on the eBay site as a primary virtual platform with great success and another business used third-party social media sites (e.g., TripAdvisor) to capture positive client comments. It is unclear why some Leaders had a relatively middle rating for ICT governance given the importance of understanding the value of business data and instigation of a recovery plan should loss occur.

The Operational businesses in this group reflected small businesses that were rated at a lower level of ICT adoption when compared to the Leaders, but ahead of the Laggards. The Operationals were noted as generally having a middle level of expertise across all three ICT domains and typically used their ICT applications to achieve operational improvements in the marketing, accounting and sales areas. Businesses that were deemed as the Operationals not only used ICT for operational purposes, but were able to add value to their business activities through what we have identified as innovative uses of ICT. For instance, the café and gallery leveraged their social media presence to enable their followers to discuss various topics and products relevant to the business. Another business had developed an interactive website, thus allowing clients to visualise the business's products, which in turn directly assisted customer purchasing decisions. They were also quite astute in the way they had developed a database to identify customer types in order to understand and subsequently engage them.

The Laggards were the least likely to have adopted ICT or even to have a knowledge of new innovations (Rogers, 2003). These businesses scored at a relatively low level across the three ICT domains compared to their counterparts in the study. All but one business scored at the lowest level in terms of having ICT skills, with most using family and friends as the source for improving such skills. Given this low classification of the Laggards, particularly in regards to ICT skills, we were surprised that several businesses did manage to engage in what we felt were innovative or value added use of ICT. Several businesses used the broad reach of the Internet to either disintermediate wholesalers or identify interesting products that could be on-sold by the business on a regular basis.

Conclusion

In this chapter the LIAISE framework was used as a lens to present findings that were based on the analysis of 19 in-depth interviews associated with the small businesses located in a UK coastal township. The use of the LIAISE framework allows the findings to highlight the important aspects of ICT adoption, its subsequent use and the benefits experienced by this group of small businesses.

Clearly, the range of different types of small business entities in this component of the study has provided particular insights into the ICT challenges and also some innovative uses that might be expected across different settings. The authors were surprised, on a number of occasions, at the greater than expected levels of knowledge and sophistication shown by some businesses in their uses of ICT, especially those businesses classified as having upper- and middle-level ICT skills.

References

Barba-Sánchez, V., Martínez-Ruiz, M. P., & Jimenez-Zarco, A. I. (2007). Drivers, benefits and challenges of ICT adoption by small and medium sized enterprises (SMEs): A literature review. *Problems and Perspectives in Management, 5*(1), 104–115.

Beckinsale, M., Levy, M., & Powell, P. (2006). Exploring internet adoption drivers in SMEs. *Electronic Markets, 16*(4), 361–370.

Burgess, S. (2002). Information technology in small business: Issues and challenges. In S. Burgess (Ed.), *Information technology in small business: Challenges and solutions* (pp. 1–17). Hershey, PA: Idea Group Publishing.

Burgess, S., Sellitto, C., & Karanasios, S. (2009). *Effective web presence solutions for small businesses: Strategies for successful implementation.* Hershey, PA: Information Science Reference.

Cragg, P., Caldeira, M., & Ward, J. (2011). Organizational information systems competences in small and medium-sized enterprises. *Information & Management, 48*(8), 353–363.

Deloitte. (2014). *Small business, big technology: How the cloud enables rapid growth in SMBs.* London, UK: Deloitte MCS.

Denison, T. (2008). *Barriers to the effective use of web technologies by community sector organisations.* CIRN 2008 Community Informatics Conference: ICT for Social Inclusion: What is the Reality, Prato, Italy.

Diallo, U., Patel, P., & Wrelton, M. (2013). *The digital imperative: Small businesses, technology and growth.* London, UK: Federation of Small Businesses/Intellect.

Eikebrokk, T., & Olsen, D. (2007). An empirical investigation of competency factors affecting e-business success in European SMEs. *Information & Management, 44*(4), 364–383.

Karanasios, S., Sellitto, C., Burgess, S., Johanson, G., Schauder, D., & Denison, T. (2006). *The role of the internet in building capacity: Small businesses and community based organisations in Australia.* 7th Working for E-Business Conference, Victoria University, Melbourne, Australia, Melbourne, Australia.

Lin, K., Lin, C., & Tsao, H. (2005). IS/IT investment evaluation and benefit realization practices in Taiwanese SMEs. *Journal of Information Science and Technology, 2*(4), 44–71.

Lockett, N., Brown, D. H., & Kaewkitipong, L. (2006). The use of hosted enterprise applications by SMEs: A dual market and user perspective. *Electronic Markets, 16*(1), 85–96.

McDonagh, P., & Prothero, A. (2000). Euroclicking and the Irish SME: Prepared for E-commerce and the single currency? *Irish Marketing Review, 13*(1), 21–33.

Rogers, E. M. (2003). *Diffusion of innovations* (5th ed.). New York: The Free Press.

Schubert, P., & Leimstoll, U. (2007). Importance and use of information technology in small and medium-sized companies. *Electronic Markets, 17*(1), 38–55.

Sellitto, C., Banks, D., Monday, A., & Burgess, S. (2009). A study of Australian small to medium tourism enterprises (SMTEs) and their ICT adoption. *The International Journal of Knowledge, Culture and Change Management, 9*(6), 1–14.

Part IV

Summary and Lessons

7   The Overall Story

Introduction

The previous chapter described how the ICT experiences of the UK coastal businesses surveyed in 2011–2012 aligned with the LIAISE framework. In this chapter we consider differences and similarities between the Australian businesses initially studied in 2007–2008 and the later surveys of the UK businesses. It is important to remind the reader that this is not a longitudinal study but rather is framed as a purposive, judgemental (non-probability) study utilising opportunity samples. As with the reporting of findings in previous chapters, we have drawn upon both the actual data and the collective experience of the authors in their research of small business adoption of ICT. The outcomes of the data collection phases across these two time periods can be viewed as reflecting the ICT adoption and use of the Australian businesses and UK coastal businesses for these two periods.

The chapter includes a summary of the data and explores the issue of how small businesses in general might have improved, remained the same or regressed in their ICT use.

Small Businesses Across the Study Period

In presenting the findings, we have divided the analysis into three key categories: ICT Skills, ICT Governance, and ICT Use and Innovation. Figure 7.1 is reproduced to remind the reader that these ICT business domains were also shown to be aligned with the LIAISE areas and were used to group the small businesses into the adopter style categories. These three domains were subsequently used to classify the respective small businesses into either a lower, middle or upper category of these three individual ICT areas.

To recap the study's population, a total of 60 small businesses were interviewed, comprising 41 in Australia in the 2007–2008 study phase and 19 in the UK in 2011–2012 phase.

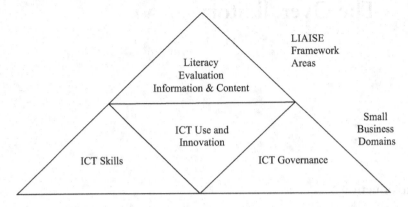

Figure 7.1 The ICT Small Business Domains and LIAISE

ICT Skills

The use of ICT and the understanding and familiarity of the technology for a business owner is addressed in this section. The degree of understanding a small business has of ICT can influence the level of technology in use. This understanding is essential in allowing small businesses to better appreciate the issues and benefits enabled by the technology, which is more likely to lead to greater adoption and implementation in the business (Burgess, Sellitto, & Karanasios, 2009).

Table 7.1 aggregates and summarises the findings from the two data collection periods, summarising how we classified the small businesses with respect to their ICT Skills expertise.

The results suggest similar dispositions across the two time periods. The following section will discuss each expertise classification for ICT skills.

'Upper' Group

Of the 41 small Australian businesses, 13 (32%) were categorised as having an 'Upper' level of ICT Skills and exactly the same percentage was found in the UK group. These small businesses often commented that they had either a formal qualification, for example, a university degree in computer science; had been using computers in a previous employment position for a number of years or had "grown up with computers". Four of these small businesses mentioned that through their previous employment role, they received formal computer training. One common theme across the businesses was that they gained 'on the job' experience through their regular use of computers and allied ICT. This group thus felt they had a relatively high degree of confidence in using their business ICT and were also identified as actively

Table 7.1 ICT Skills Expertise of Participating Businesses (2007–2008 & 2011–2012)

ICT Skills Expertise Classification	Data Collection Phase	
	2007–2008	2011–2012
Upper (Good practice users)	13 (32%)	6 (32%)
Middle (Building expertise)	21 (51%)	8 (41%)
Lower (Naïve users)	7 (17%)	5 (26%)
Total	41 (100%)	19 (100%)

seeking out new types of technologies and/or building ICT-related applications, such as their website.

This practical experience appears to be very important for acquiring ICT knowledge and the subsequent development of business-ready ICT skills. However, this practical experience was not a definitive precursor leading to good ICT business practices. Of the 13 Australian small businesses in the 'Upper' ICT Skills ranking, eight were considered to be 'Middle' or 'Lower' in their practice of ICT Governance procedures, where data backups were a manual process that was conducted intermittently. In the case of the six UK businesses, all except one of these owners were grouped in the 'Middle' level for ICT Governance practices, with most using similar technology to their Australian counterparts. Some of the UK group made use of both externally located off-premise storage as well as the common manual backup procedures. One interviewee was identified as using Apple's iCloud as part of their backup procedure.

Just over half of both the Australian and UK small businesses that had 'Upper' skill levels were also assessed as being in the 'Upper' level in regards to ICT Use and Innovation. Active social media use was found in both groups and there was a growing trend in the UK sample towards the use of Cloud-based storage solutions and of Google Analytics. The growing availability of these newer technologies may demand more of the ICT skills repertoire of small business and members of this 'Upper' group appear to be well placed to take full advantage of the situation and possibly gain competitive advantage.

'Middle' Group

Twenty-one (51%) of the Australian businesses interviewed were classified as having attained a 'Middle' level of ICT Skills, with eight (42%) of the UK businesses being located in this category.

One of the common themes identified through responses from Australian businesses was that managers understood and appreciated the benefits that ICT could offer to the businesses and this was a significant driver for ICT adoption in the first instance. Some of the managers were aware of their limitations, commenting that they had not identified all of the features a particular software application could provide. In many instances businesses employed staff or used contractors who had more expertise and knowledge than they did. The UK businesses in this category also stated that they had a basic knowledge of computers and that they would typically outsource their website requirements. Most of these businesses in both Australia and the UK had basic computing setups which focused on managing their core activities. This was reflected in the number of computers actually owned and implemented on-site, whether these machines were networked and if the business was using electronic accounting packages.

Around half of the Australian businesses deemed to have a 'Middle' ICT Skills level were considered as 'Upper' level users of ICT in regards to their ICT Governance practices. Many businesses commented that they did back up data and files either daily or weekly, with several having an off-site copy of data and the majority of this group were interested in exploring automatic backup solutions. All except two of the UK businesses were classed at the 'Middle' level for ICT Governance practices, indicating that they backed up their data on a daily basis, some taking these backups off-site, usually to their residential homes. Other businesses had automatic backup mechanisms for their ICT systems. For both groups there was a feeling that if their backup systems failed, they would be able to move back to the traditional paper-based approach in the short term.

Eight of the 21 Australian businesses that were classified as having attained 'Middle' ICT Skills were also grouped as being in the 'Upper' level in regards to ICT Use and Innovation. Most of these comments were centred on the theme of adopting automated online booking systems, as distinct from their current email booking system. Some businesses had started to use Web 2.0 technologies such as Facebook and YouTube. Half of the UK businesses were classed at the 'Middle' level from an ICT Use and Innovation perspective. The notable innovations or added-value aspects of ICT associated with this particular group included the adoption of online stores (either on their website or eBay) and extensive use of Web 2.0 tools such as Facebook, user-generated content sites and online review websites.

'Lower' Group

There were seven (17%) small Australian businesses that were classified at the 'Lower' ICT Skills level and five (26%) UK organisations that were classified at this level. When compared to the 2007–2008 Australian businesses, the UK sample appeared to exhibit a similar lack of knowledge of awareness of the development of ICT. For instance, one interviewee commented that they were unaware that their phone was a 'smartphone' until it was pointed out to them by one of the researchers in the interview. Another spoke about the lack of time to investigate and understand how ICT worked. Yet another discussed a lack of understanding of the skills they actually needed in the future so that ICT could be valued in running the business.

The majority of operator comments associated with this group indicated that they did not always use computers for their business-related activities, home-related activities also making use of the technology. A traditional 'paper is better' mindset was evident, and 'maintaining a lifestyle' was given as a key motivator for running the business in both the Australian and the UK samples.

The Australian group's ICT Governance practices were mainly mapped to a 'Middle' level where many of them backed up their data and files irregularly, or engaged a third party to do this. More than half of the UK businesses were also categorised at the 'Middle' or 'Upper' level for ICT Governance. These businesses had file and data backup procedures in place but, worryingly, several businesses did not have any formal backup procedures.

All of the Australian small businesses were classified at the 'Lower' level in regard to ICT Use and Innovation, with many of them having a simple website with no provision for interactive electronic activities such as e-sales and e-bookings. However, a few businesses did volunteer comments regarding the prospects of having such online activities and that they would need to constantly monitor their Web presence, be better equipped in regards to improved ICT skills, or to actually invest in new computers. Collectively these suggestions align with the resource poverty commonly encountered in the small business environment when it comes to ICT adoption and subsequent use (Beckinsale, Levy, & Powell, 2006). As might be expected, no small operator in the UK group was classed at the 'Upper' level for ICT Use and Innovation and did not see themselves as innovative users of ICT beyond using the Internet to identify prices of their competitors.

Comparison Between ICT Skills 2007–2008 and 2011–2012

The level of ICT Skills determined in the 2007–2008 small businesses and those studied in 2011–2012 did not change significantly. Most of the respondents that we classed as having an 'Upper' or 'Middle' level of ICT Skills either had formal training, though university education, vocational job training or by having learnt 'on the job' at a previous employer. There was little indication of managers or owners undergoing or seeking training while they were running their small businesses, which is an important issue that could be addressed in order to improve ICT uptake and use. There was little difference in the acquisition or development of ICT Skill expertise across small businesses between each of the periods that data was collected. Overall, whilst the technology advanced, there was no noticeable difference in the proportion of ICT skill levels across the two places and time periods.

ICT Governance

Good ICT Governance practices can help a small operator to avoid loss of critical files, including important customer data, that could potentially render them non-operational for a significant period of time. The ICT governance level of participating businesses is summarised in Table 7.2.

'Upper' Group

Fifteen (37%) Australian businesses were identified as having practices associated with the 'Upper' level of ICT Governance, with four (21%) small UK businesses being placed in this category. Most of the Australian and UK businesses backed up their data either daily or weekly onto a standard USB stick or a portable external hard drive. Most of the people interviewed had either undertaken formal ICT training to use within their business, had acquired ICT skills through previous employment, or had hired an ICT consultant to carry out appropriate computing work.

One UK business used Apple's iCloud and the Time Machine feature built into the Apple's operating system to enable them to back up files in real time resulting in a complete file backup being generated across each day. The feature also allows the user to remotely access the externally stored files, a feature that would prove useful in situations where the business was working from a client's premises and needed access to the client file. This type of business process involving ICT would have only been accessible to larger organisations in the past and would have been a prohibitively expensive option to the businesses interviewed in the 2007–2008 time period. However, with Cloud-based services being commonly available to small business at the time of the second data collection stage, it is perhaps surprising that very few of the UK businesses were using this approach. Cloud-based services typically involve software applications that require a licence or subscription with no need for special hardware and implementation costs and thus offer small businesses an easy to use and convenient service that provides enhanced security and privacy of data than might be otherwise

Table 7.2 The ICT Governance Level of Participating Businesses (2007–2008 & 2011–2012)

ICT Governance Classification	Data Collection Phase	
	2007–2008	*2011–2012*
Upper (Good practice users)	15 (37%)	4 (21%)
Middle (Users building expertise)	21 (51%)	13 (68%)
Lower (Naïve users)	5 (12%)	2 (11%)
Total	41 (100%)	19 (100%)

achieved (Guptaa, Seetharamana, & Raj, 2013). There is a requirement that users are aware of such services and in a position to exploit them in a way that fits with their business requirements. As more information becomes available in publication venues that are typically accessed by small businesses, this may become an increasingly popular option.

Several businesses indicated that should their computer systems fail, they could return to their traditional paper-based system for a period of time, although they recognised that this would provide a potentially less responsive business environment. Only one of these businesses had any documented policies for their employees to follow with regards to file backup and data contingency plans.

In regards to the ICT Use and Innovation domain, all but one Australian business was categorised as being at the 'Upper' or 'Middle' levels, with most of these characterised by the use of online sales and Web 2.0 applications. Two of the UK businesses were categorised at the 'Middle' level in regards to ICT Use and Innovation.

'Middle' Group

Twenty-one (51%) of the Australian small businesses were categorised as being at the 'Middle' level in regards to ICT Governance practices, with 13 (68%) UK small businesses having the same classification. The Australian group backed up their data at least weekly, sometimes monthly but, quite commonly, when the owner remembered to do it. In common with Australian businesses who were categorised as occupying the 'Middle' 'Upper' level, the UK businesses felt that they had adequate hard copies of documents, for example, bookings or invoices, to continue business operations should they lose their data. Several Australian businesses mentioned using anti-virus software in conjunction with their computer systems, and none had any formal policies to deal with malicious virus attacks. The UK group's major theme was that backups were undertaken on a semi-regular basis, to an external hard drive or USB memory stick. Some of the businesses had automated this process to overcome what they saw as a cumbersome manual process; one operator recognising the value of the data to the business stored their files on a USB memory stick that was subsequently placed in a fireproof box each night.

Within this group of 21 Australian businesses, 16 were classed at the 'Middle' or 'Lower' level in regards to ICT Use and Innovation. Retrospectively, some of these businesses may be considered to be early adopters of ICT, albeit at the basic level. For example, several had implemented online booking functions through their website, but then circumvented the automation of this transaction process by accepting payments in person. This issue of general ICT adoption at a basic level was also evident in the tentative implementation of what was perceived by some as a new Internet application in the form of social media. Eleven of the 13 UK businesses were classed as being in the 'Middle' or 'Upper' level of ICT Use and Innovation. Most of these businesses expressed a confidence in using their ICT even though they had only implemented basic ICT governance practices.

'Lower' Group

Five (12%) Australian businesses were classed as 'Lower' level of ICT Governance, with 12 (11%) of the UK sample also being classified at the 'Lower' level. Interestingly, two of the Australian businesses were grouped in the 'Upper' level in the ICT Use and Innovation ranking, suggesting that innovative approaches may be business- rather than technology-driven.

Some Australian businesses in this group did not back up their data at all, although others did back up their important data on a monthly basis. There tended to be a belief that they would not experience problems with their ICT on the basis that, so far, nothing had gone wrong. Two of the owners had one of their employees (an ICT 'champion') take responsibility for backing up data and governance practices as they did not know enough about the process. The UK businesses in this group evidenced similar patterns to the Australian businesses, updating their ICT only when it failed totally or became too slow to support their needs. One business had not implemented formal data and file backup processes despite experiencing a major incident when both of the firm's computers failed at the same time with hardware failure. As a consequence of their lack of backing up procedures, they needed to engage a data recovery service to restore the files and records.

The businesses in this category volunteered that they appreciated that they lacked the appropriate skills to manage the systems they had and had no idea how they might cope as new technologies emerged. Lack of time or major focus on the business rather than the technology were the most usually cited reasons for not addressing this lack of skills. There was a limited understanding of the benefits that the Internet could offer the business and also a failure to exploit existing ICT potential (for example, one UK business made use of a smartphone simply as a phone, overlooking the broader business possibilities it could offer).

Comparison Between ICT Governance 2007–2008 and 2011–2012

The small businesses that were classed at the 'Upper' level for ICT Governance in 2007–2008 were backing up data with external hard drives, and some had automated this process. However, by 2011–2012, the availability of Cloud services seemingly allowed small businesses grouped at the 'Upper' level for Governance to adopt this Internet application. The authors believe that more businesses will adopt Cloud technologies. This will give them greater access to their data, and allow them to be not so reliant on storing and backing up their data on their office computer. Indeed, the ICT Governance practices between the two data collection stages reflected the ICT developments during that period, particularly in regards to Cloud services that had traditionally only been affordable to larger businesses. Notably, the future adoption of Cloud-based ICT Governance practices will enable even small businesses to improve the security, privacy and availability of their business data.

In terms of ICT Governance practices, the small businesses studied in 2007–2008 period typically backed up their data manually using a hard drive or memory stick. Amongst the 2011–2012 businesses, many still used a manual approach. However, we noted that some had started to exploit automated Cloud-based technologies as a data backup option. Indeed, seamless backup procedures to an external and central location such as Cloud services were seen as only an Internet connection away and were mainly associated with businesses that we classed as 'Upper' level users in regards to ICT Governance.

ICT Use and Innovation

ICT can be used by a business simply to support their day-to-day operational needs or as a vehicle to help them to develop or leverage strategies that may help them to expand or add value to their business. This section considers the use of ICT by the various businesses from the perspective of innovation, that is, how they used their ICT in novel or creative ways. We have been cognisant of the way that technology has changed across the sample period and that what was considered as innovative in 2007–2008 may be considered less so in 2011–2012. For this reason, we have not attempted to carry out a detailed comparison between the samples, instead presenting the findings for each sample in each of the Upper, Middle and Lower categories.

Table 7.3 aggregates the findings from the two data collection periods in regards to the how we classified the small businesses with respect to their ICT Use and Innovation.

Table 7.3 ICT Use and Innovation Level of Participating Businesses (2007–2008 & 2011–2012)

ICT Use and Innovation Classification	Data Collection Phase	
	2007–2008	2011–2012
Upper (Good practice users)	15 (37%)	4 (21%)
Middle (Users building expertise)	15 (37%)	10 (53%)
Lower (Naïve users)	11 (26%)	5 (26%)
Total	41 (100%)	19 (100%)

'Upper' Group

There were 15 (37%) Australian businesses that we classified as being in the 'Upper' level with regards to ICT Use and Innovation. Many of these businesses had implemented Web 2.0 applications which included Facebook (then an emerging social networking platform) and online sales/booking functions directly enabled through their website. The majority of this group of companies recorded that ICT were an important aspect of running their core business processes, be they for marketing, accounting or sales. However, some of the more novel uses of ICT included a primary producer (orchard business) using ICT to remotely monitor the fields in which their temperature-sensitive crops were planted. This real-time monitoring alerted the company should the temperature fall below a critical point, thus allowing them to take appropriate actions. A number of businesses leveraged the visual aspects offered through social media platforms for marketing purposes. For instance, a tour company used elaborate videos to promote their tours on YouTube, while a separate tour company posted photos of the last tour on Facebook and 'tagged' entities such as their guests, venues and activities for promotion and Web optimisation proposes. Tagging of guests involved the process of linking a person in a photo to their Facebook profile (Ray, 2013) which, in effect, allowed the business to use the guest's network of links for promotional purposes.

There were five (26%) UK businesses that were classified in this group. These businesses had adopted a number of new, novel or innovative ICT applications which assisted them not only with their core business functions, but also supported some of their added-value activities. Some illustrative examples of what we deemed as new, novel or innovative uses of ICT follow.

One construction/design business made all their digital files available off-site through a mobile device when they met with their clients off-site. They achieved this using Apple's Cloud system, the iCloud. For the businesses, this resulted in reduced printing costs associated with traditional paper invoices, receipts and business documents and provided them with timely and complete access to the data contained in these documents. A company aligned with tourism in the seaside township installed networked CCTV cameras around the playing area to monitor the patrons during games for health and safety reasons. The network was linked to a central control and monitoring station. A printing company incorporated a new section to their website for local artists to upload high-resolution photos of their work. This acted as an advertising and marketing conduit, linking an artist's work with its own customers, who were subsequently able to order and pay for a piece of art online. The company then was in position to print the requested piece of artwork and surface-mail it to the customer. This component of the website generated some 15% of revenue for the company, with the potential for increased sales as the owner identified how to correctly leverage this feature of the site. One business had been established and built purely using eBay as a shopfront, managing all of its documentation via this service. Another highly proactive business viewed ICT as presenting almost too many opportunities and challenges, the owner indicating that they needed to limit the development of the ICT area and focus upon spending time on the current business activities.

'Middle' Group

Fifteen (37%) Australian companies were also classified as being in the 'Middle' level of ICT Use and Innovation in 2007–2008. Collectively, the group was engaged in the use of ICT applications at a basic level with managers or owners indicating that they had computerised most of their core activities. This included communications (through email), bookings (either through email or online through their website) or sourcing new products online. These ICT-reliant activities, although adding value to business functions, were not deemed to be at the same level of innovativeness (or value added tasks) that were undertaken by the 'Upper' level users in this category. Several businesses had started to send their customers target offers via email to entice them to buy more of their products/services.

Nine (48%) UK businesses were classified as being in the 'Middle' level for ICT Use and Innovation. This group were found to be basic users of ICT, which was mainly applied to operational functions, which included running and maintaining a website with an online store feature. Several of these businesses had a Facebook presence that reflected their business offerings.

'Lower' Group

There were 11 (26%) Australian businesses classified as being in the 'Lower' level of ICT Use and Innovation. These businesses either did not use computers, or if they did use any ICT, it was in a limited capacity. Many of these companies had a rudimentary website that they considered to be of informational value, that is, the site was used to provide details about the company, products/services provided and contact details for prospective and existing customers. Seven of the 11 businesses were classed in the 'Lower' level for ICT Skills expertise. Collectively, this group was unfamiliar with ICT in general. Seven businesses were also classed at the 'Middle' level in regards to ICT Governance practices, which reflected the notion that most businesses backed up their important files and data. However, this backing-up process was sporadic and was not undertaken on a regular basis.

Five (26%) UK businesses were deemed to be at the 'Lower' level for ICT Use and Innovation, i.e., they were not using ICT for what could be regarded as innovative purposes. This particular group identified that ICT use mainly related to adopting the Internet to source products and having a basic website. Notably, this group had a poor understanding and knowledge of how the Internet could be useful for their business.

*Comparison Between ICT Use and
Innovation 2007–2008 and 2011–2012*

Whilst the level of ICT Use and Innovation area appears to have been affected by the progressive, evolving nature of ICT between data collection periods, there was no overall improvement in these practices. The small businesses that were classified as being in the 'Upper' level of ICT Use and Innovation in 2007–2008 would arguably be considered to be classed at the 'Middle' level in 2011–2012 due to the advancement in practices. The development and subsequent adoption of Cloud technologies and Web 2.0 applications (predominately social media platforms) substantially changed the way a small business could either communicate, engage or subsequent interact with their suppliers and customers. Small businesses across the period of the study started to implement social media pages, with Cloud services becoming an important instrument for their data storage activities. The reliance on the Internet will only increase with more Cloud-based applications becoming available to small businesses.

Conclusion

In this chapter, the findings from 60 semi-structured interviews of small businesses were analysed, within the small business domains of ICT Skills, ICT Governance and ICT Use and Innovation. Forty-one of the businesses were based in either Victoria or South Australia and the interviews were conducted in 2007–2008, the remaining 19 businesses being interviewed in a UK coastal town in 2011–2012. Although the findings suggest that there was not a substantial difference in the level of ICT skills expertise, ICT Governance, and ICT Use and Innovation domains between the two periods, there are some differences in the breakdown of the findings that are worthy of note.

In the ICT Skills area, the 'Upper' (Good practice) figures for both the Australian and the UK samples indicate 32% as being in this group, suggesting that roughly a third of the sample population have, or are gaining, expertise at a level that can support their businesses. The UK sample shows a higher percentage (26% UK compared with 17% Australian) in the 'Lower' (Naïve users) and this may reflect the more heterogeneous composition of the UK sample when compared with the tourism-related business that formed the focus of the Australian sample. A report for the UK Department for Business Innovation & Skills (Baker, Lomax, Braidford, Allinson, and Houston, 2015) notes that a quarter of UK SMEs report that they do not possess basic digital skills and that those working in the primary/construction sectors were more likely to consider themselves 'poor' for most digital tasks. SMEs, especially those at the micro level, tend to be time-poor and it may be a problem for them to find ways of including skills education and training into their working patterns.

The ICT Governance combined 'Upper' and 'Middle' figures are virtually the same for both the Australian and the UK samples, as are the 'Lower' figures. There are differences, however, in the balance within the 'Upper' and 'Middle' categories. The figures suggest that although the 'Good practice users' are higher in the Australian sample, the UK group is intent on building expertise.

The ICT Use and Innovation figures follow the same pattern as for those in the ICT Governance section and suggest that the broader range of businesses in the UK sample are aware of the potential for growth through the innovative use of ICT.

At the time of our first data collection, there were only 50 million active users on Facebook (The Associated Press, 2012), but by 2015 that figure had risen to over 1.4 billion users (Facebook, 2015). Broadband infrastructure is penetrating deeper into the business community and the available speed is increasing. The power of computer technology and the wide availability of relatively cheap tablet and smartphone devices provides an opportunity for small businesses to further use ICT to help build or change their businesses. In order to capitalise on these opportunities, they will need to find avenues that will help them to improve their ICT skills and to recognise and avoid potential technological dangers. The next chapter draws on the material discussed here and considers some ICT lessons for small businesses.

References

The Associated Press. (2012). *Number of active users at Facebook over the years.* Retrieved 16 December 2015 from http://finance.yahoo.com/news/number-active -users-facebook-over-years-214600186—finance.html

Baker, G., Lomax, S., Braidford, P., Allinson, G., & Houston, M. (2015). *Digital capabilities in SMEs: Evidence review and re-survey of 2014 small business survey respondents.* BIS Research Paper Number 247, Department for Business Innovation and Skills, London.

Beckinsale, M., Levy, M., & Powell, P. (2006). Exploring internet adoption drivers in SMEs. *Electronic Markets, 16*(4), 361–370.

Burgess, S., Sellitto, C., & Karanasios, S. (2009). *Effective web presence solutions for small businesses: Strategies for successful implementation.* Hershey, PA: Information Science Reference.

Facebook. (2015). *Facebook Q1 2015 results.* California: Facebook.

Guptaa, P., Seetharamana, A., & Raj, J. (2013). The usage and adoption of cloud computing by small and medium businesses. *International Journal of Information Management, 33*(5), 861–874.

Ray, R. (2013). *The Facebook guide to small business marketing.* Indianapolis: Wiley.

8 Take-Away ICT Lessons for Small Businesses

Introduction

This final chapter of the book will introduce 10 take-away lessons for small businesses to consider when implementing their ICT strategies. Perhaps not surprisingly for the reader, these will predominantly be based on the outcomes resulting from the LIAISE analysis of small businesses throughout the book. However, an important consideration behind the lessons is also the three ICT domains that we used to assess the status of small business ICT adoption and use:

- ICT skills
- ICT governance, and
- ICT use and innovation.

As we indicated in Chapter 3, these domains are linked to the LIAISE framework and allowed us to classify the small businesses that we investigated in the two phases of this study into three categories of ICT adoption: *Leaders, Operationals* and *Laggards*. We had a good balance of all three categories of ICT adoption across the two phases (refer Table 8.1).

Obviously, there was a tendency to draw the ICT lessons that we recommend in this chapter from the ICT Leaders and, where possible, to avoid the behaviours of the ICT Laggards. Whilst the ICT adoption categories were useful to allow us to classify the ICT behaviours of these businesses, we identified aspects of the ICT practices in the vast majority of the small businesses that we investigated that could be improved. Although we identified 20 small businesses as ICT Leaders, only two (some 3% of the overall sample) were rated at the highest level in all ICT domains (ICT skills, ICT governance, and ICT use and innovation). At the other end of the scale, four of the 60 businesses were assessed at the lowest level for all three ICT domains, so at least the vast majority of the businesses had at least one commendable ICT practice.

It should be noted that we did not have any predetermined 'ratio' of performance for each ICT domain. We simply determined what we would regard as 'upper', 'middle' and 'lower' levels of practice for each ICT domain. As Table 8.2 shows, it turns out that the same proportion of

Table 8.1 ICT Adopter Categories for Participating Small Businesses

ICT Adoption Category	Australian Data Collection (#)	UK Data Collection (#)	Overall (#)
Leaders	15	5	20
Operationals	16	9	25
Laggards	10	5	15
Total	41	19	60

Table 8.2 Overall Classifications of Participating Small Businesses Across ICT Domains

ICT Classification	ICT Skills (%)	ICT Use and Innovation (%)	ICT Governance (%)
Upper	32	32	32
Middle	48	42	56
Lower	20	26	12

'upper' level ratings occurred across all three ICT domains. However, there were differences across the domains at the middle level. Our results for ICT Use and Innovation showed the greatest weaknesses by the businesses, with over one-quarter of all businesses that we assessed being rated in the 'lower' category for this ICT domain.

General ICT Lessons

1. Have an ICT Strategy

Although it was not a specific focus of the questions that we asked in our interviews, we were always looking to see how the various businesses related their ICT practices back to their business practices. Whilst we are not suggesting that small businesses necessarily need to have a formal, documented ICT strategy, they should be considering two important questions in relation to their use of ICT in their business:

- How ready is the business to use ICT effectively?
- How does existing and intended ICT use relate to the overall business aims?

'Readiness' refers to how ready the business is to adopt ICT and use them effectively. It requires an understanding of the drivers of ICT success and the barriers associated with their use. Readiness is effectively represented by the early parts of the LIAISE framework, which recognises that small businesses need to have access to the technology through exposure to adequate ICT Infrastructure, but also the skills to use it effectively (Literacy and Support). Only then will they be able to effectively Access the ICT.

The need to align ICT strategy with business strategy has been known to larger businesses for many decades. Small businesses often struggle with developing their own general business aims and objectives, without even considering how their use of ICT might match to these. As mentioned earlier in this book, ICT is often adopted in small businesses without necessarily thinking of how it fits into the overall business aims. This does not mean that ICT use does not benefit a small business; it can often provide efficiency gains that are of great benefit to the business. It can mean, however, that potential strategic benefits to be gained from strategic use of ICT might be missed. A simple analogy that is evident from many of the vignettes in this book is that the traditional small business will look to use ICT to save costs or to improve efficiencies whilst the entrepreneur will look for ways that ICT can be used to add value to the business offerings and match the strategic aims of the business. These ways of using ICT in small businesses were represented in the matrix of ICT applications that was introduced in Chapter 2.

Finally, it is important for the small business to consider Governance aspects of their ICT usage. This relates to the steps that they take to protect their important files and, particularly, how they measure the success of the ICT against their business aims and objectives. This latter component of ICT governance relates to the *Evaluation* aspect of the LIAISE framework.

The Lessons

This section begins with two general or overriding lessons that small businesses should consider if they are adopting ICT for the first time. However, the lessons still apply to even well-established small businesses that are already using ICT, when considering upgrades to existing technology, ventures into the use of ICT, or even frustration as to why existing ICT are not providing expected benefits.

Lesson 1: Match ICT Aims and Strategies to Business Aims and Strategies

A business will need to consider where it wants to be in three to five years time, whether it is looking to expand or is happy with the existing customer base or whether the business supports a particular lifestyle. All of these questions will influence the short- to long-term strategy of the business. This book is about the use of ICT and not specifically about business planning. However, if you have a business plan for your small business that sets out the business aims and its short- and longer-term objectives, then it is going to be much easier to develop ICT aims and strategies to match. Once a business plan is in place, it is then possible to identify the specific benefits of ICT that you are looking to adopt from the Matrix of ICT applications. These are repeated here:

- Improved information search
- Improved communications
- Improved decision support
- Improved recording and monitoring
- Improved work practices
- Improved relationships
- Improving the big picture

Some of these require little investment in ICT and can provide immediate short-term benefits (e.g, improved information search and improved recording and monitoring). Others, such as improving the big picture, involve longer-term strategies and require more commitment.

Lesson 2: Think About the Readiness of the Business to Adopt ICT

As we mentioned earlier in the book, many businesses suffer from resource poverty (limited time, limited knowledge, limited finances) in relation to the use of ICT. The business needs to consider devoting the time to properly learn about ICT capabilities and what they can do for the business. If ICT is thought about as a strategic resource rather than as a cost, then it is easier to justify the time spent on this task.

Once you have decided what you want to achieve from your ICT, it is a good idea for you to assess the readiness to adopt the particular technologies or applications that you are interested in. Rogers (2003), in his well-known work on the diffusion of innovations, identified the knowledge of an innovation as the first step in what he referred to as the innovation-decision process. In the case of a small business, knowledge of ICT occurs when the owner/manager or another influential employee in the business "is exposed to an innovation's existence and gains an understanding of how it functions" (Rogers, 2003, p. 169). Knowledge of the existence of ICT can come in many different ways for small businesses, such as seeing advertisements, reading trade journals, use of ICT in real life (such as with smartphones and tablet computers), seeing it in use in other businesses, talking to ICT consultants and so forth.

According to the LIAISE framework, having access to particular ICT requires the appropriate infrastructure to be in place. This is another important component of readiness. For instance, in developing countries and rural and remote areas of other countries, fast and reliable connections to the Internet are still an issue. This can make the use of the Internet for video and even voice communication unreliable. A small business may have little control over such a situation. At a local small business level, older computers may not be able to run the latest software applications that are available. As per the LIAISE framework, this effectively reduces access to the technology due to lack of appropriate infrastructure within the business.

The final, important, aspect of readiness is having the skills to effectively use ICT. Possessing ICT literacy and having appropriate ICT infrastructure provide effective access to ICT. The next few lessons relate to ICT skills.

ICT Skills Lessons

These lessons relate to the Literacy and Support aspects of the LIAISE framework.

Our classification of the ICT skills of the businesses in our study (refer to Table 8.3) revealed that we considered approximately one-third of them to have upper-level ICT skills and one in five of the businesses to have lower-level ICT skills.

Breaking this down further, Table 8.4 shows the common responses to the different questions that we asked about ICT skills across the different skill classifications.

Most of the businesses in each of the classifications were familiar with the basic ICT terms that we asked them about and described their practical understanding of those terms as being at the intermediate level. There were more instances of participants that classified themselves at the expert level as the skill classifications increased.

The main differences between the groupings began to emerge when we asked about newer technologies (remembering that we did update this list for the UK aspect of the study as this was conducted a few years after the Australian study). As the classifications moved from lower- to upper-level ICT skills, so did the level of familiarity and practical understanding of newer ICT.

Table 8.3 ICT Skills Classifications of Participating Small Businesses

ICT Skill Classification	Australian Data Collection (#)	UK Data Collection (#)	Overall (#)
Upper	13	6	19
Middle	21	8	29
Lower	7	5	12
Total	41	19	60

Table 8.4 Most Common Responses to ICT Questions by ICT Skill Classifications

ICT Skills Question	ICT Skills Expertise Classification— Most Common Response		
	Upper	Middle	Lower
Familiarity with basic ICT	Yes	Yes	Yes
Practical understanding of basic ICT	Intermediate (Expert 42%)	Intermediate (Expert 10%)	Intermediate
Familiarity with newer ICT	Yes	Some	None
Practical understanding of newer ICT	Intermediate (Expert 16%)	Inexperienced (Intermediate 21%)	Inexperienced
Can identify operating system	Yes	Mostly	Mostly
Current ICT skills OK? (self-assessment)	Yes	Yes	No
Future ICT skills OK? (self-assessment)	Yes	Range of answers (Yes, Unsure, No)	No

There were also notable differences in how businesses in the different ICT skills expertise classifications assessed the current and anticipated future level of ICT skills. Businesses in the lower classification generally felt that both their current and anticipated future ICT skill levels were inadequate. Businesses at the upper level of ICT skills classifications felt that their skills were adequate now and that they were well placed for the future. These responses have encouraged us to propose the next three (ICT skills-related) lessons for small businesses.

Lesson 3: Know About Established and Newer ICT

This lesson stems from our familiarity with and understanding of ICT questions. Note that in this lesson we are not proposing that owner/managers need to be ICT experts. However, they should have an idea of what ICT is currently available and affordable for their business and how it might be able to be employed effectively. This is all about Rogers' (2003) notion of knowledge of an innovation.

So, how can this knowledge be gained? There are a number of ways. Read the technology section of the local newspaper. Join a networking group, online forum or social networking group dedicated to ICT use in your industry, trade group, your region or even small businesses in general. Attend ICT briefings or breakfasts when presented by local industry groups. Watch what competitors are doing or speak to other small business owners about how they use ICT. Look for advertisements about ICT. When you hear about a new technology that you think might be useful, look it up on the Internet. See if there have been videos posted showing how it is being used elsewhere. These are just a small number of suggestions.

Lesson 4: Possess Appropriate Skills to Use ICT Effectively in the Business

Once the knowledge of ICT is gained and the decision made to adopt it or upgrade, it is important that the relevant skills to use it are available to the business. Note that this lesson does not say that the relevant skills have to be available within the business. That decision should relate to how important ICT is to the business. It also relies on the different aspects of ICT, in this instance hardware, software and data.

For instance, if the business is installing a new wireless network, it is unlikely to need employees to have the skills to do this. In the past, the installation of a network would have required dedicated cabling and servers to be installed. Nowadays it might require an Internet connection combined with a wireless network, perhaps using Cloud storage. If assistance is required to do this, then the business could just pay (say a consultant) for its installation.

In the same way, a small business may not need a dedicated employee to set up their website. These days there are a number of different options available to do this, from inexpensive (or even free) template options to the use of consultants to design fully interactive websites. However, an employee may be regularly required to update the content of the website, so the skills to do this should be available within the business.

The results of our study suggest that there are still a large proportion of small businesses that are not comfortable with the level of ICT skills available within their businesses. If they are not in a position to bring in employees with the required ICT skills, then the only solution left to them is to access the ICT skills elsewhere.

Lesson 5: Know How to Access ICT Skills From Reliable Sources

This lesson specifically relates to the Support aspect of the LIAISE framework. As mentioned in the previous lesson, ICT skills can be brought into the business by hiring consultants or hiring employees with ICT skills. However, it is known that small businesses often use other approaches to source their ICT skills, especially using family and friends as they offer a low-cost alternative to gaining expertise. One of the risks of this strategy is that these people, whilst well intentioned, may not have the level of ICT expertise required (for instance, they might be hobby users of the technology) or have enough understanding of the business context to be able to offer advice that is of value. It is for this reason that we caution the use of family and friends as a single source of ICT expertise, or at least recommend that the small business owner/manager should carefully consider the training and background of the person from whom the advice is being sought.

Table 8.5 shows the source of ICT skills as indicated by participants in our study, separated into the different ICT skills classification levels. The results show that most small businesses did, indeed, rely on more than one source for their ICT expertise. However, one figure does stand out quite starkly in the results. Whilst somewhere between four and five businesses out of 10 in the upper and middle ICT skills classification sourced ICT skills from family and friends, over nine out of 10 businesses in the lower ICT skills classification sourced ICT skills in this manner.

We believe that this is disturbing. Family and friends cannot necessarily be relied upon to have the ICT skills at a level suitable for the business, or to have an understanding of the business context that ICT is being applied in. Also, they are often used as a cheaper alternative to other sources of ICT expertise (Burgess et al., 2009). In this study, a slightly lower proportion of these businesses sourced their ICT skills from consultants or ICT courses. None of the businesses in the lower ICT skills classification indicated that they used the Internet to source ICT expertise or teach themselves ICT skills. This might reflect a lack of adequate search skills and/or confidence to be able to do this effectively.

It is for this reason that we recommend that when small businesses do need to access ICT skills that they do so from reliable sources, such as ICT consultants with good reputations and ICT courses. When they use family or friends, ensure that they are well qualified to offer the expertise which is being sought. When the Internet is used to gather information about ICT or source ICT skills, then ensure that the sites that are being used are well regarded.

ICT Use and Innovation Lesson

The lessons in this section are devoted to the information and content aspects of the LIAISE framework or, more simply, how small businesses

Table 8.5 Source of ICT Skills by Skills Classification

Source of ICT Skills	ICT Skills Expertise Classification (%)		
	Upper	Middle	Lower
Family or Friends	42	45	92
Consultants	37	41	33
ICT Courses	26	31	17
Books or magazines	16	14	17
Internet/self-taught	16	10	–
Other	–	10	17

use their ICT. Table 8.6 indicates how we classified businesses in this study according to their level of ICT use and innovation. There was a more even split between lower levels (little or no use of ICT), middle levels (typical uses of ICT for small businesses, such as for record-keeping or word processing) and upper levels (typical uses plus at least one 'added value' or innovative use) categories than for ICT skills.

However, the results suggest that there is a relationship between the level of ICT skills and the level of ICT use and innovation within a small business. Table 8.7 examines the level of ICT use and innovation against the ICT skills classifications. It is perhaps not surprising that the most prominent levels of ICT use and innovation in the small businesses match their corresponding ICT skills classifications. This is yet another indication of the importance of ICT literacy to the small business.

This brings us to our next lesson.

Lesson 6: Know Something About Added-Value Uses of ICT in Addition to Regular Uses of ICT

The difference between this lesson and Lesson 3 is that Lesson 3 was more about owner/managers knowing about available technologies. Lesson 6 is concerned with owner/managers knowing what ICT applications are available for the business and how they can add value (as per the earlier discussion related to Lesson 1).

Table 8.6 ICT Use and Innovation Classifications of Participating Small Businesses

ICT Use and Innovation Classification	Australian Data Collection (#)	UK Data Collection (#)	Overall (#)
Upper	14	5	19
Middle	16	9	25
Lower	11	5	16
Total	41	19	60

Table 8.7 ICT Use and Innovation Classifications by ICT Skills Classification

ICT Skills Classification	ICT Use and Innovation Classification (%)			
	Upper	Middle	Lower	Total
Upper	53	37	10	100
Middle	34	48	16	100
Lower	–	25	75	100

The most popular uses of ICT amongst the businesses were:

- Record-keeping
- Email/communication
- Reporting/word processing/publishing
- Use of the Internet for ordering/making bookings/making payments
- Social networking (especially in the later interviews)
- Use of the Internet for searching for information

There were also a number of other uses, such as industry-specific software (such as dedicated software for drafting) and online services that simulated how a product might look (such as a carpet).

ICT Governance Lessons

This series of lessons relates to the evaluation aspect of the LIAISE framework and some other, more general, governance aspects of ICT use. Overall, we rated 53 of the 60 businesses we studied to be at the middle or upper classification in regards to governance (refer to Table 8.8).

Two important ICT governance activities for small businesses to consider are how current their ICT resources are and how they protect their valuable ICT resources.

Table 8.9 shows how often businesses at the different ICT skill classifications considered upgrades to their ICT. This might include upgrades to hardware, but also operating system or software upgrades.

Table 8.8 ICT Governance Classifications of Participating Small Businesses

ICT Governance Classification	Australian Data Collection (#)	UK Data Collection (#)	Overall (#)
Upper	15	4	19
Middle	21	13	34
Lower	5	2	7
Total	41	19	60

Table 8.9 Frequency of ICT Upgrade Considerations by ICT Skills Classification

ICT Skills Classification	How often do you consider upgrading your ICT? (%)			
	Ongoing/Every 6 months–2 years	Every 3–5 years	Infrequently/ Never/Unsure	Total
Upper	42	26	32	100
Middle	52	17	31	100
Lower	18	18	64	11

188 *Summary and Lessons*

The results once again suggest that many businesses in the lower ICT skills classification are at a disadvantage, with almost two-thirds of those businesses virtually never thinking about whether they should be upgrading their ICT resources, or doing so infrequently. However, this is not a phenomenon strictly limited to those businesses, with almost one-third of the businesses in the middle and upper ICT classifications infrequently, or not, considering upgrades to their ICT resources. For that reason we introduce the next lesson.

Lesson 7: Consider Upgrading ICT Resources at Least Every Five Years

Lesson 7 is a very conservative lesson, but our study findings indicate that it should result in an improvement for many small businesses in assessing how current ICT might be able to provide better value for their business than their existing resources. The time period of five years is very conservative (it should probably be at least three years). Also, we are suggesting that small businesses should only consider upgrading their ICT resources. They should actually only do so if there are demonstrable benefits available to the business by doing so.

The next aspect of ICT governance relates to small businesses having their own backup and recovery plans if some part of their ICT should fail. This should not only cover the loss of hardware, but also software and data that is important to the business. Even in these modern times when storage capabilities fail less frequently, it is still worthwhile to have a regular routine of at least backing up (and knowing how to recover) important data, storing programs away or knowing how to source them so that they can be restored and knowing where and how to source replacement hardware if it fails. In relation to the latter point, it is important to be aware of the type of support that is offered in guarantees or warranties. A service program that requires you to return your hardware to the manufacturer may mean that you are without that hardware for some time whilst it is being repaired or assessed for replacement.

These days it is a frequent occurrence to download software or applications ('apps') online. If the software needs to be reinstalled, it is often just a matter of downloading it again. Businesses are also commonly now accessing software that runs remotely (on 'the Cloud', which means that it is really running on off-site servers). Whilst this means that the business does not need to concern itself with maintaining the software on its own hardware, it is necessary to have a reliable, and ideally fast, Internet connection to manage the link to the software and the data that is transferred.

Another common occurrence these days is for businesses to store their data on the Cloud. Again, the reputation of the service provider should be considered. How do they ensure that your data is protected? Additionally, how do they ensure that it is secure and that other parties are not able to access it? Although many of these services provide impressive data backup services, we feel that it is still useful to store data locally within the business.

Historically, a business would store its data with its hardware and then often have data backups on a remote site. Perhaps the modern equivalence to this might be that the main data of a business is stored securely on the Cloud and backups are stored locally. These can then be accessed if there is a problem with, say, the Internet connection.

Table 8.10 shows the existence of ICT recovery plans of study participants, again split across businesses with different ICT skills classifications. The results again suggest that those businesses that we classified in the upper and middle ICT skills classifications were more likely to have ICT recovery plans in place. However, there were still some businesses in all ICT skills classifications that did not have recovery plans.

This brings us to our next lesson.

Lesson 8: Develop ICT Recovery Plans That Enable Functioning Hardware and Software and Access to Data to the Extent That Operations Will Not Be Adversely Affected If Something Fails

The final two lessons for small business use of ICT relate to the evaluate aspect of LIAISE framework. We asked our study participants if they evaluated their ICT success. The answers are summarised in Table 8.11.

The responses were divided into those that indicated that they did evaluate their ICT success against those that said that they did not, or were unsure or that they evaluate the success of their ICT using "gut feeling" (instinct or intuition).

Table 8.10 ICT Recovery Plan Existence by ICT Skills Classification

ICT Skills Classification	Do you have an operational ICT recovery plan? (%)		
	Yes	No	Total
Upper	88	12	100
Middle	80	20	100
Lower	64	36	100

Table 8.11 Evaluation of ICT Success by ICT Skills Classification

ICT Skills Classification	Do you evaluate ICT success? (%)		
	Yes	No/no need to/not sure/gut feeling	Total
Upper	68	32	100
Middle	52	48	100
Lower	33	67	100

It is quite obvious from Table 8.11 that there was some relationship between the level of ICT skills classification and the likelihood that a small business would evaluate the success of its ICT investment, with those in the upper ICT skills classification more likely to do so; however, there were still too many businesses across all classifications that did not evaluate the success of its ICT investment. Thus, we introduce the next lesson:

Lesson 9: Evaluate, on a Regular Basis, the Success of ICT Investments

In this instance we consider 'regularly' to mean at least once every six months to one year.

We found that it was somewhat more difficult to get participants to list any *formal* measures that they used to measure the success of their ICT investment. However, we did manage to find some common approaches that were used to measure ICT success:

Customer-related measures

- Level of online sales or bookings
- Number of online enquiries
- Customer feedback

Website traffic-related measures

- Website hits/online usage
- Google Analytics

Cost-control measures

- Monitoring the costs of ICT
- Measuring cost savings through the use of ICT

In an earlier book dedicated to examining the small business Web presence (Burgess, Sellitto, & Karanasios, 2009), the authors suggested that it was important to think about Web presence success early, and this certainly applies to ICT use. It is better to think about how to measure ICT success before they are purchased and being used than afterwards. In Burgess et al. (2009) the authors also indicated that it was easier to measure the costs associated with ICT than the benefits. The measures for assessing success obtained from participants that are listed above are all quantifiable. Some measures of ICT success are not so easy to assess (such as better communications, faster business processes or better-quality information being provided for decision-making). In those instances, measure of ICT system usage, impact of ICT on organisational performance (which may be hard to identify) or even measures of satisfaction of ICT users might be suitable indicators (Burgess et al., 2009).

Whatever formal measures are selected, it is important to think back to Lesson 1 and ensure that those measures will indicate whether the performance of ICT is measured in the achievement of business aims; see Lesson 10.

Lesson 10: Develop Formal Measures to Evaluate the Success of ICT That Relate to the Achievement of Business Aims

Conclusion

This chapter has re-examined the results of our study of the use of ICT by 60 small businesses in Australia and the UK and proposed some lessons for ICT use by small businesses. We believe that, if adopted, small businesses will better be able to use ICT more efficiently, more effectively and with greater confidence to assist them to achieve their business aims.

References

Burgess, S., Sellitto, C., & Karanasios, S. (2009). *Effective web presence solutions for small businesses: Strategies for successful implementation*. Hershey, PA: Information Science Reference.

Rogers, E. M. (2003). *Diffusion of innovations* (5th ed.). New York: The Free Press.

ICT Lessons for Small Businesses

Lesson 1:	Match ICT aims and strategies to business aims and strategies.
Lesson 2:	Think about the readiness of the business to adopt ICT.
Lesson 3:	Know about established and newer ICT.
Lesson 4:	Possess appropriate skills to use ICT effectively in the business.
Lesson 5:	Know how to access ICT skills from reliable sources.
Lesson 6:	Know something about added value uses of ICT in addition to regular uses of ICT.
Lesson 7:	Consider upgrading ICT resources at least every five years.
Lesson 8:	Develop ICT recovery plans that enable functioning hardware and software and access to data to the extent that operations will not be adversely affected if something fails.
Lesson 9:	Evaluate, on a regular basis, the success of ICT investments.
Lesson 10:	Develop formal measures to evaluate the success of ICT that relate to the achievement of business aims.

Index

Note: Italicized page numbers indicate a figure on the corresponding page. Page numbers in bold indicate a table on the corresponding page.

Printed in the United States
By Bookmasters